RETURN TO FREEDOM

The War Memoirs of
Col. Samuel C. Grashio USAF (Ret.)

By

SAMUEL C. GRASHIO
and
BERNARD NORLING

To

The Valiant American and Filipino Defenders of
Bataan and Corregidor;
Especially the 21st Pursuit Squadron,

and

Our Commanding Officer,
Lt. Col. William Edwin Dyess

ISBN 0-912958-20-0

Library of Congress Catalog Card No. 82-060732

Cover design by LEO ASPENLEITER

Printed by
UNIVERSITY PRESS
Spokane, Washington

Contents

Foreword

COLONEL SAM GRASHIO AND PROFESSOR BERNARD NORLING have combined their talents to give us a rare insight into a phenomenal chapter in 20th Century history. *Return to Freedom* is at once a narrative of one of the most daring escape stories of World War II and at the same time it holds up to the light of history the phenomenon of unbelievable Japanese treachery and cruelty. It analyzes the human behavior of the captors and their captives, the will to live, and the will to die. It also brings into focus the inhumanity of both the Americans and Japanese in the execution of the War.

It was my honor to know fighter pilot Grashio and his idol, Ed Dyess, at Cabcaben Field on Bataan in the Philippine Islands early in World War II and I share the Colonel's admiration of Ed Dyess. He was everybody's hero on Bataan—an unusual leader who deserves more recognition than he had received.

My commander on beach defense during the siege of Corregidor was Marine Corps Captain Austin (Shifty) Shofner who was a prime mover in planning and executing the escape.

In the prison camp on Corregidor I had become acquainted with Marine Lieutenant Jack Hawkins a fourth member of the ten who were later to escape. He considered escaping from Corregidor with me but decided to wait for a more favorable opportunity than swimming the shark infested north channel back to Bataan.

Many months of dreaming and scheming went into the preparation for their flight from the Davao Penal Colony. On the escape route when they had reached the end of their stamina and endurance, it was Sam Grashio who inspired them to a strong faith in God. The spirit generated from that faith gave them the strength to carry on so that nine of the ten men were able to return to freedom and home in the United States.

Edgar D. Whitcomb
Seymour, Indiana
June 14, 1982

NOTE: Governor Whitcomb's own incredible story of escape from the Japanese is set forth in *Escape From Corregidor*, published in 1958 by Henry Regnery Company.

Preface

THOUGH I HAD KNOWN COLONEL SAMUEL C. GRASHIO casually for thirty years it was only in 1979 that I heard him describe at length what he had done, seen, and endured in the Philippines during World War II. I was amazed. While other prisoners of the Japanese had been treated even more shamefully than Colonel Grashio, I had never heard of anyone who had been involved in such a variety of wartime adventures or who had so many close brushes with death. From the ages of thirteen to sixty, in youthful escapades, as a combat pilot, on the Bataan Death March, in three different Japanese prison camps, during a sensational escape from one of these camps, while fighting alongside Filipino guerrillas, on an unauthorized mission in New Guinea, on routine flights in the United States later in the war, and in his many years of service in the U.S. Air Force after 1945, he had narrowly escaped death at least two dozen times: from Japanese bombs and bullets, American antiaircraft fire, starvation, disease, exhaustion, drowning, ambushes, terrorists, mistaken identity, defective equipment, and the foulups that are an inescapable part of war. Even a python of uncertain disposition had lain in wait for him on one occasion. My immediate response was that it was a story that ought to be told. Eventually we decided to collaborate in the writing of what are essentially the war memoirs of then lieutenant, subsequently colonel, Grashio.

Samuel Grashio spent a year in Japanese prison camps. Scores of such prisoners of war have long since written their memoirs, or had them penned by others. Nonetheless, most such books relate the personal experiences of a single individual, embellished somewhat by references to those who were jailed with him, but with only minimal effort to link any of this to the general course of the war itself. Few have considered what other prisoners have endured in other places, at other times, or in other wars. Thus it has seemed to us that a fine opportunity now exists to attempt a war memoir with more dimensions than most: to not only make comparisons of the experiences and thoughts of Samuel Grashio with those of other prisoners in World War II but with those in the Korean and Vietnam conflicts as well.

The reader of a collaborative work sometimes wonders who wrote what. While I (Norling) "wrote" this book in the usual meaning of that word, both of us, alone and together, went over every line, discussed, added, subtracted, and revised, so the final product can justly be ascribed to both of us. The frequent references to religious convictions and to prayers, especially in difficult circumstances, are Colonel

Grashio's own. Another person could not possibly know in advance how he would respond in some desperate situation, or what construction he might put on his survival afterward.

The main source for most of the book is Colonel Grashio's personal recollections. He did not keep a diary during the war but he did assemble an extensive collection of newspaper clippings during its latter stages when his experiences and exploits were described at length in many newspapers. These materials have provided an excellent corrective to the human memory, as have books by four of the men (Ed Dyess, Melvyn McCoy, Steve Mellnick, and Jack Hawkins) who were in prison camps with Colonel Grashio and who took part with him in the only mass escape from the Japanese in the whole war. Several other books by men who were in the same camps have also proved particularly valuable.

In the text there are periodic references to American military unpreparedness, to international politics in the 1930s, and to American and Japanese strategic thought. Much of this was not known and digested thoroughly by Lieutenant Grashio *at that time*. He learned about some of these matters quickly, from painful experience in the war; he became conversant with the rest only after 1945. Nonetheless, these subjects are mentioned occasionally in the early chapters of the narrative in an effort to make more intelligible what sort of situation American soldiers were sent into in 1941-42.

The book is written in the first person throughout. Thus "I", "me", and "my" ordinarily refer to Samuel Grashio. The only exceptions are in this Preface where "I" indicates Bernard Norling, and in a number of references to Eve Hoyt, a personal friend of mine who survived three years in Santo Tomas prison in Manila but whom Colonel Grashio never knew.

Sometimes persons are referred to by different military ranks in different parts of the narrative. This may be confusing but it is unavoidable. Many officers held a permanent rank and a temporary one at the same time. Nearly everyone was promoted at least once, usually several times, during the war and afterward. The American and Filipino guerrillas regularly promoted themselves and each other, with scant reference to regular military procedure. Thus it was possible for an American officer to have a permanent rank of First Lieutenant, a temporary rank of Major, and to be a "Colonel" in the guerrillas, all at the same time. Hence references to rank are often approximations.

I am indebted to the University of Notre Dame and to an understanding departmental chairman, Reverend Marvin O'Connell, for giving me leave from teaching for a semester, which greatly speeded completion of the book; and to my friends, Dr. Ralph Weber of Marquette University, and Drs. Charles Poinsatte and Jack Detzler of

St. Mary's College, all of whom read the manuscript and offered numerous suggestions for improvement.

Colonel Grashio would like to thank Reverend William Kelly, John Evoy S.J., and Dr. Francis J. Polek, Professor of English at Gonzaga University, all of whom read and criticized the manuscript; Colonel Eugene P. Cunneely USAF (Ret.), who encouraged him to write his memoirs; and particularly Reverend Armand Nigro S.J., without whose persistent urging this book probably would never have been written.

Bernard Norling
South Bend, Indiana
April, 1982

Prayer the escape group recited
in the jungle swamp:

The Memorare

Remember oh most gracious Virgin Mary,
Never was it known that anyone
Who fled to your protection
Or sought your intercession
Was left unaided.
Inspired by this confidence I fly unto you
Oh Virgin of Virgins my Mother.
To you I come, before you I stand,
Sinful and sorrowful.
Oh Mother of the word Incarnate,
Despise not my Petitions,
but in your Mercy and Kindness,
Hear and answer me . . . Amen.

Chapter One

The War Begins

When I GOT OFF THE SHIP IN MANILA on November 20, 1941 with the other pilots and ground crews of the 21st and 34th Pursuit Squadrons of the U.S. Army Air Corps, Pearl Harbor was only two and a half weeks away. Yet I did not have a care in the world. Writing at the end of the war and long afterward, many high ranking military officers, journalists, and "old Asia hands" of several nationalities claimed that knowledgeable people everywhere in the Far East knew throughout 1940-41 that war with Japan was inevitable; they were uncertain only about when and where it would begin. Maybe they did, but I certainly did not "know" it.

During my adolescence I had wanted to be a pilot in the simple, straightforward way some boys want to grow up to be President, others to become professional athletes. Aviation still had a lot of glamour in the 1930s. People in small towns and rural areas still dashed outdoors to scan the skies when they heard the hum of an unfamiliar motor. World War I "aces" like Captain Eddie Rickenbacker and Baron von Richtofen were still mentioned in casual conversation. Young boys read about their exploits and dreamed of themselves in the cockpits of biplanes flashing out of the clouds at 100 m.p.h. to riddle enemy fighters with machine gun fire.

My youthful fascination with aviation had been stimulated further by a close friend, Paul Giesa, who was obsessed with flying. In 1938, after being out of high school two years, Paul and I had entered Gonzaga University in our home town of Spokane, Washington. Two years of college was required then to qualify as a flying cadet and Gonzaga had a federal contract to run a flight training program. We also joined the 116th Observation Squadron of the Washington Air National Guard in 1939 because this looked like the only way near penniless youths like ourselves would ever actually get to fly. In due course I received my private pilot's license, and proceeded through what were for me nine extremely enjoyable months of flight training at Ontario, California and at Randolph and Kelly Fields near San Antonio, Texas. On April 25, 1941 I was commissioned a 2nd Lieutenant, and became a fighter pilot in the Army Air Corps.

Though it is somewhat embarrassing to admit now, during flight training and when I was assigned to Hamilton Field near San Francisco in the months afterward, I thought of flying only in the narrow sense: taking to the air in the best World War I movie tradition, embellished with goggles and helmet, scarf waving in the breeze. I thought little about *why* I was training and flying so much. Of course I knew that war had been going on in Europe ever since September, 1939 but in flying school I thought of it mostly when a fellow cadet of Greek lineage would needle me about what his countrymen were doing to the Italian troops Benito Mussolini had so injudiciously sent to invade Greece.

My mistaken perception of the world deepened soon after the 21st Pursuit Squadron sailed from San Francisco on November 1, 1941. Our ship was the President Coolidge, a former luxury liner then being used as a troop transport. Life was lovely: there were no duties, the food was magnificent, and we did not even know where we were going! Only after docking at Honolulu and then setting off still further westward did we deduce that PLUM, the codeword for our reassignment, meant Philippines, Luzon, Manila; that our destination was the Philippines. Though we formed a convoy west of Guam, picked up a naval escort, and were blacked out at night the rest of the way, nothing happened that might have suggested, even remotely, that a real war was not far off. Quite the contrary. On board the Coolidge there were a number of senior officers who had just graduated from the National War College. Having little to do, I listened to them extensively. To a man they were convinced that there would be no war with Japan because the Japanese would not be so stupid as to start a war they would be certain to lose within a few weeks.

Thus in my first days in the Philippines I was merely excited to be in such an exotic foreign place. Everything was new: the steaming, oppressive tropical heat, the pungent odors of the Orient, the delicate flavor of papayas with a little lime juice squeezed over them, the excitement of watching Jai Alai played in a beautiful stadium.

There is a hillbilly ballad called "The Cold, Hard Facts of Life." I began to awaken to these only on December 6 in a theater at Nichols Field, where I was stationed, a few miles south of Manila. There Colonel Harold H. George, a senior air officer, solemnly warned us that war was imminent. The Japanese had 3000 planes on Formosa, only 600 miles away, he told us, and they had already been flying reconnaissance over the Philippines for several days. He concluded that fate had probably destined us to be a suicide squadron. In retrospect, one would suppose that such a pronouncement would have shocked me like an icy shower on a hot day. Not so. I was stirred, to be sure, and rendered temporarily thoughtful, but I still offered to bet Ed Dyess, our Squadron Commander, five pesos that there would be no war with Japan. Ed took the bet at once and laid another five that war would begin within a week.

Vindication of Ed's judgment required only two days. About 2:30 A.M. on December 8 the officer of the day, Lieutenant L.A. Coleman, a classmate of mine in flying school, banged on the door of the officers living quarters and yelled at us to report at once to the operations tent at Nichols Field. We dressed in a rush, jumped into a waiting vehicle, and sped away. At Nichols, Dyess announced enigmatically that there was an emergency, but ten minutes later he told us to go back to our quarters. It seemed to me that I had just fallen asleep when Coleman began banging on doors again. This time he shouted at us to get dressed, that Pearl Harbor had been attacked! It was about 4:45 A.M. We dashed back to Nichols. This time Dyess confirmed that Pearl Harbor had indeed been heavily bombed by the Japanese. He ordered us into our new P-40E pursuit planes, and directed us to start our engines and stand by on the radio.

It was only now that I began to think seriously about the prospect of war with Japan, and about our chances of winning. I knew that our pursuit pilots, while eager, were inexperienced, like myself just a few months out of flying school. Reflection on the number and state of our planes was even more sobering. We had trained in P-35s, planes sufficiently primitive that their landing gear had to be wound up manually. Even so, the P-35 was a good little plane, a pleasure to fly and sufficiently maneuverable that it might actually have been better in combat against the marvelously maneuverable, darting Japanese Zeros than its replacement, the P-40. Be that as it may, we now had P-40s. They too were good planes: sturdy, reliable, with excellent speed in level flight, good protection for the pilot, and ample firepower, though only moderate maneuverability. But the consideration of overwhelming immediate pertinence was that none of us had ever flown one! In fact our P-40s were so new that only eighteen of them had been taken out of their crates and had their six .50 caliber machineguns divested of the thick greasy cosmolene in which they had been packed. Of the eighteen, none had been flown for more than three hours. Four had never been off the ground at all, and the remaining fourteen had not been completely slow-timed. I felt rather like a member of a football team being told on Day One of practice that the opening game of the regular season would be tomorrow.

The true state of American air defense in the Philippines was much worse than I knew at the time. Though our P-40s were new, most U.S. planes there were outdated, with badly worn engines. Most were lightly armed with guns that were either worn out or so new that they had never been boresighted and fired. Some pilots had had as little as fifteen hours training in pursuit planes. There were only two complete bomber crews with as much as one hour of training above 20,000 feet—this sixteen months after the Battle of Britain in which air battles had taken place as high as 30,000 feet. On December 7, 1941 there were in all the Philippines only about 100 first class planes ready for combat, so few that General Lewis Brereton, Commander of the U.S. Far Eastern Air Force, hesitated to ask for more lest he thereby invite a Japanese attack to destroy them! Even so, there were not enough airfields to disperse these few planes properly, nor any camouflage to hide them. Most of the runways were short, all of them were sod rather than concrete, some were near swamps, and most were too soft to handle B-17 bombers. There was no defense system worthy of the name anywhere in the Philippines, no radar detection system on Luzon, the big northern island, and no air raid shelters in Manila. The air warning system depended heavily on Filipino watchers who had never been taught aircraft identification. Communications were equally primitive, dependent on the ordinary civilian telephone system. Everything connected with gunnery was woefully inadequate. Ammunition was in such short supply that pilots sometimes went into combat without air-to-air firing training. All the target practice I had ever had in California, for instance, had consisted of firing a few bursts at silver slicks on the ocean. It was all sadly typical of American unpreparedness in all branches of the service everywhere in the Pacific.

Disgruntled G.I.s used to say that standard operating procedure in the U.S. Army was "Hurry up and wait." Now we did exactly that. After the initial alert we cut our engines, got out of the cockpit, sat under the wings, and waited as seemingly endless hours dragged by. Suddenly about 11:30 A.M. we received an urgent call to prepare for action, though just what action was unspecified. Soon Dyess divided our eighteen P-40s into three groups and led two of them, Flights A and B, into the air. I was to lead the remaining six, Flight C, and follow him, but a couple of our planes developed minor engine difficulties that delayed us just enough that we lost contact with A and B Flights. Only about 11:50 did my flight actually get into the air. Our first deed was practical, yet tragicomic: we flew to Laguna de Bay, a huge lake just south of Nichols Field, and for the first time tested our .50 caliber machineguns by firing short bursts into the water. More of the fruits of unreadiness appeared only minutes later. Two pilots in my flight reported that their engines were throwing so much oil on the windshields that they couldn't see. They could only go back to Nichols. This left four of us: Lieutenant Gus Williams flying on my wing and Lieutenant Johnny McGown on Lieutenant Joe Cole's wing. By now Flights A and B were not only out of sight but for reasons unknown out of radio contact as well. Since I had received no orders other than to get into the air and follow the other flights our isolation was complete, if not necessarily splendid. Since I had to do something I radioed Joe Cole that we should fly towards Clark Field, sixty miles north. Clark was the major airfield on Luzon, and most of our B-17 bombers and P-40 pursuit planes were there. Thus it seemed a logical target for Japanese planes flying in from the north.

We arrived over Clark Field about 12:20 P.M. . It was a gorgeous day. The sky was blue and the air smooth as glass. Observing the idyllic look of the whole area I still could not feel that I might become personally involved in a shooting war at any moment. To the reader it must seem incredible that anyone could have been in such an abstracted condition eight hours after Pearl Harbor. All I can reply is that I accepted that fact of war only when it hit me in the face, and that there were many like me. A maintenance man with the 19th Bomber Group at Clark Field recorded that most of the men with him ate breakfast in silence after hearing that Pearl Harbor had been bombed. Many simply did not believe it. He added that he was, himself, so dazed by the sudden, unexpected bombardment of Clark Field a few hours afterward that, even though slightly wounded, he did not fully accept the fact that we were at war with Japan until about 1:00 A.M.-2:00 A.M. on December 10 when Japanese planes began to bomb Manila.

Observing nothing unusual at Clark, C Flight flew westward towards the China Sea. Suddenly I spotted planes at about our altitude (10,000 feet), moving south. We closed in, pulses, racing. No sweat! They were only some other P-40's. Before we could get close enough to tell which squadron they belonged to, however, our earphones were suddenly filled with hysterical shouts from the tower operator far below, "All P-40s return to Clark Field. Enemy bombers overhead." These ominous words were almost immediately intermixed with the terrifying "whoomp" of bombs exploding. To my utter astonishment, the formation of P-40s continued serenely on a southerly course, climbing gradually. Obviously they had not heard the frantic order to return to Clark. What had happened to their radios? It was just the second snafu on a day that was to be filled with them.

Right at this crucial juncture Joe Cole radioed that his engine was throwing oil so badly that he could not see out of his windshield. Like the other two who had experienced the same trouble less than an hour before, he had to return to Nichols Field. This left McGown, Williams and myself. We turned back towards Clark. In the distance I got my first glimpse of the spectacular destructiveness of war. It was astounding! Where the airfield should have been the whole area was boiling with smoke, dust, and flames. In the middle was a huge column of greasy black smoke from the top of which ugly red flames billowed intermittently. The Japanese had hit an oil tank! Momentarily, I thought how utterly, abysmally wrong the senior officers on the Coolidge had been, a reflection almost immediately replaced by pity for those on the ground who must be going through hell. I said a quick prayer, asking God to help them and thanking Him for sparing me, at least for the moment, from being on the receiving end of Japanese bombs. The sixteenth century Holy Roman Empire Charles V is supposed to have remarked, after some political disaster, "Fortune is a woman, and she does not love old men." Maybe so, but she certainly loved one young man many times in the early days of World War II. I was one of the few pilots aloft when the Japanese hurricane broke over us. Though I did not know it at that moment, some of my friends and classmates had already been killed while struggling courageously to get their planes off the ground.

About 12:50 P.M., directly over the field, I noticed several enemy dive bombers perhaps 800 feet below us and 2000 feet above ground, bombing and strafing. All our flight training had been directed towards moments and opportunities like this. I signaled my wingmen to attack. Just then a lonely enemy dive bomber shot out of the smoke maybe 500 feet below. I looked at once for McGown. He was nowhere in sight. Gus had disappeared too! Instead, about 100 yards behind and above me were two Zeros, closing in. They opened fire. I veered sharply to the left. My plane shuddered as a cannon burst hit the left wing and blew a hole big enough to throw a hat through, as Ed Dyess put it later. For the first time that day I had the hell scared out of me. Momentarily, I was sure I was going to die on the first day of the war. Instinctively, I began to pray again, this time with greater fervor than before. Prayer comes easily when the end seems near; and if there are few atheists in foxholes they are equally rare in the cockpits of fighter planes in raging dogfights. I also remembered what Ed had told us so many times: never try to outmaneuver a Zero; go into a steep dive and try to outrace it. I pushed the throttle wide open and roared for the ground. The wind shrieked past me and the earth flashed upward at horrifying speed. According to the book, I was courting suicide. Technical manuals specifically warned against attempting a power dive in an untested plane, and I was in a P-40 that had been in the air a grand total of two hours. But with two Zeros on your tail the admonitions in technical manuals are not the first things you think about.

My luck held. When I tried to pull out of the dive at treetop level just west of Clark the plane responded magnificently. Glancing back, I was overjoyed to see the two Zeros falling steadily behind me. the superior diving capability of the P-40 had saved my hindquarters. To be sure, the Zeros pursued me relentlessly as I raced for Nichols just above the treetops, but their tracers flashing past my cockpit were increasingly wide of the mark, indicating that I had passed beyond their effective firing range. About midway between Clark and Nichols they gave up and turned back. I breathed a prayer of thanks, only to break out anew in a cold sweat. Would I be able to land with that gaping hole in the wing? I radioed Nichols tower for advice. I was told to climb to 8000 feet above an uninhabited area and simulate a landing. Wheels and flaps down, I did so. The hole in the wing presented no problems. Nevertheless, many curious and doubtless apprehensive people stood along the runway when I came down about 1:30, the first pilot to make it back to Nichols from combat.

The reception I got was immensely heartening. Sergeant Gibson, one of our fine maintenance men, who was later to die in prison camp, rushed over and hugged me joyfully. The act was typical of the warm feeling between officers and enlisted men in our outfit. One of the features of flight training I had liked best was that I had had no dealings with disgruntled draftees, only with youthful volunteers who shared my own enthusiasm for flying. Then at Hamilton Field I had been assigned to a unit in which most of the enlisted men were not draftees either, but older career men. After six months we all felt close to one another.

When I got out of my plane I don't remember what I said or did. Ed Dyess wrote later that my first words were, "By God, they ain't shootin spitwads are they?"

As for Dyess himself, he had already saved my life, at least indirectly. Indeed, one of the biggest breaks I ever got in my many years of military service was to get William Edwin Dyess as my first commanding officer after graduation from flight training. There were only about thirty squadron commanders in the entire U.S. Army Air Corps at that time, all first rate men. Ed Dyess, the youngest of them all was the most inspiring military officer I have ever known. He came from the little town of Albany in west Texas. He was impressive in bearing: tall, husky, handsome, with deep piercing blue eyes. He was intelligent, magnetic, and fearless: a natural leader who commanded respect without being intimidating. He was the best flyer in the outfit he led, a superb trainer of his fellow pilots, and a man who regularly saved the toughest assignments for himself. His pilots and enlisted personnel revered him and would have followed him anywhere. Had he survived the war he might have become Chief of the U.S. Air Force one day, for he had all the essential qualities. Already he had saved my neck by teaching me how not to deal with a Zero.

The Zero was an amazing airplane in certain ways. It was so light and flimsy that a few bullets could blow it apart. One knowledge-able American officer called it, partly in jest, partly in awe, "a flying engine with machine guns." It was propelled by an exact copy of the powerful American Wright Whirlwind engine; hence its extreme maneuverability and capacity to climb with incredible speed. Claire Chennault, the maverick commander of the Flying Tigers, had learned all about Japanese Zeros and Nates in the Sino-Japanese War of the late 1930s. In 1939 he sent the Military Intelligence branch of the War Department a lengthy report of the characteristics and capabilities of both planes, with detailed advice on how to deal with them in combat. But Chennault was not a popular man in the upper echelons of the

Army Air Corps in those days as all he got was a letter of thanks, with the notation that "aeronautical experts" said it was not possible to build an airplane to the specifications of the Nate. Nothing at all was said about the Zero. Though pilots trained by Chennault or associated with the Flying Tigers knew all about the strengths and shortcomings of the Zero, and had been trained to cope with both, most U. S. pilots simply assumed that any Japanese weapon must be inferior to its American counterpart and so were fatally surprised when they first encountered Zeros. Whether Dyess had somehow seen or heard of Chennault's report, or whether he merely deduced the qualities of the Zero from study and intuition, I never knew; but it was typical of him that he did know. In training he had warned us repeatedly never to try to outmaneuver a Zero; just to take our shots, if we had a chance, and then high tail it out of the area.

The debacle at Clark Field was one of the most controversial episodes of World War II. Here, eight hours after the attack on Pearl Harbor, the Japanese found half the U.S. Far Eastern Air Force lined up, wing tip to wing tip, on an unprotected field. In a few minutes they destroyed thirty medium bombers and observation planes, all the parked P-40s, and all but three of the B-17s. Many attempts have been made to pinpoint responsibility for the disaster but they all dissolve in a sea of conflicting accounts and recriminations as highly placed people in both Washington and the Philippines have sought to defend their reputations.

For a long time after the disaster, and lesser catastrophes elsewhere, stories circulated that these remarkably successful Japanese attacks had been set up by years of espionage supplemented by the activities of Filipino Fifth Columnists. There were tales of mysterious signals, flares suddenly appearing around the perimeters of U.S. installations immediately preceding attacks, even of a Filipino bartender near Clark Field who was supposed to be in regular contact with Japan via short wave radio.

About such tales, all I can say is that I heard them all. Grubby spies have had a lot to do with the outcome of many wars in the past, though it is always difficult and often impossible to prove this since neither spies nor their employers are in the habit of leaving behind filing cabinets full of records for interested parties to consult. That some Filipinos were pro-Japanese when the war began is incontestable, though they were vastly out numbered by those who were pro-American. Overall, it seemed to me that the calamities that befell us in the first days of the war were due mostly to three considerations: 1) The Japanese had planned their operations skillfully, 2) American forces were grievously short of everything, not the least of which was time, and 3) Sheer muddle, a constant factor in human affairs.

It had been well said that confusion is the first weed that grows on the field of combat. The chaos at Clark Field on the afternoon of December 8 was wondrous. Command, leadership, discipline, even simple order, had vanished utterly. Officers, enlisted men, and civilians had scattered headlong in all directions. Wryly typical was the action of a Filipino civilian who had been hired to run a mechanical ditch digger along the edges of the field. He was digging trenches for men to jump into to avoid bomb fragments and bullets when the first Japanese attack came. He displayed so little faith in the utility of his activities that he promptly abandoned both his machine and his newly dug trenches and dashed into the jungle.

Those of us who managed to get back to Nichols Field, either with our planes or without them, now feared that Nichols was likely to be blasted at any moment just as Clark had been. Since we had only a few planes left it was vital to save them. Dyess was directed to deploy the P-40s of the 21st Pursuit Squadron to Clark that same afternoon, on the assumption that the Japanese would not think it worth their while to bomb Clark again so soon. The manner in which he handled the operation was typical of both his personal character and professional skill. He told the rest of us he would land first, we should observe carefully what he did, wait until he had gotten his plane out of the way, and then follow him exactly. Down he went onto a field covered with several inches of dust as fine as flour and pockmarked with bomb craters. He landed perfectly. We followed, one by one, as instructed, and got every plane down safely. That night we survivors, still half-dazed, slept in the jungle.

When we awoke at dawn, somewhat recovered from the shock of the previous day's disaster, it occurred to someone that we might be caught napping again so we were ordered to take our P-40s up to 15,000 feet and get into position ready to attack. When a plane taxied to takeoff position the cloud of dust that rose exceeded in size and density anything I had ever seen prior to the clouds caused by the bombing of the day before. Moreover, the field was full of bomb craters. Thus three minute intervals were prescribed between takeoffs. Even so, there were several accidents. One pilot lost his engine, careened madly into the jungle, and was killed. I got airborne without mishap but Bob Clark, who followed me, did not allow enough time for the dust to settle, lost his way, and crashed blindly into a parked B-17 bomber. There was a sudden flash of light, a violent explosion, and hail of bullets all over the area as flaming gasoline from the plane's ruptured tanks set off the six loaded .50 caliber machine guns it carried. Bob was killed instantly.

My own promising start proved short lived. "Pappy" Boyington, the famous Marine ace who shot down nearly fifty Japanese planes, claimed that slipshod maintenance, carelessness in takeoffs, getting lost in clouds or fog, and other operational mishaps killed far more pilots than combat. The accuracy of his judgment had already been brought home to me a couple of times in training back at Hamilton Field. Once I had been up in a P-36 over the Sacramento Valley when magneto trouble developed and the engine cut out. That time I had managed to get down safely, and later flew the same plane without incident. Another time I had started to take off when a mechanical failure in the rudder bar assembly caused me to ground loop and shred the right wing tip, though I did stop the plane without further damage. Rejoicing inwardly at my good fortune, and momentarily confused, I had simply relaxed inside the plane and made no immediate effort to get out even though gasoline was spilled all over the area. For that mental lapse Captain Casey Vincent, the 35th Pursuit Group Operations Officer, had given me the most merciless chewing out I ever received from anyone. He had described to me with unforgettable vividness what my fate would have been had the least spark been struck during my siesta.

Now, on the second day of the war, capricious Fate nearly leveled me again. At about 9000 feet my engine suddenly started cutting in and out and losing power. Down I came, trying desperately to identify the problem and to restrain my own panic. Soon the engine cut in again, then went out again, then cut in once more. Gradually I regained control of the plane in the sense that I felt reasonably sure I could land, though it was clear that I could not maintain flying speed. The sticking point was that there was a certain identification procedure for landing which specified entry corridors. This I would have to ignore if I was to get the plane down at all. So in I came from an unexpected direction. Our antiaircraft batteries, understandably trigger-happy after the events of the day before, promptly opened fire on me. Fortunately, their marksmanship had not improved overnight. I got down unscathed, but separated from Dyess and the other pilots of the 21st Pursuit Squadron, all of whom landed at an auxiliary field north of Manila. Subsequently, they and our enlisted men, who were still at Nichols Field, were moved to a new field being constructed near Lubao over on the Bataan peninsula some fifty miles northwest of Manila in Pampanga Province. Such was the chaos of those wild days that it took me a month to find them, and then I did so only by accident.

With one full day of the war now behind me I could take comfort in the thought that I had not been killed by either friends or enemies. Had I been able to foresee the future I might have felt some kinship with those G.I.s who stormed ashore in Morocco in November, 1942 amid gunfire from their own navy, or with General Patton's troops who were both shelled by their own navy and bombed by their own air force when they disembarked on the beaches of Sicily in 1943. Had I known it, I might have been consoled further by the reflection that such foul-ups did not occur only in the American Army; that on the first day of the African campaign in 1940 an Italian A.A. battery shot down their own War Minister, Marshal Balbo; that planes from the British aircraft carrier ARK ROYAL attacked one of their own cruisers May 26, 1941 while chasing the German battleship BISMARK; and that even the Germans, notorious for their "efficiency," had bombed and shelled their own troops on more than one occasion. Whoever first coined the phrase "fog of war" knew what he was talking about.

Grisly irony was added to the whole episode when another pilot took my plane that afternoon, after it had been supposedly repaired. The engine failed him just as it had me. The only difference was that in his case it was on the takeoff. Thus he had no time to experiment or maneuver. There was just a crash and he was dead. It is much the intellectual fashion in our time to assert that all important developments must have profound and complex causes stretching well back into the past. I don't believe it. Many times my life has been affected by trivial, even accidental, events. This was such a case.

In the next few weeks confusion was rampant all over the Orient. Everywhere the Allies seemed dazed at the tempo of the Japanese operations, incredulous that the enemy could attack in Hawaii, Guam, Wake, Borneo, Java, Malaya, Singapore, Hong Kong, and several places in the Philippines almost simultaneously. Each day seemed to bring news of some fresh disaster. The Japanese themselves were amazed at their successes, which were due in about equal proportion to their own careful preparations, to Dutch, British, and American unpreparedness, and to surprise. Though I did not realize it at the time, the only ray of light amid the gloom was that these conquests came so easily that the victors assumed that their present equipment and tactics would suffice for all future operations.

As nearly as I can figure, forty years later, I must have subconsciously absorbed the spirit of these recurring disasters and the confusion that accompanied them for my few clear recollections of the two weeks after December 9, 1941 are random. I remember walking on Clark Field one day in the company of a Filipino Scout when Japanese planes appeared suddenly and flew over so low I could see the faces of the pilots and rear gunners. They strafed and dropped fragmentation bombs. I dove into a nearby slit trench but the Scout stood defiantly in the open, firing his .45 at the enemy. Though his act reminded me of stories about hunting bears with switches it did display one thing unmistakably: properly trained Filipinos are brave men.

I also recall going back to Nichols Field one day in a truck, then walking to an apartment complex called Los Tamaros Courts where some of us newly arrived officers had been housed a few days before. Now the whole area was demolished, but my faithful Filipino houseboy,

Pete, was still guarding what was left of my possessions. I gave him all of them on the spot and never saw him again.

Enemy bombardment of Manila was only sporadic, but there were several air raid warnings a day and civilians seemed to be in perpetual panic, scurrying about like agitated rabbits. How easily one forgets that in war areas life is quite as grim for civilians as for soldiers. One pitiful instance sticks in my memory. One day an air raid warning sounded. I looked about anxiously for cover. The most promising close place was a church so I bounded up the steps. At the top was a small Filipino girl, perhaps thirteen or fourteen. She was standing in the open, as motionless as if graven in stone, utterly terrified, simultaneously wetting herself and crying as if her heart would break. Some things touch one immediately and viscerally, without reason. Bombs or no, I stopped and hugged her, and told her to follow me and then dashed inside.

At another time I recall going to nearby Fort McKinley. Though the Japanese had already destroyed much of what we had on Luzon, American authorities were feverishly determined to prevent them from getting anything useful that might be left. There was a lot of communications equipment at McKinley that could not be moved readily so several of us seized crowbars and smashed everything in sight.

Steve Mellnick, who was to escape from prison camp with me a year later, was once involved in a somewhat similar episode, half-funny, half-tragic, and wholly infuriating, since it illustrated even more vividly how years of American slackness in preparing for the defense of the Philippines was now suddenly succeeded by frenzied destruction. During the last days of the defense of Corregidor Steve was one of those assigned to burn $10,000,000 in U.S. currency to prevent the Japanese from getting it. He observed with interest that the Andrew Jackson $20, bills burned faster than the Lincoln fives. He also described dumping tons of Philippine silver pesos into the deepest part of Manila Bay to balk the Japanese.

Readers may find it hard to believe that I cannot remember where I stayed in Manila during these tumultuous days, nor with whom I was associated. The only regular companion I had was Lieutenant Leo B. Golden, a classmate (Class 41C) at the Advanced Flying School at Kelly Field. Leo's fate was to be heartrending. Like so many American soldiers who survived combat and prison camp, starvation and disease, brutality and humiliation, Leo was to die near the end of the war in a pathetic way that mocked all sense of appropriateness: on board an unmarked Japanese prison ship, sunk by an American bomber. Perhaps Leo and I stayed at Santo Tomas University, though I have no recollection of this. Both of us were equally unclear then about where we should be or what we should be doing since the breakdown in leadership and routine had been so complete ever since

December 8 that neither of us had any orders. On Christmas Eve Leo heard that a ship was loading. Neither he nor I had any idea what ship, nor what its destination might be. All we knew was what news reports said: the enemy was breaking down through our lines and would be in Manila in a few days, perhaps hours. Figuring we had nothing to lose by going anywhere *else*, we slipped aboard the ship about midnight. Next morning we found ourselves off Mariveles, a small port on the southern tip of the Bataan peninsula, about thirty miles west. It was Christmas Day, 1941.

NOTE: Of course I and the distinguished passengers aboard the COOLIDGE were not the only ones who were oblivious to the possibility of war in the Far East. The unpreparedness, both material and psychological, of the British and American governments, armed forces, and general public, was notorious and appalling. As one example out of scores that might be cited, when General Lewis Brereton arrived in the Philippines on November 3, 1941, to assume command of the U.S. Far Eastern Air Force he observed that training schedules were "still based on the good old days of peace conditions in the tropics," and that the usual gaiety prevailed in Manila high society. Ironically, the night before the devastating Japanese attack on Clark Field there was a gala party for that same General Brereton. Lewis R. Brereton, *The Brereton Diaries*, p. 21. Cf. also the official Army historian Louis Morton, *The Fall of the Philippines*, p.72-73; and Sidney Stewart, *Give Us This Day*, pp. 13-23, on the same subject.

General Brereton, *ibid.*, pp. 8-9, describes the sorry state of air defenses in the Philippines. For more details about the deplorable condition of *all* Philippine defenses on the eve of the war Cf. Douglas MacArthur, *Reminiscences*, pp. 104-110; Morton, op. cit., pp. 12, 24, 26-30, 46-47, 50, 71, 85, 94, 131, 288-289, 496; and W.F. Craven and J.S. Cate, *The Army Air Forces In World War II, I, Plans and Early Operations*, 1939 to August, 1942, 186-189. Such citations could be multiplied endlessly from both official records and the testimony of those who were in the Philippines on the eve of the war.

For an indication of the bewilderment of many servicemen at the sudden outbreak of war Cf. Carlyle G. Townswick, *Too Young to Die*, pp. 13-15.

Claire Chennault, *Way of a Fighter* pp. 57, 94, 113, 116, 136-137, describes the qualities of the Zero and the Nate and gives his side of his many differences with Washington in the years before the war. Tom Harmon, the ex-Michigan football star who served in a unit in China attached to the Flying Tigers, says all the pilots trained by Chennault were familiar with the high quality of the Zero and knew how to deal with it. Cf. *Pilots Also Pray*, p. 132.

For a vivid description of the breakdown of everything during and immediately after the bombing of Clark Field Cf. Walter D. Edmonds, They Fought With What They Had, pp. 101, 111-112, 119, 130-140.

Steve Mellnick describes the destruction of American and Filipino money in Philippine Diary, pp. 11-14, 38, 116, 150.

Chapter Two
The Bataan Campaign

WHEN LEO GOLDEN and I got off the boat at Mariveles we were orphans. Nobody back in Manila knew what had become of us, we had arrived at our present destination by the merest chance, and we had no orders. We heard that some Air Corps people were at Little Baguio, near Cabcaben, a few miles east, so we started to walk in that direction. In the middle of the day we ran into the 803rd Engineering Battalion. Its officers generously invited us to share a Christmas dinner, which proved to be delicious. Afterward, they gave us precise directions to the Air Corps unit. We found it later in the day and were soon sent to meet our buddies of the 21st Pursuit squadron. Among them was Ed Dyess, whom I hadn't seen since December 8. My spirits soared at once.

Had I known more about the inadequacy of Philippine defenses my elation would have been muted. To be sure, the U.S. High Command had long considered the possibility of a Japanese attack and had devised various plans to thwart it, though none of these had suited General Douglas MacArthur when he was appointed Commander of all U.S. Army forces in the Far East on July 27, 1941. His objections or his own plans, mattered little. When the Japanese attack came all he could do was try to rush as many American and Filipino troops into the Bataan peninsula, which is surrounded on three sides by water and where some defensive preparations had been made. Here, now, were 75-80,000 troops, mostly Filipinos, encumbered by another 20-25,000 civilian refugees, all short of everything.

Nobody was more short of more "essentials" than those of us in the Air Corps. Indeed, one disgruntled soul suggested that a telegram be sent to Washington: "Please send us another P-40. . .that one we had was all worn out." It would not have been an inappropriate request for we began the air defense of Bataan with only nine planes, though there were several times that many pilots. Since it was clear that most of the fighting would now be on the ground, infantry training was improvised for the air crews. It had to begin with the absolute fundamentals since many of us had never fired a rifle in our lives. My own previous acquaintance with even a shotgun had been pitifully limited: a bit of skeet shooting in flight training in order to learn how to lead a moving target. Now we practiced firing obsolete rifles and dabbled in other aspects of infantry training. Most of the pilots were disgusted in varying degrees at the prospect of being turned into instant imitation infantrymen specializing in beach defense. Perhaps I, too, would have resented this decline in my social position had it lasted longer; but my entire career as an infantryman consisted of one reconnaissance mission, on foot with Tech Sgt. "Speedy" Nelson, to look for places along the southwest coast of Bataan where Japanese landings might be attempted.

In a few days I was reprieved. An order came from General George to report for flying duty again at Bataan Field, two or three miles north of Cabcaben. A new provisional outfit was being formed, composed of the more experienced pilots who had survived the disasters at Clark and Iba Fields, and elsewhere. As things turned out, we flew mostly reconnaissance missions until the end of the whole Bataan campaign. Our main concern was to keep some planes flyable; not to risk them in combat unless presented with some exceptional opportunity to damage the enemy. Though I had some harrowing adventures, and was eventually taken prisoner with everyone else, I was profoundly grateful that I got to fly rather than endure the tribulations of the beleaguered ground troops.

In my first month on Bataan all the ground action took place thirty miles away in the north end of the peninsula. In the south, save for one series of attempted landings which will be described later, the Japanese were content to harass us. They would bomb our airfields, our engineers would repair them, and the Nips, with characteristic punctuality, would then repeat the bombing at the same time the next day.

Around Manila in the first days of the war, and again on Bataan, it was brought home to us how grievously Americans had underrated both Japanese planes and their pilots. Though the pilots were not particularly imaginative or adaptable, many of them were veterans of the campaigns in China where they had become experts at set pieces. I once saw the leader of a flight of four Japanese dive bombers drop out of formation and attack one of our antiaircraft batteries. He immediately drew fire from all four guns in the battery, who thereby revealed their positions. At once the other Japanese pilots peeled off, one by one, in perfect order, each picking out a different A.A. gun. In one graceful, synchronized dive they silenced the whole battery and sped away. Fortunately for us, the quality of enemy pilots declined steadily throughout the war. Just why the Japanese High Command chose to throw in all their aces from the first day instead of holding some in reserve to train and inspire replacements, I never knew. Probably they hoped to win the war so quickly that it would not matter. It was a grave error on their part.

In January, 1942 several Filipino officers told their President,

Manuel Quezon, that they could defeat the Japanese on Bataan if only they had all the planes they needed. While one must admire their courage and optimism, their judgment was faulty for the primary causes of the fall of Bataan were lack of food and diseases that derived from malnutrition.

Before the war and in its first days, the performance of various branches of the Services was decidedly uneven. The Ordnance Department, for instance, had shown admirable foresight by storing huge stocks of munitions in the Bataan peninsula before the war. The Quartermaster Corps, by contrast, had done nothing comparable with food. There were immense quantities of food stored in Rizal Stadium in Manila when the war began, but it never seems to have occurred to anyone to move it post haste to Bataan, even though all the prewar military plans called for a last stand to be made in the peninsula. Commander Melvyn McCoy, who was later to escape from prison camp with me, recorded grimly that after the fall of Corregidor the Japanese had compelled him to help load all this food onto trucks for their use. Months before, 100-150 supply trucks, that might have been crammed with this food and equipment, were driven into north Bataan empty. Even there they might have loaded 2000 cases of canned food at Tarlac supply depot or vast stocks of rice abandoned at Cabanatuan. Some food was seized in these various places by individual Americans who never turned it in, much more fell to the Japanese, and the invaders destroyed some of it during bombing raids. For years afterwards there were wrangles about why these immense stocks of food had been largely overlooked; about how much of what had been issued, when, and to whom; and how much had been used, destroyed, or allowed to fall to the enemy. I cannot pretend to know who should be blamed, and in what degree, for the whole fatal foul up. Most likely it was due to nothing more complex than the incompetence, panic, and muddle so evident everywhere in the Philippines in the first weeks of the war.

On January 8, 1942 there was about 3000 tons of canned meat and fish in the peninsula, supplemented by inadequate supplies of rice. This constituted rations for 100,000 men for thirty days. Without control of the sea, air, or highways we could get no more. (Rickety planes, which we called the Bamboo Fleet, would occasionally fly in pittances from Cebu and other southern islands, but the amounts were insignificant in the context of the whole campaign.) On January 8 everyone was put on half rations, some 2000 calories per day. This was subsequently cut to 1500 calories in February and 1000 in March (at a time and under conditions when men needed 3500-4000 calories to maintain their health and strength.)

Hunger brings out the worst in people. It has been alleged that individual men and units cheated on food in every way possible: they stole, hijacked, and hoarded food, and submitted inflated rosters, all

17

in a desperate effort to fill their shrinking bellies. Perhaps they did. If so, it would not be surprising. Still, I must record that I did not see such conduct on an appreciable scale. It was common knowledge that rear echelon troops usually ate better than those on the front lines and that the Corregidor garrison was better fed than the men on Bataan. Beyond that I cannot generalize. It has also been charged that much bitterness developed between Filipino and American soldiers in the front lines because the Filipino soldiers, being smaller physically, received smaller rations. If this was true I never knew it, though I was not in a good position to observe since my career in the infantry lasted only a few days. Most of the Americans and Filipinos I saw got on well.

Our semi-starvation diet began to undermine my strength and energy noticeably after about three weeks. Like everyone else, I tried to do something about it. I scrounged for bananas in the jungle, and found quite a few. Occasionally I found a few mangoes. Now and then I was able to get on the Conopus, a submarine repair ship anchored off Mariveles, and get a few cans of sweetened condensed milk. When it was boiled in the can and then mixed with shredded coconut the result was a rich, tasty luxury. Unhappily, I couldn't get to the Canopus very often. Many men formed hunting parties. They scoured settlements and jungle alike to kill and eat anything that moved: chickens, domestic pigs, wild pigs, deer, carabao, and cavalry horses; soon followed by dogs, cats, monkeys, iguanas, even snakes. I never joined any of these hunting expeditions though on occasion I helped eat what had been gleaned. I drew the line on snakes, but this required no exceptional fastidiousness since I never saw more than three or four snakes during my whole tour in the Philippines. One of them was crawling one day on the ceiling of Ed Dyess' tent. In the best Texas frontier tradition Ed brought it down with one shot from his .45. To my knowledge, it did not end on anyone's menu. Iguana I tried once. It tasted good, rather like chicken, but iguanas were so scarce on Bataan that they were negligible as a potential supplement to regular rations. Many carabao were killed and eaten though the energy required to consume carabao meat counterbalanced whatever nourishment was secured. Though these huge, patient beasts were valuable draft animals, their meat was hard, stringy, and leathery even when it had been soaked in salt water and pounded remorselessly. This was particularly true of old carabao, and most of those on Bataan were senior citizens. Ed Dyess said that the best recipe for carabao was to boil it in a pot with a stone. When the stone melted the meat was cooked. Our main fare was either canned salmon or this indestructible carabao, supplemented by steadily diminishing allotments of rice. Of the latter, one wit remarked, "Rice is the greatest food there is. Anything you add to it improves it." Another observed to a friend that the quality of the rice must be deteriorating since the worms in it were not as fat as they had once been.

If hunger was the most important cause of the eventual fall of Bataan diseases were a close second. Our two worst medical scourges were malaria and dysentery. Both are wearing, wasting maladies that sap vitality and enervate the human spirit. Most of the time at least half of the men had malaria; perhaps 80% did when surrender came.

For this sorry condition there was little excuse. I never received a medical briefing for the tropics and, so far as I could tell, nobody else in the Army Air Corps did either. Though the Philippines are simultaneously saturated with malaria and close to the Dutch East Indies, the world's foremost quinine producing area, stocks of quinine were pitifully inadequate. The same was true of mosquito nets, shelter halves, and blankets. Once the Japanese swept over the East Indies, in the first month of war, Allied access to quinine was cut off. Eventually, British and American scientists developed an adequate substitute in atabrine, but this took considerable time. Meanwhile the U.S. Government responded to the crisis in a way best termed "interesting." Washington negotiated an agreement with Costa Rica to plant 2,000,000 cinchona seedlings there, though it would be from fifteen to twenty years before the resulting trees would produce the bark from which quinine is derived.

I was lucky. I got malaria only later, in prison camp. On Bataan I was vexed chiefly by persistent dysentery and one bad case of dengue fever. The latter malady was like a severe attack of flu, in its early stages. I experienced intense pain behind my eyes. Chills and fever then alternated for two or three days. Finally, I entered a longer stage in which my muscles ached and all my bones felt like they were being broken.

The misery produced by hunger and disease was accentuated by shortages of hospital supplies and clothing, and by myriads of flies, lice, bedbugs, and mosquitoes. Hanging over everything were enormous clouds of choking dust and a horrendous, everlasting stench rising from filth of every variety. The grimmest places were the hospitals. Most of us could at least get around and look after our needs most of the time. Not the luckless patients who were packed into the primitive field hospitals. There they moaned or screamed in pain from wounds and diseases, or both, that the medical staff could do little about from lack of drugs and equipment. I never returned unshaken from a visit to a hospital.

While I was flying reconnaissance in south Bataan the ground war heated up in the north. In war, blunders are seldom confined to one side. We were lucky that both General Homma, the Japanese Commander in the Philippines, and his superiors in Saigon and Tokyo, misjudged the situation on Luzon in several important particulars. In its first two weeks the Japanese campaign went so well that

19

Field Marshal Terauchi in Saigon decided that Homma would not require the entire fifty days that had been allotted for the conquest of the Philippines. Consequently, many of his best troops were detached and sent to bolster the invasion of Java. They were replaced by mediocre soldiers originally slated merely for garrison duty. The Japanese had already missed opportunities to destroy most of the American and Philippine forces as the latter had raced headlong around the north end of Manila Bay into Bataan. Now they were confident that even their new third rate troops could smash their way down Bataan's east coast and drive 25,000 demoralized Filamericans into the sea.

Now our position was precarious, to be sure, but it was not nearly as hopeless as the enemy assumed. To start with, the Bataan peninsula is naturally strong defensively. It is about 35 miles long, north to south, and 15-20 miles wide. Running down its middle is the southern end of the Zambales mountain range, whose highest peaks are Mt. Natib (4220 feet) in north Bataan and Mt. Bataan (4700 feet) in the extreme south. In between are many lesser peaks. The foothills of the range fall sharply into the seas on the western side. On the eastern side swampy, cultivated lowlands several miles wide separate the mountains from Manila Bay. The mountains are steep, rocky, and indented with scores of deep ravines and rushing streams. All of the peninsula, save for a few villages and the cultivated lands, is covered with dense tropical rain forest. Some huge trees tower hundreds of feet in the air. In 1941 a hard surfaced highway ran from Manila around the north end of Manila Bay. It then became a dirt road down the east coast of Bataan to Mariveles at the tip of the peninsula. From here it meandered up the west side of the peninsula for some twenty-five miles where it simply stopped. There was one cobblestone crossroad that ran east-west across Bataan about fifteen miles north of Mariveles between the foothills of the two extinct volcanoes, Mt. Natib and Mt. Bataan. Otherwise, only obscure jungle trails penetrated this forbidding primeval wilderness.

Bataan had only two natural weaknesses. In the north the slopes of Mt. Natib and environs were so steep and difficult to negotiate that defenders on one side of it could not cooperate with, or even maintain contact with, those on the other side. And of course Bataan was a cul de sac. From its southern end there was no place to retreat.

Pouring into this natural, if flawed, stronghold were about 100,000 assorted American infantrymen, engineers, sailors, grounded airmen, Filipino police, Philippine Army regulars, and civilians; not the mere 25,000 the Japanese had assumed. Most of the troops were badly trained and poorly equipped, to be sure, and the Americans had not had time to fortify Bataan properly, but these deficiencies were less desperate than the Japanese had supposed. Our troops were disorganized but not demoralized, and more equipment had been salvaged than the Japanese thought.

Most of this force, numerically, consisted of Philippine Army troops. Some American officers regarded them with contempt. One grumbled that they were good at only two things: saluting and eating three meals a day. When the war began that judgment was sadly accurate; but also cruelly unjust, for the men were not unwilling to learn. The troubles were elsewhere. Nobody had ever figured out how to deal with the training and command problems posed by the dozens of dialects the men spoke. Worse, time had been too short. Most of the Filipino common soldiers had been through nothing more demanding than a few months of leisurely instruction in close order drill. None, in any rank, had ever had any combat experience. Most had never even fired their antiquated rifles. They had little artillery and only a few third rate tanks.

Personally, I was always impressed by the loyalty of these men. It seemed to me that all they lacked was training. Their brothers, the Philippine Scouts, who were part of the American Army and who had been properly trained, were respected by American officers for their bravery, skill, and doggedness. In fact, during the Bataan campaign, Philippine Army troops did improve appreciably as they gained combat experience though they had neither the time nor the opportunity to become first rate soldiers.

Still other Filipinos proved invaluable to the American and Filipino armies. They were primitive peoples, Igorot mountaineers from north Luzon and Negrito tribesmen from around Clark Field. They adapted quickly to the terrain of Bataan and became guides and scouts of amazing skill.

When the Japanese began their initial attacks around Mt. Natib early in January they still clung to their prewar conviction that the decisive battle for Luzon would be fought somewhere near Manila. Consequently, they did not push hard enough. American and Filipino resistance was surprisingly stiff. The defenders inflicted eight casualties on the Japanese for each one they suffered in return, and the invaders began to succumb to heat, hardship, and disease. By the end of January the Japanese offensive had ground to a halt. The invaders had lost 7000 men from fighting, and had another 10,000 sick. Moreover, their commanding officer was on the verge of a nervous collapse. Six weeks would pass before they would be ready to attack once more.

While these struggles were taking place in north Bataan we in the south were not vacationing. Beginning January 17, the Japanese made four amphibious landings on peninsulas on the southwest coast of Bataan. One was on Longoskawayan Point, only two miles west of Mariveles. Rumors circulated that other Japanese had slipped into the area anywhere from two to five years before. Supposedly, they had then secretly built concrete gun emplacements and cached food and ammunition underground, all in anticipation of future war. Like the stories about Japanese agents "marking" targets around Clark Field and Manila, I heard all these tales but I never saw any evidence for any of them. The official U.S. Army History says the invaders were pushed out of the area before their own higher headquarters even knew they had landed. This hardly supports any supposition that they were only now implementing some scheme they had carefully worked out before the war. Our ground troops said most of the Japanese they saw seemed at least as confused as our side; like us, lost in the jungle most of the time.

Opposing the invaders was a motley aggregation of U. S. infantry, sailors, marines, and "airmen who had lost their planes," supplemented by Philippine Scouts, Philippine Army regulars, and constabulary forces. The airmen were mainly members of my old 21st Pursuit Squadron, commanded by Dyess. Though some of them were overheard still inquiring how to fire their rifles, even after having undergone instant infantry "training," the locale vexed them more than unfamiliarity with the tools of infantrymen. The jungle was incredibly dense and crisscrossed with streams. Heat and humidity were paralyzing. In this tropical hell a fierce struggle raged for more than two weeks. Gradually Filipino and American forces forced the enemy back to the brink of sheer cliffs that fell off to bare beaches below. Here the unprotected Japanese could be simultaneously bombed and strafed from the air, shelled by artillery based on Corregidor only a few miles to the east, and riddled by naval guns on U.S. small craft standing offshore. The carnage was frightful. Many Japanese soldiers were so desperate and panicky that they leaped off the cliffs to their deaths. Others scrambled down the face of the cliffs and crawled into caves. There, their fate was grim. Either they were decimated by machine gun fire directed at them by Dyess, Lieutenant I.B. (Jack) Donaldson, and others of the 21st, in the offshore boats, or they were blown to bits by dynamite lowered over the cliffs by Philippine Scouts.

We pilots got into the battle too. Somehow our Intelligence got some remarkably accurate information: on February 1 at about 10:30 P.M. a Japanese ship would tow thirteen landing barges, crowded with 1000 troops, into nearby Aglaloma Bay. At the appointed hour our shore batteries abruptly shone their searchlights onto the barges, turning them into sharp silvery silhouettes against the black waters of the South China Sea. As targets they were perfect. The other pilots and I, singly and in two-ship formations, flew back and forth over them, no higher than 200 feet, strafing every barge repeatedly, from end to end, with .50 caliber machinegun bullets until we ran out of ammunition. Most of the barges sank. It seemed to me at the time that every last enemy soldier must have died either from the gunfire or from drowning, though many years afterward I read an account that stated that about 400 Japanese troops did manage to get ashore, where all but three were soon killed by our troops. This is the only estimate I have ever seen that presumed to be more than a guess. All things considered, the battle of Aglaloma Bay was one of the most effective operations undertaken by our meager Philippine Air Force. For me it was the most satisfying.

When it was all over, around 2:30 A.M., General George was ecstatic. He grabbed each of us in a Russian-style bear-hug, and recommended all of us for Silver Stars.

The sweeping, if local victory, coming amid so many larger disasters, was a great tonic for our forces. It was especially so for the "beach defenders," my buddies in the 21st and 34th Pursuit Squadrons. They acquitted themselves splendidly in the unfamiliar role of infantrymen and seagoing machine gunners, even though the price had not been low. We were all saddened when several men in my old outfit were either killed or grievously maimed by Japanese dive bombers. Of those whom I knew well, Corporal Freeland lost both his legs, Sergeant Harangody lost one leg and Sergeant Fowler was killed. What all of us ought to have pondered was the implication of virtually every Japanese soldier preferring death to capitulation. Before many weeks had passed plenty of us would wish that we too had chosen to fight to the death rather than surrender to our foes.

Long before the end of the Bataan campaign it was obvious that the Japanese were extremely brave soldiers, indeed fanatical in a sense unknown in the western world. If they knew where our land mines were sown they would throw themselves on the mines and detonate them to speed the passage of their comrades. If they encountered barbed, electrified fences they acted similarly. Oftentimes they would do such things as play dead and then shoot Americans in the back, shoot at American soldiers engaged in burying Japanese dead, feign injury and then shoot American doctors who sought to minister to them, or offer to surrender and then mow down U.S. or Filipino soldiers who went out to receive them. One of our best and most respected pilots, Lieutenant Marshall Anderson bailed out of his P-40 on January 19, Japanese pilots shot him and his parachute to pieces, an act which later caused our pilots among Dyess' beach defenders to fight with exceptional zeal against the Japanese on the ground.

Japanese soldiers delighted in infiltrating our lines at night, a tactic which especially unnerved Filipino troops. On these nocturnal excursions they would ambush patrols, murder sentries, pick off officers, and steal food and equipment. Sometimes they would don Filipino or American uniforms to confuse Filamerican troops. Occasionally they would shoot long strings of firecrackers over our lines in the middle of the night in an effort to induce us to fire back and thus reveal our positions. At other times they would employ sound trucks to play nostalgic songs at night, or to broadcast groans, shrieks, or other unearthly noises, all in an effort to keep us from sleeping and to erode our morale. All such actions are part of war, of course, but to us our foes seemed unnecessarily enthusiastic about waging war by every means human ingenuity would devise.

Much worse, it soon became apparent that many Japanese were savagely cruel. While I did not personally witness Japanese atrocities at this stage of the war, many others did and there was much talk about them. Many corpses, some American, some Filipino, floated around the entrance to Manila Bay with their arms and legs tied together, riddled with bayonet stabs. It was equally commonplace to find the bodies of one's comrades, tightly bound, obviously tortured, disemboweled, with their severed genitals stuffed in their mouths, Even Filipino messboys who had worked on the *Canopus* were bayoneted by the Japanese and their bodies piled in a heap onshore.

The effect such Japanese savagery on Americans and Filipinos is not hard to imagine. The Filipinos were particularly infuriated by reports that our foes had mutilated Filipino women. Soon they began to set booby traps, to plan ambushes, and to organize anti-sniper patrols. If they managed to capture a Japanese they would interrogate him with what Steve Mellnick called "oriental practicality." Few Americans took Japanese prisoners at all.

How to react to such enemy cruelties is a good example of the soul searching questions that are an inescapable part of war, both ethically and in the "practical" order. Sidney Stewart, a fellow survivor of the Death March and of Japanese prison camps, admits that he once shot a prisoner. He says he was reluctant to do it but could not take the man with him and was even more reluctant to let him return to the Japanese lines. Apparently, some refinement like "kneecapping" did not occur to him. What I would have done in Stewart's shoes in 1942 I cannot say for sure. I have always been grateful that I never had to make such a painful decision.

Looking back long afterward though I am sure that to respond to enemy savagery in the spirit of "an eye for an eye, a tooth for a tooth," while understandable in human terms, is not an intelligent way to wage war. In war the rational objective is to induce the enemy to surrender on terms of one's own choosing, not merely to kill as many of his soldiers as possible. To gain a reputation for cruelty only causes the foe to be cruel in turn, and fearful in the bargain. In hopeless situations enemy soldiers then fight to the last man, adopting the attitude that "at least I'll take a few with me." If one takes no prisoners no useful information is gotten from the foe. Each battle against him tends to be as hard as the last. This lengthens the struggle and adds to one's own casualties. On the other hand, if one is known to treat prisoners well, enemy soldiers in desperate circumstances have an inducement to surrender and save their lives. A soldier is taught to reveal to his captors only his name , rank, and serial number. If he is wise he will heed the injunction. Indeed, as some have observed, if Eve had responded to the blandishments of the serpent by giving only her name, rank, and serial number, we should still be living in the Garden of Eden. Nonetheless, many people like to talk, many can be led to do so, and some can be frightened into it, all without actual employment of violence. Information gleaned from prisoners of our enemy dispositions, plans, capabilities, and weaknesses can shorten war and reduce their cost. In the treatment of enemy prisoners I do not believe either side fought the Pacific war intelligently, though on our side this was mitigated by the refusal of most Japanese to surrender no matter how hopeless their circumstances.

Many days we did not think about Japanese atrocities or about flying either. We just sat around camp thinking about our empty stomachs. Only occasionally did we attempt an offensive mission. One such instance came early in February when six of us took off at night to strafe Neilson Field near Manila. Though we did not learn of it until long afterward, we came near to being killed due to one of those foul ups which plague all armies. In this case, somebody forgot to notify Corregidor that we would fly over at 8:00 P.M. . Had not General Richard Sutherland, MacArthur's Chief of Staff, guessed correctly that we were Americans rather than Japanese the whole U.S. Far Eastern Army Air Corps probably would have been shot down by the Rock's A.A. batteries.

In the actual attack I flew top cover while the other pilots came in low and strafed. At the time we could only guess whether we had hit anything worth mentioning. Long afterward I learned from Filipino reports that many Japanese planes had been destroyed or damaged, that Japanese casualties had been heavy, and that so much havoc had been wreaked that the enemy had changed his whole defense system around Manila. Had I known this at the time, how much more painful would have been a thought that occurred to all of us pilots in those days, if only we had sixty P-40s instead of six!

Sometime later, around the middle of February, after Neilson Field had been raided and the Japanese driven off the southwest Bataan coast I flew a different sort of mission that left me saddened.

Back in flight training nothing had received greater stress than integrity, that an officer never lied or shirked responsibility. I had had the point brought home to me personally with particular sharpness one weekend in Ontario, California when I was confined to quarters for some misdemeanor which has since slipped my mind. On Saturday night an underclassman had come to me with the information that four of our compatriots were in a mellow condition in a tavern in nearby Pomona. They had no way back to the base, he said, and they wanted me to come and get them. I reminded the messenger that I was confined to quarters. He insisted that I accompany him. Eventually I relented, donned my flying suit and boots (merely because they were handy), and went along in his car. When we arrived at our destination our well fortified brethren refused to leave the tavern unless I went in after them. I hesitated, then entered in full flight regalia. They now insisted that I have a drink with them. Quite some time later all hands were in the street save myself. Since I was in a better state of repair than the others, I had already gotten into the driver's seat in the car. At that awkward juncture a city policeman came by. He took a look at all of us, then asked me, the presumed driver, to get out and walk a straight line along the curb. He was observing me intently when three of our instructors suddenly appeared. I was petrified. Back at the base they could easily make out a report that would wash me out. All my dreams of becoming a military pilot would be shattered. Though I worried for several days not a word was said, then or afterward. Only weeks later did the episode surface. At graduation ceremonies Captain Robert L. Scott, later to be the author of *God Is My Co-Pilot*, publicly asked who was the cadet who had attempted to walk a straight line in full flight gear on the occasion described. I raised my hand. Nothing followed. In retrospect, I was convinced that Scott and others knew who it was and had asked the question on the most public of occasions expressly to test my integrity.

Now my integrity, and that of another, were to be tested in a different way under much more trying conditions. One day I was assigned to undertake a routine reconnaissance mission over the China Sea with an officer much my senior in age, rank, and experience. I had flown on his wing for some time when I spotted two Japanese planes below us. I signaled to my partner. He motioned acknowledgement and flew several circles, but did nothing. Eventually he directed me to follow him home.

I was sorely perplexed. Nobody likes to blow the whistle on a superior, much less to gain a reputation for such conduct. Yet I was certain that a splendid opportunity to strike at the enemy had been deliberately ignored. Finally I concluded that duty compelled me to at least discuss it with General George. The General listened to me carefully, and said little, and quietly reassigned the man elsewhere.

This action was typical of General George. Like Dyess, he was a natural, obvious leader. Unlike many officers, he often consulted his men before making an important decision. When the decision had to be made he invariably acted unobtrusively and with primary concern for humanity and common sense.

General George was always concerned about the welfare of his pilots too. Whenever one of us returned from a mission he was there to meet us as soon as we stepped out of the plane. He would do anything he could to make our lives a little easier. On one memorable occasion he persuaded the nurses from the field hospitals at the tip of the peninsula to join the pilots for a party. He got some alcohol from cooperative medics and even found a piano player. We mixed the alcohol with "lemon powder" of indeterminate origin and character. The resulting drinks would not have taken any prizes for their subtle blend of rich flavors but they did not lack strength. The party was the highlight of the entire Bataan social season, indeed our only entertainment for three months.

Ed Dyess never believed in sitting idle if there was some way to strike at the enemy. On March 2 he learned that several Japanese ships had entered Subic Bay, about thirty miles northwest of us. He persuaded General George to let him go after them. This was in no sense an ordinary mission. Twice Ed attached a 500 pound bomb to a P-40 fighter plane, in a bomb rack designed by a warrant officer and flew off alone to face a Japanese flotilla. The action was typical of him. He could have ordered someone else to go, but his natural inclination was always to spare his men and undertake the most hazardous assignments himself. It was one of the main reasons our whole outfit, officers and enlisted men alike, admired him. In this instance, he did so much damage to both ships and harbor installations by bombing and strafing that Radio Tokyo announced on March 4 that the Bay had been raided by three flights of four engine bombers with fighter escorts.

After two runs at the enemy Ed directed Lieutenants Crellin, Stinson, Burns, Fossey, Crossland, White, Posten, and myself to finish the assault properly with fragmentation bombs. What ensued was one of the hairiest experiences of my life. By now most of the few planes we possessed had been patched together from pieces of previous wrecks. My plane on this occasion carried three thirty pound frag bombs under each wing. I got off routinely, flew to Subic Bay, sighted the half-laden Japanese barges I was supposed to bomb, maneuvered myself into position, and hit the bomb release handle. I glanced down but did not see any splashes. Puzzled, I assumed that I must have missed my targets or looked in the wrong place for the detonations. Disappointed, I headed back towards Cabcaben Field. It never occurred to me that the bombs might not have dropped!

Back at Cabcaben, Captain Ozzie Lunde, the tower observer, radioed me in tones of repressed panic, "Don't land! Your flaps are down! Your bombs are hanging! Bail out!" To say I was unpleasantly startled would be a gross understatement. If even one of the bombs should drop while I was attempting to land the war would be over for me. Yet the last thing I wanted to do was bail out for I was virtually certain to land either in the jungle where I would likely be hung up in the top of some 200 foot tree, or in Manila Bay which had an abundant population of sharks. Moreover, there were Zeros in the vicinity.

When a crisis occurs in the air a pilot cannot ponder a dozen courses of action at his leisure: he must do something and do it quickly. Just why he does a certain thing and not something else he seldom knows for sure, either at the time or afterward. What I did first was instinctive; I said some prayers. At the same time I flew back the few miles from Cabcaben to Mariveles, which had a longer runway. (It was just as well that I did not know that three of the other pilots had preceded me to Mariveles and that all of them had been caught by a strong tail wind and blown off the far end of the runway as they had landed.) I decided not to attempt the usual "three point" landing in which the pilot throttles back the engine and noses the plane up just as its wheels touch ground, for if I made a rough "touchdown" the plane would surely bounce and thereby increase the risk that a bomb would fall off. Instead, I decided to come in "power on," to "touch down." This is an easier way to land, one less likely to jar the bombs, but it requires a longer runway and much breaking, which is hard on tires. The field was lined with onlookers who had already watched my predecessors overshoot the runway following conventional landings. As soon as they saw I was going to come in "power on" they scattered like autumn leaves.

Providentially, my landing was perfect! I touched down at the very near end of the runway, braked hard, and managed to stop the plane before reaching the far end. Miraculously, the bombs remained attached to the racks. Afterward Ed Dyess wrote that I knew how badly we needed the plane and so chose to land it rather than bail out and let it crash. It was generous of him to say this, and of course I did realize how sorely we needed every plane, but my main concern was to save my neck. I just decided that to try to land was a better risk than to use my parachute. My guardian angel rode in with me.

This episode illustrates how many of the hazards of flying owed less to the enemy than to our straightened circumstances and to factors indigenous to the Philippines. As an example of the former, none of the landing strips on Bataan were as long as we pilots would have liked, nor were they laid out ideally. Thus takeoffs and landings were always more dangerous than they would have been in other places. How dangerous was evidenced by what happened to an under classmate of mine, Lieutenant Bob Ibold of Phoenix, Arizona. Bob was a fine pilot and close friend. One day, loaded with bombs, he went off a narrow runway on the takeoff. The bombs exploded, injuring him severely and leaving his face badly scarred. Though he recovered from these injuries, Bob was like so many I knew in the Philippines: he escaped some spectacular death only to perish ignominiously on some dreadful prison ship or in a wretched Japanese camp. In Bob's case it was the latter. After the war his remains were returned to the United States for burial. His parents asked me to serve as escort officer from Fort Worth, Texas to Denver for burial, an honor that moved me deeply.

How considerations peculiar to the Orient could complicate the lives of pilots was illustrated by another episode which nearly killed Lieutenant Bill Baker of St. Louis, one of those who had won a Silver Star with me at Aglaloma Bay. One night Bill came in to land at Cabcaben, a field laid out so that one took off towards Manila Bay and landed towards jungle and mountains. At the last moment for "touch down" a carabao wandered onto the runway directly in Bill's path. In desperation, he gave his plane full throttle. He barely cleared the carabao immediately in front of him, and the trees and hills at the end of the runway. He regained his flying speed, circled, got clearance, and came in to land again, only to have the same carabao saunter out onto the runway again. This time he could not climb fast enough. He hit the mountain with a thunderous crash, amid a blinding flash of light and fire. Somehow he wasn't killed. The next morning when I saw him in the hospital he was swathed in bandages from head to foot, with only peepholes for his eyes. Like Bob Ibold, Bill's luck was bad afterward. He died in a Japanese camp in Akobe.

On March 10, 1942 General MacArthur left Corregidor. Eventually he made his way to Australia. His departure occasioned some bitter remarks about "Dugout Doug" from men who had long envied the Corregidor garrison for what they presumed was the easier life of the latter or who blamed MacArthur for the inadequate defenses of the Philippines. There were also gripes that the General had taken along the family's Chinese maid and, according to "latrine rumors," even a refrigerator. I never shared that discontent. Like most G.I.s at all levels I felt somewhat let down to learn that The Chief was no longer with us, but it seemed to me mere common sense to save him for the rest of the war rather than to let him fall into the hands of the enemy.

Whatever else might be said about MacArthur, he had a marvelous capacity to inspire others. An example of this came only a few days after his departure. Several of us were ordered to fly over Manila and lesser places to drop leaflets designed to keep up the morale of the Filipino people. MacArthur tried to explain to them why he had left. He also called upon them to be courageous, and promised that U.S. forces would return soon to rescue them. "Soon" proved to be three years, but the faith of the Filipinos remained undiminished throughout.

Shortly before General MacArthur left Corregidor he made a

decision that probably saved my life. By early March we had all been on semi-starvation rations for two months. Fewer than half the pilots could fly at all. The rest of us were so exhausted after a mission that we had difficulty getting out of our planes. One day General George went to General Edward P. King, at that time MacArthur's Chief of Artillery, and told him the pilots simply could not fly any longer unless we had proper food. King was later to prove himself an uncommonly courageous man. He must have been persuasive as well, for MacArthur readily agreed to send us extra food from the slim stocks on Corregidor. Dyess then called in several sergeants from our outfit and asked them what the enlisted men would think if the pilots got extra food. The sergeants were quite as aware of the realities of the situation as anyone else and, though famished themselves, accepted the arrangement at once. Ed said later that he had never been more proud to be an American. I was equally touched.

In a couple of days we were feasting on canned corn beef hash, ham, peas, bread, pineapple juice, sugar, and coffee, supplemented by vitamin pills. The effect was miraculous. Our weight, health, and spirits bounded upward. Without this bounty I don't believe I would have survived the Death March. Those of us who got extra food were crucially stronger than most of our comrades during that travail. My normal weight when the war began was about 135 pounds. When Bataan fell I was some fifteen or twenty pounds underweight, thin, and weakened; but nothing like the 85 pound scarecrow I subsequently became in prison camp.

Another event took place at about the same time that affected me deeply. For some time Captain Joe Moore, Commander of the 20th Pursuit Squadron (later Lieutenant General, Senior Air Force Officer in Vietnam), had been flying a light plane at great risk to various southern islands in the Philippines in an effort to get extra food for the pilots. When he could he also brought back mail and Red Cross messages from Cebu. On March 9, Joe delivered the only mail I ever got on Bataan. It brought the news that my wife Devonia had given birth to our first child, a baby girl.

After the costly Japanese attack in north Bataan had bogged down in February there was a "six weeks lull" in the land war. We had no illusions about its significance. We had not been delivered. The enemy was merely making his preparations, this time more carefully, to resume the assault.

By the end of March the shortages of food and medicine that had prostrated so many Japanese troops six weeks earlier had been remedied though only for the time being, as events would show. General Homma now had 50,000 healthy troops, some 15-20,000 of them newcomers, 150 new field guns, sixty bombers and, most significantly, three new senior staff officers. The last reinforcement was a clear indication that Tokyo's patience with Homma's slowness had run out. A maximum effort to end the Bataan campaign would begin soon.

Opposing this host were some 80,000 Americans and Filipinos. Despite our superior numbers, our prospects were forlorn. At least three quarters of the men were weak from malaria, 35% had beri beri, 30% had bacillary dysentery, 10% had amoebic dysentery, and many suffered from hookworm. Some 24,000 sick and wounded were jammed into hospitals and aid stations. There was no quinine; indeed little medicine of any kind. Sanitation hardly existed. Daily rations had shrunk to a pitiful ounce-and-a-half of meat or fish and four-to-eight ounces of rice. Only four planes were left: a shot up and patched up P-40, two worn out P-35s, and a fourth plane impossible to designate since it was composed entirely of remnants from other wrecked aircraft. Efforts had been made during the six week lull to train Filipino troops and to strengthen the defenses of south Bataan but the men were too weak and sick to accomplish much.

On April 1 our forces still had plenty of artillery shells to fire at the enemy, but mere numbers were deceptive. As ever early in the war, many were duds. Most of the rest were of only limited effectiveness when fired out of or into dense jungle for they usually hit trees. About all that was left was hope, and it was ebbing fast.

The Japanese grand assault began on April 3. It was Good Friday, the anniversary of the death of Christ, for our side, for them, the anniversary of death of the legendary first Japanese emperor Jimmu Tenno. For me, personally, April was also a special month. I was born on Easter Sunday, April 1, 1918, graduated from flight training in April, became a prisoner in April, escaped from Davao in that month, and was promoted to major then.

The offensive began like a hurricane. Japanese aircraft, unhampered by our four plane air force, rained bombs onto everybody and everything. Enemy artillery roared incessantly. Shells seemed to burst everywhere. It is hard to say which we hated worse, the bombs or the shells. Since I was in the rear area, out of range of Japanese artillery most of the time, I feared bombs more, though a person could at least see Japanese planes coming and anticipate bombs. Infantrymen at the front dreaded artillery fire more because it descended without warning. Soon the incessant shelling and bombing caused fires to break out in dry cane thickets. The heat from the sun and the fires combined was paralyzing. Clouds of dust and smoke hung in the air interminably. Into this enclave of hell the enemy now poured wave after wave of assault troops.

Within five days our forces disintegrated. Leadership and discipline vanished. Sick, starved, dazed, terrified men abandoned arms and equipment and milled about aimlessly. Many were so tired they fell asleep as soon as they sat down. Nobody knew what anyone else was doing since communications had broken down everywhere. Plans made in higher echelons had little relevance to a fluid situation in the field. Defensive positions were abandoned almost as soon as they were occupied. Some Filipino troops had to be driven to their positions at gunpoint. Traffic control vanished as roads became jammed with men and vehicles headed in every direction. The Japanese strafed jungle trails crowded with stragglers pouring southward from battle areas and men from the south hoping to escape captivity by fleeing northward into the bush. Few seemed to care what happened anymore. It was confusion beyond my wildest imagination; bedlam even worse than that at Clark Field on December 8.

This utter chaos that engulfed us in the final stages of the Bataan campaign stimulated much post-war discussion of American and Filipino morale. That morale did collapse in the first days of April is unquestioned. But what of the charges that it had long been sinking towards collapse, that men had jeered openly when MacArthur ordered them to fight and promised reinforcements? That some did compose and sing satirical songs is well known. One of the best of them, written by war correspondent Frank Hewlett went

"We're the battling bastards of Bataan;
No mama, no papa, no Uncle Sam;
No aunts, no uncles, no nephews, no nieces;
No rifles, no guns, or artillery pieces;
. . .And nobody gives a damn."

Another, sung to the tune of "Battle Hymn of the Republic," went thus:

"Dugout Doug MacArthur lies a-shaking on the Rock,
Safe from all the bombers and from any sudden shock;
Dugout Doug is eating of the best food on Bataan,
And his troops go starving on."

"Dugout Doug is ready in his Chris-Craft for the flee
Over the billows and the wildly raging sea.
For the Japs are pounding on the gates of old Bataan,
And his troops go starving on."

Perhaps it was the memory of songs such as these that caused General MacArthur to assert that many of the men on Bataan cursed Japan and American impartially, in the belief that their own country had deserted them. Edgar Whitcomb, who served on Bataan, remarked ambiguously that those who prayed and died there did so for a cause they hoped was right but which they never truly understood. Surveys done after World War II indicated that most G.I.s in that titanic conflict had little real understanding of the issues and interests for which it was waged. Most fought simply because they were ordered to do so, because they did not wish to let down their fellows, or because there was seldom any alternative. When the official Army historian was preparing his volume on the fall of the Philippines he wrote to many officers who had served on Bataan and Corregidor and posed numerous questions to them. He said he received a vast array of answers, but that two themes were prominent in all of them: self-justification, and bitterness at what they believed to be abandonment by their government. . ."

Such appraisals have always seemed to me too dark. Surely nobody ought to have been surprised if hungry, beleaguered men, short of supplies and facing death or imprisonment, should have thought and spoken bitterly of staff officers, rear area troops, "brass hats in Washington," even the merely well fed anywhere, especially when none of these parties came to their aid; but this is not proof that most of us on Bataan had long been near despair. Both the actions and the testimony of many who served there indicate the opposite. I used to hear, for example, that most of the men in the 31st Infantry, especially its Regular Army personnel, were misfits and "eight balls." Possibly they were in the peacetime army; but they certainly were not such on Bataan. There they fought heroically until the final collapse. Sidney Stewart, who went through the whole campaign; Juanita Redmond, an Army nurse who was one of the last people to be taken off Bataan; even Whitcomb, acknowledge that for weeks on end virtually everyone expected U.S. reinforcements to arrive within a few days.

For a long time I, like most of the others, believed that help would come soon. Only gradually did realism intrude. Of course I knew that our Pacific Fleet had been smashed at Pearl Harbor. I had experienced the destruction of Clark Field. Our present plight was evident. Still, sobering though such reflections were, they never caused me to despair. I never supposed that our leaders had betrayed us. It seemed to me that they had done about all they could. I was disgusted in varying degrees by the many kinds of unpreparedness I had seen in so many places but I did not equate it with treason. I did not hate our government or imagine that there were no significant differences between America and Japan. I don't believe most others did either. On the contrary, both at the time of surrender and later on the Death March I saw many men cry when compelled to watch Japanese soldiers desecrate the American Flag. If some G.I.s know little about why the war was being fought, after Dec. 8, 1941 there had been no unclarity in my mind about it. We had been struck dastardly blows by Japan, to which the only possible response was war; and in war sane people try to win. Most people, even professional soldiers, do not really like combat. Most, like myself, were often scared during the war. But, it seemed to me, most others on Bataan accepted the necessity of war, as I did, and bore its burdens reasonably well. Maybe I would have been more disgruntled had I known more fully just how inadequate U.S. defenses were, but even if I had I don't think I would have abandoned all hope that the world's greatest nation would eventually find some way to rescue us. Doubtless some realized quite early that the best we could do was just hang on as long as possible, delay the Japanese, and thereby help our homeland buy time to prepare for a long struggle, but most of us accepted this in our hearts only slowly. Even at the end, nobody wanted to surrender. We had seen and heard too much to have any illusions about the humanity of the Japanese. We surrendered only when further resistance became impossible.

Perhaps the clearest indication of how long I remained hopeful is that the thought of becoming a prisoner of the Japanese did not even cross my mind until a few days before we surrendered. I had thought many times about the likelihood of being killed or wounded, and I surely *should* have pondered the possibility of being made a prisoner of war, but I simply did not do so. What this proves, if anything, I am not sure; the visceral optimism of most Americans perhaps.

A more complex question concerns the kind of information about the war that high political and military authorities chose to divulge. Throughout the Bataan campaign General MacArthur assured us regularly that help from the United States would arrive shortly. He could hardly have believed this. Afterward, Carlos Romulo, who was in charge of MacArthur's press relations, and who regularly broadcast "inspirational" messages of this sort to Filipinos and Americans alike, would only comment evasively that he did not know the truth of the matter himself. Still, it is hard to criticize the Supreme Commander for wanting to encourage his troops. There is no doubt either that such propaganda was important in keeping up the morale of the Filipinos. Long after most of us Americans had at least begun to harbor doubts about these optimistic forecasts, the faith of the Filipinos remained high, doubtless because they had revered MacArthur in the years before the war.

Even now I am still not sure what to think of such practices. It is disheartening to reflect that such exaggerations and evasions show with devastating clarity what our rulers, civilian and military, really think of us. In wars and other major crises, governments at once assume not that they should tell the truth but they must "calm" and "reassure" everyone, that ordinary people have to be fed a constant diet of good news. Whether such news reflects reality is, to the rulers, unimportant. That democratic governments act thus as readily as authoritarian regimes indicates that, at bottom, all rulers regard their people as children and not very bright or brave ones at that.

The crux of the matter, though, is not whether we should be indignant but whether our masters are correct. P.T. Barnum, the nineteenth century circus impresario, once said, "Nobody ever went broke because he underestimated public taste." Regardless of the cynicism to that remark, it is sadly instructive to observe what certain professionals assume about the public. Politicians have to estimate accurately the temper, taste, and level of intelligence of most people or they lose elections. Advertisers must reckon these matters accurately or they do not sell the wares of their employers. Entertainers must judge them correctly or they draw no crowds. Reflection of the whole phenomenon is not heartening. In our particular case, though I am loathe to admit it, I believe that without the glowing rumors and gilded news the Bataan campaign would have been shorter. Most people simply must have something to hope for, no matter how illusory the hope may be objectively.

Most journalists are remarkably single minded about their proper role in dilemmas of this sort. They assume, in wartime and peacetime alike, that they have a natural right to learn all they can about everything, everywhere, and to publicize it at their own discretion. If they grudgingly cooperate with military censors they often regret it afterward and complain that they have been reduced to mere propaganda agents. Like so many of humanity's problems, those involved in manipulating news appear to have no good solution. There is only a choice of evils.

When it became obvious to all that the end was near on Bataan, Ed Dyess received a phone call from Lieutenant Colonel K.J. Gregg, a Senior Air Officer left on the peninsula. He told Ed to get on board an incoming plane and fly south to the island of Mindanao for eventual evacuation to Australia. I was with Ed in his command post at the time and heard his reply: "We haven't surrendered yet. I can't leave my men." Shortly afterward he took me aside and began to speak to me quietly, almost solemnly. He said he knew I was married and had two daughters (my wife had a child by a previous marriage). Then he asked me if I wanted to leave. I parried the question by asking him what he intended to do. He repeated what he had told Colonel Gregg: "I'm staying." I replied at once that I would stay too. Later that day Ed made the same offer to Leo Golden, who was also married and who had a son. He got the same response.

I would like to claim that Leo and I acted out of some profound sense of military duty, but that was hardly the case since, whatever our dispositions, our military duty was not clear. Even had we been able to foresee the future, would it have been our "duty" to stay on to the end and become prisoners of the Japanese in the expectation, or the off-chance, that we might set some example of personal heroism for future generations to admire? But of course we might not act heroically at all! At least as likely, we might merely be killed. Would it have been more truly our "duty" to do the more natural thing: save our skins and hope to come back to fight the Japanese another day? I don't know about Leo, but I did not even think of subtleties of this sort. I chose to stay for the most direct of reasons: my deep respect for Ed Dyess, the man who had already taught me so much about loyalty, leadership, unselfishness, and courage. If remaining on Bataan was good enough for Ed, it was good enough for me.

Ed's conduct here contrasted sharply with that of some others who were prominently placed. I was amazed to see some colonels pull rank on each other ruthlessly in order to get on board anything leaving Bataan in its last days. I suppose I shouldn't have been: self-preservation is the most powerful of all human instincts.

On April 8, the day before Bataan surrendered, I had my last chance to escape. Ed asked me to undertake a reconnaissance mission to some islands far to the south. I was to take a P-40 with a belly tank of gasoline to extend my range as far as possible, and to leave at dawn the next morning. My objective was to look for Japanese naval forces along my flight route. If I saw any I was to plot them on my navigational chart, showing their number, type, and location, which way they were heading, and the time. When I reached the island of Culion, perhaps 150 miles south of Bataan, I was to check my fuel. If I still had more than half a tank I was to continue the reconnaissance southward until only half a tank remained. Then I was to turn at once and fly straight back to Bataan. Any data I collected would be used primarily to establish safe routes for evacuating Important People from Corregidor to locations south.

Sometimes I slept soundly before missions, sometimes not. This time I couldn't sleep for hours from uncertainty, foreboding, and endless second guessing. I knew Bataan was about to collapse. What would come after that? The thought was gut-wrenching, yet I was unable to imagine anything clearly. I wondered if I would ever see my newly-born daughter whose name I didn't even know. I thought about my wife Devonia, and my step-daughter Patricia, and how few had been the days we had been able to spend together after our marriage in June, 1941. Had I been mad to stay on Bataan when Ed Dyess would have sent me out? Even now, should I quietly forget about returning to Bataan and simply fly on south to Cebu, or even Mindanao, if my fuel allowed? When the officer of the guard awakened me at dawn I could not have slept much, and I felt like I had not slept at all. I was never less ready, mentally and emotionally, to fly a mission.

What carries a person through at such times had to be training, habit, example. I remembered what I had been taught in flying school about self-discipline. I thought about what Ed Dyess would have done in the same circumstances. By the time I was dressed the adrenalin was flowing to such a degree that I could not eat breakfast. I started towards the revetment where my P-40 was parked. Suddenly a whole family of monkeys who had miraculously escaped the stew pot ran across the trail ahead of me single file. My nerves were so taut they startled me half out of my wits. In mystery novels they would have composed a collective omen of some sort, but if they were so here I missed the point. Now, forty years later, I cannot imagine why I still remember them so vividly.

The flight itself was anticlimactic. For a time it was positively enjoyable during interludes when I could keep from thinking. Up there at 10,000 feet over the China Sea the sky was clear and blue and the air was balmy. No bombs were falling, no artillery shells were bursting overhead. There were no foxholes. Nobody, racked with awful cramps of dysentery was racing or crawling for a vacant space at a latrine.

But such reveries were quickly interrupted by others more grim and compelling. Would I get back to Bataan at all? If so, what would I find? Zeros waiting to jump me? Would I have enough gasoline left to have any chance against them? How much more secure I would feel if a couple of my buddies were flying formation with me now; doubly so whenever we neared Bataan again!

I saw some Japanese ships along the way and recorded the required data on my charts. At length I looked at my fuel gauge. It was halfway down. I had to make, or not make, that dreaded 180 degree turn. The temptation to keep going nearly overwhelmed me; but I turned, set course for Cabcaben airfield. I was almost back when the action started. The tower observer radioed me that the field was under attack, that I should not try to land but should circle around Corregidor where I would be under the protection of its guns. This was precisely what I had prayed would NOT happen. It was not that circling Corregidor was particularly hazardous but that I was almost out of fuel. There were three airfields on Bataan peninsula. Two of them, Bataan and Cabcaben, were so close together that enemy pursuit at either made landing at the other extremely dangerous. The third field, Mariveles, at the southern tip of the peninsula, was only three or four minutes away. I had just decided to try to land there when I got the All Clear from Cabcaben. The signal must have set a world's record for brevity for just as I touched down a new Japanese attack began. At the risk of his life a maintenance man dashed out and towed my plane away. I sprinted for a foxhole, tripped over a tent stake, and fell into the foxhole, a sequence of events quite in harmony with our generally distracted condition by then.

That afternoon the enemy broke though our lines. Here was a perfect opportunity for Ed Dyess to take my plane, fly the last mission out, and avoid becoming a prisoner of war. Instead he assigned the plane to I.B. (Jack) Donaldson with orders to drop bombs on Japanese lines, then fly south to Ilo. Thus Donaldson got away while the rest of us were captured the next day. My flight had been the last by a P-40 into Bataan.

When General MacArthur escaped to Australia he left orders to fight to the end. Though one general, Clifford Bluemel, actually did try to counterattack, nothing came of it. By now despair engulfed everyone and disintegration had proceeded so far that to reverse it was impossible. Everywhere units were mixed together hopelessly. Men either shuffled about aimlessly or adopted the suicidal expedient of fleeing into the jungle. On the big southern island of Mindanao, where the enemy controlled little more than the seacoast, many did escape into the jungle, where they joined guerrilla bands and continued the war. On Luzon the situation was different for the Japanese garrisoned every important part of it. I knew only one man who fled into the jungle, did something noteworthy, and survived to tell about it.

Bataan fell on April 9, 1942. General Edward P. King, who had been appointed Commander of the forces on Bataan, knew he would be blamed for any capitulation; that he might even be court-martialled after the war. Undaunted, he faced facts: the situation had become hopeless. To save the lives of Americans and Filipinos in the field and in hospitals he sent emissaries, carrying white flags, towards the Japanese lines.

It was an omen of things to come that the emissaries were repeatedly bombed and strafed by Japanese planes. Other disquieting signs appeared in quick succession. General Homma refused to meet , insisting that he would deal only with his equal, General Johnathan P. Wainwright, the Commander of all U.S. and Filipino forces in the Philippines. Homma's Operations Officer, Colonel Nakayama, saw King instead. When asked for a guarantee that Japan would honor the provisions of the Geneva Convention dealing with the treatment of prisoners the only reply he elicited, ultimately, was "We are not barbarians." Despite this bleak beginning, King decided to take a chance that the conquerors would in fact honor the Geneva Convention even though they had never signed it.

My personal reaction was relief that the ordeal was over at last, followed quickly by second thoughts when Japanese planes continued to bomb and strafe after the surrender had taken place. Confirmation of our barely stifled doubts and fears was to come with dismaying speed.

Ed Dyess had refused to leave Bataan before April 9 because he considered it his duty to stay until his men were evacuated. Once surrender came, however, he felt his obligations had ceased. Now, like everybody else, he wanted to get out. Somehow, in the late afternoon he got a command car. He wanted to get to Mariveles because he had heard that a submarine or B-17 might be there to evacuate the pilots. Five of us and a driver started off through Little Baguio.

Of all the distracted, frenetic American activity on this last day of the war on Bataan, the only part of it that could be called military was wholesale demolition. Amid constant Japanese bombing and shooting, groups of G.I.s raced around in the half-light and darkness burying records, flags, supplies, and souvenirs taken from the Japanese. When gasoline tanks were set afire they exploded with horrendous noise and force. Fireballs rolled up mountainsides and culminated in huge, ugly, terrifying mushroom clouds. One explosion actually tore the top off a hill, raining rocks and chunks of earth as big as houses into Mariveles harbor. Shrapnel, either demolitions or from enemy bombs, whizzed about continuously. When we drove into this inferno of fires and explosions it seemed to me that the end of the world had come. As our driver barreled recklessly across the Dantesque landscape everything came to a grotesquely fitting climax: all of South Bataan was shaken by a sharp earthquake.

Somehow we got to Mariveles early in the morning of April 10, thoroughly unraveled and exhausted. We were anxious to contact the rumored submarine or B-17 but soon realized that they were phantoms. Dyess then told Leo Golden and me to look for food and whatever gasoline had not been blown up by the demolition squads, while he and Lts. W.G. Powell and L.A. Powell searched for a boat in which he hoped we could escape to Corregidor and eventually to the south. Leo and I located one fifty-five gallon drum of gasoline, another about half-full, and three or four cases of canned tomatoes. It mattered little, for when we rejoined Ed and the Powells they had been unable to get the boat.

Nothing was left now but to try to rejoin our outfit. Cold reality enveloped us within a few minutes. We met a Japanese tank and staff car. We stopped at once, threw up our hands, and waved white handkerchiefs. A Japanese soldier standing in front of the tank motioned for us to drive closer. We did, and again alighted with our hands up. A Filipino interpreter who was with the soldier complained that we were violating surrender instructions because we still wore sidearms. The Japanese then jumped down and, without a word, proceeded to club Dyess mercilessly. For good measure he then stole two rings of mine, a crash bracelet, and a pen and pencil set. Then he motioned for us to get back into the car and resume driving towards our outfit. As we proceeded our captor pulled close to our vehicle, smiled inexplicably, and threw my jewelry back into our car. But as soon as we stopped other Japanese lined us up in groups of 100 and stole my possessions all over again, save only my flying ring which I managed to tie inside my underwear. I learned later that an ex-Notre Dame football player, Mario (Motts) Tonelli, who subsequently became a close friend, had a similar experience. When he surrendered, his Notre Dame ring was stolen by a Japanese enlisted man. A Japanese officer observed the act, smashed the enlisted man in the face, and returned the ring to Tonelli, explaining that he had graduated from USC in 1935, the same year Tonelli had played in his last USC-Notre Dame football game.

Such episodes as these indicated the unpredictable, even whimsical, side of the Japanese. though their military tactics were often predictable, when it came to personal conduct one never knew what they might do. They could be kind, indifferent, savage, reasonable, unreasonable, all by fits and starts, in no discernible pattern. Later, on the Death March, Dyess, in rage and bewilderment at the mercurial dispositions of our guards, threw his flight ring, which meant a great deal to him, into Manila Bay simply to prevent any Japanese from ever getting it. I tore up a cherished picture of my wife for the same reason.

Maybe I should have reflected that for the preceding eighteen months I had enjoyed a phenomenal run of luck. I had escaped death several times in flight training; had survived the Clark Field holocaust, Japanese Zeros, bombs, and bullets; had emerged unscathed through American anti-aircraft fire; cheated the Grim Reaper on all my Bataan flying assignments; brought in a plane loaded with bombs where three predecessors had gone off the end of the runway; and had even avoided dying from disease or starvation. But good fortune does not last forever. Lady luck looked away from me the next year.

In a narrow military sense the battles of Bataan and Corregidor were the most humiliating defeats ever inflicted on American arms up to that time. Their importance though lay elsewhere, in the realms of psychology and mythology. Like the defense of the Alamo, they created a legend. As a species we human beings are fortunate in that we tend to gradually forget defeat, disaster, pain, injury, and unhappiness. In addition, Britons and Americans seem to have a special cast of mind which enables them to eventually convince themselves that some unmitigated disaster was really a glorious chapter in the nation's history. Thus Bataan came to be regarded as a symbol of indomitable American courage, the soil from which a generation of national heroes sprang.

Perhaps it was just as well, for we badly needed some national heroes early in 1942. Our civilian and military leaders knew this too, as did the ubiquitous journalists. Among them they created the legend of Colin Kelly, the first Congressional Medal of Honor winner in the war. Soon after Kelly's death I was able to visit his co-pilot, Lieutenant Robbins, who was in the hospital recovering from extensive burns suffered when their plane was hit. Robbins, who parachuted to safety, told me what had happened. They had dropped some bombs near a Japanese ship; indeed they had probably hit it, though they did not sink it. On their way back to Clark they were shot down by some Zeros. Kelly ordered his crew to bail out and then rode the plane down to his death. He was a brave man and a capable pilot but his real accomplishments were less than those of several others who flew the same day. Yet he became an instant legend because those highly situated thought we needed a legend at a time when the war news had been consistently bad.

NOTE: For varied explanations of the food shortage on Bataan and assertions about American and Filipino responses to it Cf. Melvyn McCoy and S.M. Mellnick, as told to Welbourn Kelley, *Ten Escape from Tojo*, p. 36, Louis Morton, *The Fall of the Philippines*, pp. 368-376; Stanley Falk, *Bataan: The March of Death*, pp. 34-35; and John Toland, *The Rising Sun*, p. 266.

Colonel Ernest Miller, a tank commander on Bataan, pays an especially generous tribute to the Philippine Scouts in *Bataan Uncensored*, pp. 145-147, 200, 204-205. Most Filipinos considered membership in the Scouts to be a high honor.

Louis Morton, the Official Army Historian, gives a detailed account of the savage ground fighting that preceded the battle of Aglaloma Bay. Cf. *The Fall of the Philippines*, pp. 298-316, 338. The claim that 397 out of 400 Japanese soldiers died rather than surrender at Aglaloma Bay is made by John Morrill and Peter Martin, *South From Corregidor*, p. 181.

Sydney Stewart, *Give Us This Day*, pp. 29-37, describes his mixed feelings about shooting a Japanese prisoner.

American morale in the last stages of the Bataan campaign had been judged variously. John Toland, *Not In Shame*, pp. 158, 267-268, 280, and Douglas MacArthur, *Reminiscences*, pp. 135-136, portray it darkly: Louis Morton, *The Fall of The Philippines*, p. 591, only slightly less so. Edgar Whitcomb's comments in *Escape From Corregidor*, pp. 43ff, 67, are more equivocal. One man who was certainly disenchanted, not to say absolutely furious, was General W E. Brougher, the Commander of the 11th Division of the Philippine Army. Brougher spent three years in several Japanese prisons, his Diary, published a whole generation after the war, contains the angry allegation that 20,000 American troops were sent to certain death, or to a living death in prison camps, by high ranking officers who knew the Philippines could not be defended. He called it "a foul trick of deception... played on a large group of Americans by a Commander in Chief and a small staff who are now eating steak and eggs in Australia. God damn them!" D. Clayton James ed., *South to Bataan, North to Mukden: The Prison Diary of General W.E. Brougher*, p. 32. It always seemed to me that the American government and people, rather than MacArthur and his associates, were mainly responsible for the inadequacy of Philippine defenses. Like myself, Sidney Stewart, p. 41, thought the judgments of Toland, General MacArthur, and Morton unduly severe.

Juanita Redmond's observations, like Whitcomb's are open to more than one interpretation, though hers indicate a spirit of resignation rather than anger or despair. She relates that doctors, nurses, corpsmen, and patients alike made bets about how many days it would be before U.S. aid arrived, as though they were afraid to entertain the thought that it might not come. When she and other nurses were told that they must leave for Corregidor they were shocked because they were now forced to believe consciously what they had long known subconsciously must come someday. *I Served On Bataan*, pp. 73-74, 123.

Another American who was as oblivious as I to the possibility of becoming a prisoner was Gwen Dew, a newspaperwoman who went into Hong Kong shortly before the war began. Afterward, she said in *Prisoner Of The Japs*, p. 105, that she had known that the outbreak of war was a distinct possibility, had realized that she might be killed or wounded, and had accepted this; but that had even the possibility of being imprisoned by the Japanese occurred to her, she probably would have been unable to face it.

Chapter Three

The Bataan Death March

Prisoner of War! . . . it is . . . a melancholy state. You are in the power of your enemy. You owe your to life to his humanity, and your daily bread to his compassion. You must obey his orders, go where he tells you, stay where you are bid, await his pleasure, possess your soul in patience.—Winston Churchill, *A Roving Commission.*

Prisoners see war without the glory and the glitter. The comradeship of the combat zone is far from them. They meet brutal men, and their own fiber coarsens.—Frederic R. Stevens, *Santo Tomas Internment Camp*, p. 331.

As THESE QUOTATIONS INDICATE, the lot of prisoners of war has seldom been happy. The Ancient Romans used to chain prisoners together and parade them through their capital city in triumphal marches. During the Third Crusade at the end of the twelfth century the English King Richard the Lionhearted once massacred 2000 Moslem captives because the Egyptian sultan Saladin had displayed typical oriental slowness in negotiation. Saladin retaliated by killing all the Christian knights he had taken. Yet the two rulers were on such good personal terms that when Richard fell ill Saladin sent him his personal physician accompanied by presents of fruit and ice. It was only their prisoners that each regarded as mere pawns. Acting similarly in the chivalric tradition, another English King, Henry V of Shakespearean fame, on the eve of the battle of Agincourt (1415) ordered that all French prisoners in English hands, save only noblemen, should have their throats cut. The noblemen were spared because they could be held for ransom. In fact, one of the reasons England waged the Hundred Years War (1337-1453) against France was because restless English knights hoped to grow rich from capturing their French opposite numbers and holding them for ransom. Swiss troops of that era were regarded by contemporaries as especially fearsome because they showed little interest in this method of growing rich: they simply killed captured knights. Maiming and mutilation of prisoners was commonplace, for a variety of reasons. The age old hatred of Greeks and Bulgars for each other was exemplified by the action of the Byzantine Emperor Basil II in 1014 after a battle on the River Struma. He divided 14,000 captured Bulgarian soldiers into groups of 100, blinded 99 of each 100 men, put out one eye of each remaining hundredth man, and left it to the half blind 140 men to lead their 14,000 totally blind comrades back to Bulgaria. In the late middle ages armored knights who fought in the accepted "chivalrous" manner, on horseback, clad in armor, bearing lance or sword, looked with boundless hatred and contempt on the commoners who fought on the ground with such deadly new missile weapons as the crossbow, longbow, and primitive musket. With such weapons, low-born men could kill mounted "gentlemen" before the latter could come close enough to strike back. The usual response of knights who survived was to murder any of the foot soldiers who were captured or, more commonly, to castrate them or cut off their hands. Gian Paolo Vitelli, a famous late fifteenth century mercenary soldier, routinely blinded and cut off the hands of any musketeers he captured. Barbarism towards prisoners was routine when the enemy was perceived as scarcely human, as was the case in the wars that raged intermittently for centuries between the Turks and the Christians of Balkan Europe. Prince Eugene of Savoy (1663-1736), one of the outstanding soldiers of modern times, had in his private library a number of books on military subjects bound in the tanned skins of Turkish spahis and janissaries.

Not until the eighteenth century, a more civilized age than our own, did it become customary to treat prisoners humanely. After the battle of Narva in 1700, most of the Russian prisoners taken by the victorious Swedes simply walked away after the Swedes became too drunk to guard them. The youthful King of Sweden, Charles XII, who loved war so much that he was known in his own lifetime as The Madman of the North, then received the few Russians who remained and gave them back their arms. To him, war was sport. Sixty years later, the Duke de Broglie, then a Marshal of France, took the English Marquis of Granby prisoner after the battle of Corbach. He then sent Granby to the de Broglie castle where he lived as an honored guest of the family until the Seven Years War ended three years later. In gratitude for such good treatment Granby had his portrait painted by Joshua Reynolds, the most prestigious English artist of the day, and presented it to the de Broglie family.

The twentieth century, in this sphere as in so many others, has seen a reversion to the barbarism of ages past. The Nazi Germans froze, starved, and otherwise put to death millions of Russian prisoners, not to speak of countless civilians as well. The Russians replied in kind. Something like 1,000,000 German prisoners of the Russians have never been accounted for at all. Spanish fascists on the Russia front often cut off the noses, ears, fingers, and other appendages of Russians captured in combat. In return, the Russians bayoneted Spanish prisoners, tortured them, mutilated them, nailed their heads to the frozen ground with ice picks, stripped them naked in midwinter, and blew off their heads with hand grenades. The French tortured Algerian rebels in North Africa, and were tortured by them in return. North Koreans maltreated United Nations' prisoners in the Korean War, and North Vietnamese tortured American prisoners atrociously in the Vietnam War. The horrible genocidal massacres of our brutal century; Armenians by Turks, Jews and Slavs by Germans, Hindus and Moslems by each other, East Pakistanis by West Pakistanis, Ibos by Hausas in Nigeria, Cambodians by their own rulers and North Vietnamese, to cite only the more glaring cases have not involved prisoners of war in the narrow sense. Nonetheless, the victims have been in almost exactly the same position as war prisoners: helpless unfortunates in the hands of a powerful enemy whom they cannot ignore and from whom they cannot escape.

If this melancholy recital indicates anything it is that the human tendency to be cruel to our fellows is innate; that the crust of civilization is thin and easily broken, in our age quite as readily as in the past. Against this historical background cruel Japanese treatment of American and Filipino prisoners in World War II does not appear exceptional. But few Americans study the history of other times and peoples with any care, or see anything to be gained by so doing. Thus we are repeatedly surprised when some atrocious or distasteful practice, which has been commonplace in other parts of the world for centuries, is abruptly thrust into our consciousness. A good example was the reaction of Martin Boyle, a Marine taken prisoner on Guam at the beginning of the war. The mere fact of becoming a prisoner of war and being left ravenously hungry for the first time in his life was so shocking that he was unable to remember anything that happened in the next seventeen days.

Now, quite suddenly, with little psychological preparation, I too became a prisoner of war.

The horrors of the Bataan Death March have been described many times. The March was a macabre litany of heat, dust, starvation, thirst, flies, filth, stench, murder, torture, corpses, and wholesale brutality that numbs the memory.

It has long been common knowledge that painful or disagreeable experiences fade in one's mind while pleasant episodes are recalled with clarity. Nonetheless, the degree to which this is true still surprises me. Now, forty years later, I remember many individual incidents on the hellish Death March, I cannot recall their sequence in any but the most general way. Those which are described below did not necessarily happen in the precise order in which they appear here.

45

They are merely the most vivid memories I retain of that satanic week. Unless otherwise indicated, the events described are things that happened to me or that I saw; not just atrocities I heard about or read about afterward.

Something like 75-80,000 men began the Death March, many several days later than others. Since the prisoners were strung out for many miles along the east coast road of Bataan the experiences of different individuals and groups varied considerably. Hence the many differences in accounts of the Death March. During the March itself I had no reason to assume that other prisoners, miles ahead or behind, were being treated any differently than I was or those whom I could see. In prison camps afterward I compared notes with other survivors. Since the war I have read books and articles by survivors, and about them. I now believe that what was endured by those near me on the March was somewhat worse than the average, though not decisively so.

The general impression which overwhelms all others about the Death March is of the savage brutality, the arbitrary cruelty, of our Japanese captors. Of course the March would have been difficult and wearing had the Japanese been humane. Most of us were weak and underweight from three months on short rations and sick with anywhere from one to four tropical diseases. The heat and humidity were fearsome: 95 degrees or thereabouts most of the days, with close to 100% humidity. Since it was the dry season in that part of the world we marched through clouds of dust caused by the constant passage of Japanese vehicles. Only once, near the end of the ordeal, did some rain fall in the night so we could wet our parched mouths and throats, catch some water in our canteens, and cool our burned, feverish bodies. All this would have been bad enough in itself. It was made infinitely worse by the systematic brutality of our guards.

We learned early on the first day what the Japanese had in store for us. We were divided into groups of a hundred and told to march four abreast. Two Japanese guards were assigned to each hundred prisoners. Almost immediately word began to pass through our ranks that a general search was coming; to get rid of anything Japanese. The warning was ominous, and accurate. The guards bore an instant and venomous animosity toward anyone who had any Japanese money or articles. Probably they assumed that such things must have been taken off the bodies of dead Japanese soldiers. I soon heard that an American captain who had Japanese currency in his pockets had been beheaded. Though I did not actually see this atrocity I saw many others. Those with Japanese articles in their possession were battered unmercifully with fists and rifle butts or were bayoneted on the spot. The Japanese loved to use their bayonets. Guards shot or bayoneted to death anyone who could not keep up on the March.

Often they jabbed men callously to force them back into line. Many times they bayoneted Filipinos who tried to help us or who merely appeared alongside the road.

When the guards searched us they picked us clean. Some of the men who came into the P.O.W. camps from Corregidor and elsewhere weeks later were able to bring money, personal affects, even books. Not us. All I managed to hide was my flying ring. A few doctors secreted a little medicine: others had all theirs taken by the conquerors. With their habitual caprice, the Japanese did not look for such things as maps, or orders, or code books, which might have had military value, but merely for loot: watches, rings, currency, medals, and other personal effects.

If there was anything the guards enjoyed more than bayoneting their victims it was beating us with fists and gun butts. I saw American officers forced to stand at attention while Japanese privates beat them in the face without mercy, and then forced them to bow to their tormentors when the battering was finished. I saw a little Filipino beaten to a pulp because he tried to give a drink of water to a dying American. I saw scores of fellow prisoners clubbed into insensibility for some minor infraction of marching discipline. The Japanese particularly loved to beat up big men, perhaps because the sight of towering occidentals intensified their inferiority complexes. Ed Dyess, who was about 6'2", was beaten repeatedly by the guards while I, much smaller, was overlooked most of the time. Anyone who wore a steel helmet was beaten, seemingly because the Japanese regarded helmets as war material. Soon after the March began I suspected that such would be the case and threw my helmet away. Dyess, who was marching with me at the outset, did not, for he wanted to protect his head from the burning sun. A guard came along and knocked his helmet off with a gun butt. He then gave Ed a fierce beating, and kicked him into a ditch. I made a halting gesture to come to Ed's aid and for my pains was kicked back into ranks.

Perhaps the most valuable thing I ever learned in flight training had been to obey orders promptly and cheerfully. I am sure it saved my life when I was a prisoner of the Japanese for realists learned early when dealing with them that it was essential to be obedient and submissive. Lloyd Stinson, a friend and classmate of mine who spent 42 months in prison camps, said the Japanese respected someone who stood up for his rights. Royal Arch Gunnison, an American newspaperman who was interned with other civilians at Santo Tomas in Manila, and later in Shanghai, said patience, persistence, and politeness eventually enabled one to secure concessions from the Japanese. Lloyd and Gunnison must have been around milder and more humane guards than I ever was. Any I ever saw demanded instant and respectful compliance with orders. Any captive of the Japanese who was undisciplined, uncooperative, or rebellious rarely survived to boast about it. I once saw a captain who had been slugged in the face by a guard instinctively clench his fist, then catch himself and snap to attention. It was too late. The guard had seen the momentary gesture. He hammered the captain's face to a pulp.

Within a few hours on our first day our captors took away whatever food we had and refused to give us any in return. Though water from springs and streams was plentiful they would not let us drink it or fill our canteens. Instead they took away the canteens of many prisoners and gave what water some of them contained to their horses. All they would let us drink was the muddy, filthy, scummy water in occasional carabao wallows alongside the road. Even then when men were so close to madness from thirst that they would race to drink this vile liquid, the guards would sometimes club them back into line. Occasionally we would straggle by artesian wells bubbling with cool, clear water. Then some men would truly go mad and rush for them. Their usual fate was to be shot in the back, or beaten unmercifully. One day a case of milk fell off a passing truck. Prisoners swarmed over it like ants. The Japanese leaped in among them, swinging their fists, kicking, and flailing with rifle butts until all the parched and famished wretches had been pounded back into line.

Hunger was nearly as bad as thirst. The first time I got anything to eat was at the end of the third day of the March. It was one rice ball. A maintenance man in our outfit, Jack Donohoe, found a bag of Japanese horse feed, full of weevils. So famished was he and another man that when we stopped for the night they built a fire cooked the mess, and ate it.

Even harder to endure were the purely gratuitous indignities visited upon us by our merciless captors. For instance, a steady stream of Japanese tanks and trucks loaded with combat troops rolled south along the road as we proceeded north. They were being massed in the south for an attack on Corregidor. Japanese soldiers in the trucks would abruptly stick out rifle butts or bamboo sticks in order to hit prisoners in the face as they went by.

Another case related to one of the two hospitals in south Bataan. It had been bombed in the fighting, and many of its patients were scattered out of doors when the March began. Japanese guards swept them up impersonally with the rest of us and marched them down the road. Sick men staggered along for a mile or two. One legged men tried to keep up on crutches. One Filipino with both legs amputated dragged himself through the dust on his stomach, with his arms alone. No Japanese truck ever stopped to pick up such pitiful creatures. They just gradually died on the road or in the ditches, or were shot, bayoneted, or clubbed to death by the guards.

Before we had gone many days there were so many bodies,

both American and Filipino, that the sweet, sickly, overpowering stench of human corpses was always in our noses. Since hundreds of these bodies were found many miles from where any fighting had occurred it was plain that the murders had taken place on the March.

The imaginations of our captors were inexhaustible when it came to devising ways to increase our suffering. They delighted to march us through the hottest part of the day or, if we did not march then, to give us the "sun treatment" instead. This particular atrocity consisted of forcing half-dressed men, most of them without head covering, to sit in the sun for hours, and then stand in the sun for more hours. The experience left one drained physically and in spirit, dehydrated, and half-mad from throbbing, paralyzing headaches. Then, while we sat dazed and starved, the Japanese would mock us by throwing up their hands in imitation of surrender and laughing. Sometimes they promised us food, and then refused to give it to us. At other times they would eat their own food in front of us. Once, I believe it was on the second day out, the guards even turned us about in the hottest part of the day and marched us nine miles back the way we had come. Many thought this was a purely gratuitous cruelty. I suspected at the time that they wanted to keep us for a while in the south end of the peninsula, mixed with their own troops and near two hospitals, to dissuade the U.S. garrison on Corregidor from firing artillery onto the area while the Japanese were moving their own men and supplies into it.

Though the Japanese treated us atrociously, our worst scourges were medical. The most agonizing of these was dysentery. Sores form on the intestinal walls of the victim. His guts ache constantly, and his stools are a mass of water, fecal matter, blood, and mucous. In our cases, the frightful cramps of dysentery were intensified by ordinary hunger pangs. Many men cried almost constantly from the dreadful combination of the two. I acquired dysentery for the first time on the second night of the March. I believe it was the cruelest affliction I have ever endured. Overall, chronic semi-starvation was the worst problem with which most American prisoners had to cope, but its pains were less intense than those of dysentery. When one is ravenously hungry even the worst food seems flavorful and satisfying, and it is one of the quirks of our nature that once one's stomach is full memories of hunger pass away rapidly. Now, long after the war, I recall that I was hungry most of the time but I find it difficult to recapture the feeling of being hungry. By contrast, I have never forgotten the awful, gripping, gnawing cramps of dysentery or the mixture of fierce pains and aches that accompany the high fever stage of malaria.

By the third night of the March, dysentery, diarrhea, and tropical ulcers had become widespread among the prisoners, most of whom already had malaria. It was bad enough that the Japanese never allowed the slightest medical attention to be given to us. Worse, they regularly crammed us into small areas at night. On one occasion they forced about 10,000 men into a rice field approximately 150 x 200 yards. We were packed in so tightly we could not stretch our legs. We simply collapsed en masse, each on his own filth and maggots, and fell into an exhausted stupor. Such treatment virtually guaranteed that anyone who did not already have dysentery would soon acquire it. This was one of several occasions when I prayed that I would die.

Most of the time, by contrast, I clung tenaciously to life, though my reasons for doing so were by no means constant. At first I thought a good deal about my wife and children, my parents, sisters, and friends back home, and wanted to live for them. Sidney Stewart, whom I did not know but who also endured the Death March, wrote afterward that the experience filled him with such a black, deadly hatred of the Japanese that he was determined to live if only to spite them. Ed Dyess responded similarly and told me we had to survive if only to someday gain revenge on our torturers. As always when I was around Ed, some of his spirit rubbed off onto me. This was particularly the case after we passed a lot of Japanese trucks and other vehicles of American make. Some of these had been imported from the U.S.A. before the war, others captured during the fighting in the north. Either way, both of us were reminded anew of all the American equipment and scrap iron that had been sold to Japan. Sheer resentment strengthened our will to endure.

Apart from motives, I believe I did survive the Death March mostly because the human mind, soul, and nervous system can absorb only so much shock. Atrocities that are numbing one day make little impression when they are repeated a dozen times for many days. To see a friend from my outfit, Leroy Cowart, try on a pair of new shoes, and then see a guard take away both the new shoes and the old ones, thereby compelling him to march barefoot until his feet became infected and worn away, is a shattering experience if one has never seen anything like this before. But the memory of it fades quickly when one also sees a Japanese tank deliberately swerve to crush an American into the roadbed. And that memory pales when one sees a half-buried prisoner rise in his grave only to be hit on the head with a shovel and then buried alive by another prisoner with a Japanese bayonet at his throat. By the time the Death March ended many were close to insanity from having witnessed atrocities or having been forced to take part in them. It is a wonder that more of us were not entirely mad. Colonel Ernest Miller, who had commanded the 194th Tank Battalion on Bataan, said afterward that he believed most of us survived the Death March precisely because we were already hungry, sick, and miserable; that had we been healthy and strong the abrupt transition to the atrocious conditions we experienced on the March would have destroyed us psychologically. Had someone suggested this to me at the time I would have thought him crazy, but looking back long afterward I believe Miller is right.

Most people would expect that it would have been the youngest men who would have endured such horrors as the Death March most successfully. This does not seem to have been the case. Stanley Pavillard, a young doctor from the Canary Islands who was captured in the fall of Singapore and sent with British prisoners to Siam to build the Bangkok-Rangoon Railway, said those English soldiers who were married survived the rigors of camp life in that ghastly region better than single men because they had more to live for. My impression was similar. It appeared to me that, as a group, older men had a greater will to live. Maybe it was because their characters had been formed more completely; maybe it was merely that a higher percentage of them had wives and families and so they had a greater incentive to endure. One thing was certain: we pilots who had gotten special rations in March were stronger than the other men and withstood the ordeal better.

The most painful violence I suffered took place somewhere in the middle of the March. Leo Golden, who was walking beside me, paused to dig up a couple of wild turnips. A guard saw him hand one to me and swung a bamboo stick at his head. Leo ducked and it hit me across the face, splitting my mouth and breaking off a tooth. The pain was agonizing, but I had to endure it for more than a week for no dental care existed on the March. Later in Camp O'Donnell one of the camp dentists held my head while a dental surgeon, Dr. Irons, yanked out the rest of the tooth with a pair of pliers. The experience was excruciating momentarily but relief was almost immediate. Fortunately, infection did not set in.

Estimates of the character of the Japanese guards have varied widely. It has been said that rear echelon Japanese troops were harder on prisoners than front line troops. Probably they were since many guards came from the dregs of the Japanese army. Some front line troops, though, were harsh because in their minds they were still fighting the war. It has been claimed that Japanese who had lived in Hawaii or America before the war were more cruel to Americans than soldiers who had never been outside their native Japan because the former had experienced American race prejudice against orientals. Others have maintained the opposite: that Japanese who had lived abroad were more urbane and humane than the ignorant, xenophobic common soldiers from Nippon proper who had absorbed military and nationalist indoctrination undiluted. Few of these alleged differences were apparent to me. General Wainright said only one Japanese had ever treated him kindly. My experience was better than that. I knew a few who were decent and humane, though most were brutes.

Some have said that the guards on the March treated everyone alike; others that officers of high rank fared better. Certainly the latter was true in some cases. Though I never actually witnessed this, several generals did not have to walk at all but were driven all the way to Tarlac in trucks and were usually treated courteously on the way, though one of them, General Brougher, Commander of the Eleventh Division of the Philippine Army, recorded that a Japanese private slugged him when he refused to surrender his money. As for those of us who had to walk, our captors treated all of us worse than dogs. If anything, they were especially harsh to lower ranking officers. Among the greatest delights was to humiliate American officers in front of enlisted men, and to humiliate Americans before Filipinos.

It has been alleged that the Japanese were more brutal to Americans than to Filipinos because of their general animosity towards occidentals and their desire to avenge racial slights; conversely that they were harder on the Filipinos because they thought the latter had betrayed their oriental heritage by aiding the Americans. There might be more truth in the latter hypothesis for there is no doubt that far more Filipinos were killed and maltreated than Americans, but one cannot make too much of this since Filipinos outnumbered Americans about four to one. I do think Americans endured the Death March a bit better than Filipinos, on the average, because our ordinary diet all our lives had been better than theirs. We were not merely bigger than Filipinos but somewhat stronger and tougher too. Overall, the Japanese were brutal to everyone.

One thing those who survived the Death March will never forget, and that other Americans should never forget either, is the innumerable kindnesses of the Filipino people to all the captives. If they could, they would slip us food. Some survivors said afterward they owed their lives to a rice cake, a handful of peanut brittle, or some other morsel passed to them surreptitiously on the March by some Filipino. Even when they could not give us food or water Filipinos standing along the road in the villages through which we passed would smile, make the V for Victory sign or, sometimes, unable to control themselves, would burst into tears at what must have seemed and endless procession of emaciated derelicts. Sometimes when we passed through towns a Filipino soldier whose uniform had became a mere assortment of rags precariously attached to his scarecrow frame would slip into a crowd of civilians. Almost at once some young Filipino woman would hand him her baby and stand beside him, converting him into an instant civilian to the Japanese guards who had momentarily looked away. Old Filipino women often wore full skirts that reached to the ground. Occasionally, a Filipino soldier, or even an American, would see a guard preoccupied elsewhere and scoot under such a skirt. The women would never move until the troops and guards had passed. All such acts by Filipinos required real heroism for if the Japanese caught them they would be clubbed with rifle butts, impaled on bayonets, tortured or, most commonly, shot on the spot. I never knew an American who went through any part of the war in the Philippines who did not come away impressed by the humanity and generosity of the great majority of the Filipino people. If any colonial people ever deserved their independence, and earned it, it was the Filipinos.

By contrast, the Japanese never seemed to realize how much animosity they had created for themselves among their fellow orientals. Some of their unpopularity must have been due merely to the fact that most Japanese were poor. Unlike Europeans and Americans, they had little money to give to "natives" and little to buy what the latter had to sell. Some of it was surely due to the rapidity and ease of their conquests, which heightened their arrogance. The crucial factor, though, was simply their swinish conduct. They were much harsher to other Asians than occidentals had ever been. The commonest and most superficial manifestation of this was their penchant for slapping people. While slapping was a common practice in the Japanese army, other east Asians regarded it as deeply insulting. The Japanese also requested people to bow bare-headed to Nipponese soldiers, a demand especially hateful to Moslems who wore skullcaps for religious reasons. Within a few months it was clear to non-Japanese orientals that for them the Greater East Asia Co-Prosperity Sphere was going to mean exploitation, executions, torture, rape, beatings with fists and clubs, and general humiliation.

The last two days of the March, before we reached the railroad junction at San Fernando, several miles north of the head of Manila Bay, were probably the worst, though few specific details stick in my memory. Guards had been changed frequently from the first day so they were always fresh while we exhausted wretches whom they goaded grew successively weaker. Scores fell by the wayside every hour now. As we stumbled along blindly we could hear shots in the rear as Japanese "buzzard squads" finished off fallouts and stragglers. Fortunately for me, when the March began I had a good pair of shoes. Many did not, and thousands had no shoes at all. For them, the last nine miles to San Fernando were ghastly. There the road had been surfaced with asphalt. It had been badly broken up by the Japanese trucks and tanks, and was sticky in the blazing sun. Barefoot men whose feet were already blistered, torn, and raw from several days' marching had to walk on the equivalent of hot coals. How they made it I cannot imagine.

I have often been asked if I ever tried to escape during the Death March. I never did. I seldom even thought of it. Guards were always about. Japanese vehicles moved up and down the road continuously. Even if one could slip away from the guards without being shot in the back, then what? I was sick and weak already. If I went into the jungle I would not know where I was nor where I should try to go. The mosquitoes would probably drive me mad if hunger, disease, or the Japanese did not kill me first. Soon I was so weak even the possibility of escape faded from my mind.

"Resting" at nights was often as horrifying as marching in the daytime, if not in precisely the same ways. Near the end of the Death March some 1500 of us, suffering from dysentery, were crammed into an old sheet iron warehouse perhaps 150' x 70'. It was like the Black Hole of Calcutta. There was an open latrine in the middle towards which most of the men struggled but which few reached. The filth and stench, in the heat that may have reached 125 degrees, was worse than in the vilest pigsty imaginable. How long I stayed there I do not know for sure; probably two or three days. I recall being given a ball of rice to eat on one occasion: I may have been fed another time or two. All that saved me was that I happened to be close to the only water tap in the place so I got plenty of water to drink for the first time on the entire March.

For many years I believed this iron adjunct of Hell was in San Fernando, the town where we were finally put on trains and shipped twenty-five miles north to Capas; but it must have been in Lubao, another town several miles to the south. Steve Mellnick and Melvyn McCoy, my compatriots in our eventual escape from the Japanese, say it was in Lubao, and add that the Japanese prevented those of us packed inside from bursting its walls by stretching a cable around it. Since they were not on the Death March and so could not have known this from personal experience I would be inclined to trust my own memory save that Stanley Falk, the author of the best academic study of the Death March, also says it was in Lubao, though he does not mention the cable. I don't recall seeing a cable around a building anywhere but since I was inside in semi-darkness there could well have been one I could not see. The whole question, minor in itself, indicates chiefly that I was so close to total physical and mental collapse during the latter part of the March that half the time I did not know where I was.

Many other men, too, were barely alive when we were at last loaded onto a train headed north to Capas. That ride was an experience hardly less wearing or degrading than the March itself. The railroad cars were undersize: 33' x 8' and 7' high, with small gratings at either end for ventilation. Into each of these tiny cars some 100-115 sick, shattered men were packed like cord-wood. The stink was so overpowering I feared I would suffocate. In addition, my broken tooth throbbed constantly. Some of the cars had steel sides. These became fearsomely hot, veritable sweat boxes. It took about four hours to negotiate the twenty-five miles but most of the men were so overwhelmed by the heat and stench and so cramped that they had little sense of either time or movement. Some of us fared a little better. On some cars one door was opened. Those prisoners near it could get a little fresh air and occasional cakes or bananas passed up to them by Filipinos along the track. Colonel Robert Gaskill, later our chief medical officer in Camp O'Donnell, says that by this time the desperate, starving men lied, cheated, and stole from each other like a pack of wolves. In his car the strongest men forced their way up to the open door and ate everything tossed up to them, refusing to pass anything back to their fellows. I cannot say what went on in the car carrying the Colonel: in my car some vestiges of civilization remained. We rotated places, so I was able to get up to the door part of the time. There I saw several prisoners simply jump off the slow moving train and escape when guards were not looking, and I saw one man commit suicide by jumping off when the train crossed a trestle.

One for whom this ghastly trip was the last mile was Lieutenant Colonel K.J. Gregg, one of the finest officers I knew during the war. He was a man who had ordered Dyess to leave Bataan, only to have Ed refuse to abandon his men. Gregg was really cut from the same cloth as Dyess. In the wild confusion that prevailed on April 8 he was one of the few officers who had stayed at his post to the end. When the train stopped at Capas, Colonel Gregg could no longer walk. Two or three Americans managed to carry him to Camp O'Donnell but he died just after getting inside the camp gates.

As for the rest of us, our spirits picked up when we got into the fresh air again. For some reason, the capricious Japanese were at the moment less brutal than usual. Quite a few men managed to secure food from friendly Filipinos, or to get drinks from buckets of water set out along the road by other Filipinos when we walked the last nine miles from Capas to Camp O'Donnell. Perhaps 7000 had died since we had left south Bataan.

After the war, when tempers had cooled, memories had dimmed, and Japanese war records had become available, academic historians began to publish accounts of the Death March and the events surrounding it. Historians are trained to be cool, impartial, and judicious. They are expected to divorce themselves from the passions that convulsed the souls of those about whom they write. They are admonished to base their accounts on hard, documentary evidence. Of course nobody with either intelligence or feelings is ever going to be entirely impartial, but historians are expected to aspire to the ideal. Some of those who described the Death March years afterward explained it more in terms of Japanese unpreparedness and incompetence than deliberate cruelty. Their case should be considered.

Many times in the history of warfare, victors have simply not known what to do with prisoners. Sometimes their own food supply has been so limited that to feed the prisoners would have required them to starve their own troops. Oftentimes they have had too few men available to guard the prisoners. Thus the mere presence of many prisoners of war could impede military operations and handicap a victorious army. Many times, in such circumstances it has seemed that there was nothing obvious to do with the prisoners save kill them. The Japanese were faced with a problem somewhat like this when Bataan fell. They had expected to secure something like 25,000 Filamerican prisoners in reasonably good health about the end of April. Instead they suddenly had on their hands, on April 9, somewhere between 65,000 and 80,000 sick and hungry American and Filipino soldiers plus perhaps 25,000 more Filipino civilians. They were in no way prepared to deal with such a horde.

On the personal level, one of the tragic ironies of the Death March was that the Japanese commanding general on Luzon was Masaharu Homma, the most westernized and lenient of all the Nipponese top commanders. He had undertaken military studies in England before 1914, had been an observer with the British Expeditionary Force in France in World War I, had been Japanese military attache in London, had served in India, and had received a British military decoration. In Japan he was regarded as pro-British and pro-American. He had suppressed a propaganda pamphlet which accused the U.S. of exploiting the Philippines. Homma said it was inaccurate, that America had supervised the archipelago quite well. He had urged his own government to make an even better record in the Philippines. Once the war began he ordered his troops to respect the customs, traditions, and religion of the Filipinos, and resisted efforts of Field Marshal Terauchi to compel him to change his policies. After the war Homma was accused of war crimes, put on trial, convicted , and executed. His career and fate illustrate sharply one of the two dilemmas that occur regularly in war. The first is to what degree should a commanding officer be held responsible for the deeds of subordinates? The other is whether, and to what degree, underlings should obey the orders of superiors when they deem those orders illegal, unreasonable, or incompatible with civilized usages? Neither issue has ever been resolved satisfactorily, despite the well intentioned efforts of those who devised and implemented the War Crimes Trials of the Germans and Japanese in 1946.

In mid-April, 1942, however, General Homma's thoughts were not on prisoners. For weeks he had been prodded by superiors in Tokyo to wind up the Philippine campaign rapidly. Now he was engrossed in plans to attack Corregidor. Dealing with prisoners was turned over to subordinates.

Initial Japanese plans for processing prisoners were sensible enough. They were to be gathered at Balanga at the end of the first day and fed. Since Balanga is about halfway up the east side of the Bataan peninsula this would have meant a march of from five to twenty-five miles for the prisoners, depending on where they happened to be when they surrendered. The average walk would have been about fifteen miles. This was not grueling by Japanese standards for their troops were expected to march fifteen to twenty-five miles per day. It was not unreasonable by American standards either, where ten to twelve mile days are expected but of well fed men in good health. From Balanga the Filamericans were to be hauled in trucks or marched from town to town in eight-to-fifteen miles stages, and fed and watered regularly, until they reached San Fernando. Here the men would be put on trains and hauled to Capas. Then they would walk the last nine miles to Camp O'Donnell.

Everything went wrong from the first. Nothing was ready even for 25,000 prisoners since the surrender had come three weeks earlier than expected. There were three or four times as many prisoners as had been anticipated. Their health was bad. They were half-starved, at a time when Homma's own troops were short of both food and medicine. Several different Japanese officers were supposed to supervise various aspects of getting the prisoners to Camp O'Donnell but responsibility was divided among them and no one of them dominated the others. Consequently, bureaucratic confusion of the usual type was rampant. King had offered to use American vehicles to transport the men to O'Donnell, but after the systematic sabotage of April 8 there were far fewer vehicles and much less gasoline available than he supposed. Even so, the Japanese, for reasons unknown, refused his offer. They had fewer vehicles of their own than were needed and these, understandably, they wanted to use to prepare their own assault on Corregidor rather than to transport prisoners.

On the actual March guards were vexed to the limits of endurance. In the old Japanese army orders were to be obeyed implicitly and discipline was enforced with physical violence. Any Japanese soldier might require any inferior to wash his clothes, run errands for him, even cook his food, and might enforce his will by slapping, kicking, and slugging. On the Death March I had been shocked the first time I saw Japanese beat up American officers, but at least such acts had not seemed difficult to understand: cruel people were being brutal to enemies. I was shocked in quite a different way, left in wonder really, the first time I saw how our conquerors maintained discipline among themselves. A Japanese noncom called a subordinate before him and, in the presence of all the prisoners, slapped and beat the man unmercifully. Though I did not know it then, the whole Japanese military regimen was so harsh that it was not uncommon for recruits to commit suicide while in training. This kind of treatment, not unnaturally, made Nipponese soldiers unfeeling towards others. Guards had orders to keep prisoners in line and moving. When men straggled or fell out the guards responded, as they would have to their own stragglers, with blows and kicks. When they gave orders, the prisoners, who did not know the Japanese language, looked on in bewilderment. The guards then became enraged at what seemed to them insubordination. They shouted anew and struck or stabbed for emphasis. As everything grew worse, the tempers of the guards grew shorter. To them, their "problems" seemed only to multiply. They responded with increased cruelty. Much responsibility for the ensuing horrors must be shouldered by lower ranking Japanese officers. Had they supervised the guards more closely and ordered them to treat prisoners more humanely undoubtedly the latter would have done so. That the officers ought to have acted thus is clear for brutality towards prisoners had been specifically forbidden in every soldier's manual issued since 1904 and in all Japanese Army Regulations. No less a person than the Emperor himself had commanded his troops to treat prisoners of war with "utmost benevolence and kindness."

The root of the trouble was that there was an implicit contradiction between these formal statements and the whole training and spirit of the Army. The psychology of the ordinary Japanese soldier was the crucial factor in the treatment of those who endured the Death March. That psychology had been formed in any Army that had been engaged for two decades in trying to neutralize people of intellectual and moral sensitivity in Japan, in trying to root humane impulses out of Japanese life. Ordinary soldiers had been taught that a prisoner of war is a traitor who leaves his comrades to defend their country and risk their lives while he surrenders and saves his own. To be taken prisoner while still able to resist was such a shameful, even criminal, act that it deserved to be punished by death. Significantly, the Japanese language does not contain a phrase for surrender. Soldiers had even been taught that they had a duty to kill their own wounded rather than allow them to become prisoners. Any soldier who found himself captive of the enemy was terrified lest his family learn of his disgrace. Hence, when tens of thousands of Americans and Filipinos not only surrendered but asked to have their names reported to their own governments and families the ordinary Japanese soldier regarded such conduct as contemptible, despicable. He promptly lost all respect for such men and felt no qualms about beating or killing them. This immense difference between Japanese and western psychology was illustrated clearly by remarks Japanese soldiers made to some of the prisoners. Two Nipponese sergeants who knew English told Colonel Miller that while we Americans had fought bravely on Bataan we should never have surrendered. Even though nothing tangible would have been accomplished thereby, the Japanese would have respected us for fighting until annihilated. Generals Wainwright and Brougher were asked repeatedly by their captors why they had not followed the honorable course in defeat and committed suicide? Nobody ever asked me that question. Had he done so, I would have been speechless.

To sum up the argument: while the behavior of Japanese troops during the Death March was inexcusably cruel under any interpretation, yet the cruelty was rooted less in deliberate malice than in initial unpreparedness, divided responsibility, preoccupation with other problems, lack of essential food and supplies, failure of officers to supervise their subordinates properly, psychological incomprehension, and ordinary bureaucratic mixups.

This whole thesis acquires further plausibility if one recalls the inept and haphazard way the Japanese attempted to deal with larger matters connected with the war. While the Japanese Army planned particular campaigns capably, especially at the beginning of the war, army and navy leaders and civilian politicians were perpetually at odds throughout the war, to such a degree that the government never formulated long range plans or a general strategy. Essential features in the war effort were never coordinated. Replacement of used up or destroyed war material was never systematic. Nobody seems to have given much thought to just what weapons should be built to defend the nation's newly acquired empire, or to the size of the merchant marine that would be required to exploit its natural resources, or to how that merchant marine was to be defended against American planes and submarines. In sum, Japan never produced an Albert Speer.

The same modified chaos prevailed when the Japanese attempted to administer the vast territories and 150,000,000 new peoples they had acquired so suddenly. They had made no plans to train and supply the teachers, technicians, overseers, officials, even propagandists, essential for a smooth transition to the New Order. Everywhere they bungled relations with their newly acquired subjects. They exploited native labor mercilessly, treated native nationalist movements maladroitly, and became entangled in red tape that produced such anomalies as a glut of rice in one place while native laborers starved elsewhere. The whole task was doubly so when that system had become dominated by coarse, arrogant militarists who represented the most brutal and unimaginative elements in Japanese national life.

It is wryly enlightening that a Japanese private who was captured in Burma at the end of the war and who spent the next two years at hard labor in a British prison camp should have been convinced that the indignities visited upon him were due to deliberate British malice, while the English translator of his book remarks that anyone familiar with the British Army would recognize at once that they were chiefly the product of muddle and accident.

Of course there is no doubt that a trained researcher who writes long after an event and who can balance the recollections of participants with official records is better situated to render an impartial account than one who writes in the heat of the action or from personal memory afterward. Even so, there is no necessary contradiction between the two modes; nor are immediate impressions necessarily inaccurate. Written records cannot reflect looks, tones of voice, and gestures that indicate intentions unmistakably. A participant in an event or an eye witness remembers these vividly. A scholar, writing long afterward, cannot know them or feel them.

At the time of the Death March, I and most of the others who endured it had no doubt about why we had suffered so much. We had been at the mercy of subhumans who were more cruel than any beast. That some of our misery might have been due to the surprises and foul-ups inseparable from war, any fair person would admit afterward. It is quite possible, for instance, that with the best will in the world, our captors might not have been able to feed us for a day or two. But there is no reason other than sheer malice why they could not have let us stop periodically to drink from streams that ran along the road and to wash ourselves. The pace of the March was not rapid; in fact if our thirst had been quenched and our bodies cooled we could have marched faster. There was no rationale for the "sun treatments" save the sadistic desire to make us suffer. Striking at men's heads from moving trucks had nothing to do with administrative inefficiency; much to do with hatred and meanness. Beheading men for trifles, burying them alive, and forcing them to sit and sleep in their own body wastes was not due merely to unrealistic planning. While it was probably true that General Homma did not know how sick most of the prisoners were, and it may have been true that some of his lieutenants did not know either, the fact remains that they should have known. South Bataan is one of the most malarious regions in the world. When Homma's own army pushed into it in the first week in April the Japanese promptly developed 28,000 cases of malaria. The thought should have at least crossed the minds of Homma and his subordinates that American troops might be in a similar state, especially since Japan now controlled access to the quinine of the East Indies. After the surrender of April 9 it should have been apparent to anyone that most of the prisoners were underweight, sick, and exhausted. It should have been obvious that a marching schedule that was reasonable for healthy men could be cruel to an extreme degree for unhealthy ones. I have always believed that the true explanation of Japanese excesses is that the victors were intoxicated by the speed and scope of their successes. They were sure they were going to win the war. They thought they would never be held accountable for their deeds; indeed that all the captives, as they called us, would die before long and the outside world would never learn what had been done to us. So most of them gave free rein to all the cruel impulses that flowed from the Bushido tradition and from their accumulated hatred and resentment of occidentals. All indications are that had the Japanese home islands been invaded all Allied prisoners in all Japanese camps would have been executed.

Lieutenant Jack Hawkins, USMC, who eventually escaped from Davao prison camp with me, and who spent three weeks on Corregidor with thousands of others crowded together in the sun, with insufficient food and water, agrees with me. At the time, he says, he attributed his treatment to administrative confusion rather than deliberate malice. He changed his mind when he was in Cabanatuan prison. There he realized that the Japanese were uninterested in whether prisoners lived or died. That Jack's grim judgment is essentially correct is, I think, indicated by Japanese conduct in many other places. The crimes they committed in China, especially in 1937 and after, were legion and highly publicized. The Bataan Death March was not the only one of its kind. Though it involved more men than any other, there were others that were far worse statistically. On one in Borneo 2970 prisoners set out but only three survived!

Thus did the Japanese spread on the pages of history one of the most terrible indictments ever written by a people against themselves. Eventually they reaped a whirlwind from their vile deeds, for the Death March became for Americans and Filipinos a symbol of Japanese depravity and fixed their determination to repay these bestial crimes a hundredfold. Probably the firebombing of Japanese cities in the spring of 1945 would have taken place anyway. Perhaps the atomic bombs that obliterated Hiroshima and Nagasaki would have been dropped in any event. One cannot know. But it is certain that memories of the Bataan Death March made it easier for American political and military leaders to make the decisions that resulted in those holocausts, and easier for the American people to cheer the results.

NOTE: What looters value in war indicates much about the level of intellectual and cultural discernment that exists in different societies and among various groups in those societies. An incident that occurred in Berlin in the spring of 1945 indicates that Russian and German looters did not differ much from their Japanese counterparts.

During the war Hitler's propaganda chief, Josef Goebbels, decided to keep a careful diary of events so he could write the definitive history of the war afterward thus assure his own immortality. Though Germany was short of every kind of raw material, Goebbels' secretaries typed his memoirs, triple spaced, with wide margins, on the most expensive paper available.

At the very end of the war when Allied troops overran Berlin some Russians found the filing cabinets in which Goebbels had stored all his private papers. The ignorant muzhiks wanted only the *cabinets* to send back to Russia with everything else they were stealing, so they dumped out the bound papers without a glance. Sometime afterward a German junk dealer came along and saw the new binders. Certain that they could be sold, he undid the strings and dumped out over 7000 loose sheets of paper. Then either he, or somebody else, struck by the high quality of the paper, concluded that it too might be sold, and tied several bundles with ropes. Nobody seems to have looked at the *writing* on the paper until it finally passed into the hands of Frank E. Mason, a newspaperman who had once been U.S. Military Attache in Berlin some twenty-five years before. He began to read a few of the sheets. At once he realized their value as historical source material. Thus were *The Goebbels Diaries* preserved for posterity or at least parts of them were. Nobody knows how much of the paper one or more junk dealers got. Cf. Louis P. Lochner ed., *The Goebbels Diaries*, 1942-43, pp. v, viii, 3-4.

Many ex-prisoners have testified to the hatred other Asians bore the Japanese and, by contrast, the good will they displayed towards the enemies of Japan.

Commander John Morrill USN was aided in a dozen ways by scores of Filipinos when he and seventeen men sailed from Corregidor to Australia. Morrill and Martin, *South From Corregidor*, pp. 109-121, 129-141, 150-151.

Edgar Whitcomb, who lived to become Governor of Indiana, was fed and helped many times by Filipinos as he made his escape from Bataan through the mountains of Luzon. Whitcomb, *Escape From Corregidor*, pp. 110-111, 125-128, 134-142, 153.

Royal Arch Gunnison, an American newspaperman, had a Filipino chauffeur whom he had known for only a month. Yet for eight and half months the man came every single day to Santo Tomas prison to bring food to Gunnison and his wife. Even though he was poor himself he refused to accept a penny for it. Gunnison, *So Sorry, No Peace*, pp. 87-88, 134-136.

Eve Hoyt, an American newspaperwoman in prewar Manila, has told me many times of the numerous kindnesses shown her by Filipinos when she was in Santo Tomas.

Two of my close wartime friends have related similar experiences. Bert Bank, *Back From The Living Dead*, pp. 23-24, 55, 61-63; and Edward Haggerty, S.J.,*Guerrilla Padre In Mindanao*, pp. 43-62.

One American escapee from a Japanese prison in Shanghai made his way 700 miles across country to Chungking. Dozens of times he was aided by Chinese civilians who knew they would be tortured or killed if their deeds became known. They took the risk because they hated the Japanese implacably for their earlier crimes in China. Quentin Reynolds ed., *Officially Dead: The Story Of Commander C.D. Smith*, pp.169-230, 235-236.

Though they were never prisoners, General Chennault and Tom Harmon said much the same about the help Chinese civilians would give to downed American pilots. Chennault, *Way Of A Fighter*, p. 169; Harmon, *Pilots Also Pray*, p. 173.

James Bertram, imprisoned by the Japanese in China and then put to work on the docks in Japan, found the Chinese as friendly as they dared to be; and also that both Chinese and Korean dock workers hated the Japanese even more than war prisoners did. Bertram, *Beneath The Shadow: A New Zealander In The Far East*, 1939-1946, pp. 119, 164.

Agnes Keith wrote movingly of Chinese, Malay, Japanese, and other East Indians who, at great risk to themselves, smuggled food and medicines to the civilian internees on Borneo. Keith, *Three Came Home*, pp. 45-69, 81-83, 92.

Ernest Gordon of the 93rd. Scottish Highlanders came close to being worked to death building a railroad for the Japanese along the River Kwai. He noted that local Thais, like the Filipinos and Chinese, risked their lives to give the prisoners food and medicine. Gordon, *Through The Valley Of The Kwai.* p. 109.

The clearest evidence that the Japanese grossly underestimated the number of prisoners they would take when Bataan fell can be gathered from a Tokyo communique of April 14, five days after General King's surrender. It claimed that 40,000 U.S. and Filipino troops had been taken. In war the winners customarily exaggerate their victories and the vanquished minimize their losses. Thus the Japanese who expected to take 25,000 prisoners, claimed 40,000; while the American government, knowing that the true figure was far higher than this, announced that 38,850 had been lost, Cf. Stanley Falk, *Bataan: The March Of Death. Falk*, pp.194-198, explains in detail why he thinks between 5000 and 10,000 prisoners died on the Death March, and why it is unlikely that a more precise figure will ever be established. Total casualties were, of course, much higher, but they are impossible to determine since nobody knows how many prisoners (especially Filipinos) escaped along the way, how many such escapees survived, how many of the deaths in Camp O'Donnell should be ascribed to the Death March and how many to conditions in the camps, or how many of the sick should be listed as "casualties." General MacArthur, *Reminiscences*, p. 129, estimates "25,000 casualties," but does not attempt to break down the figure.

It must be emphasized that those writers who stress Japanese incompetence in their accounts of the Death March do not overlook or condone its brutalities. Cf. Toland, *Rising Sun,* pp. 296-301; Toland, *But Not In Shame,* pp.310-329; and Falk, pp. 56-91, 125-153, 212-236. Falk was a research assistant to Louis Morton, the author of *The Fall Of The Philippines*, one of the volumes in the Official History of the U.S. Army in World War II. Falk's own book, drawn considerably from Japanese sources, was done originally as a doctoral dissertation. It is an excellent "academic" history. Toland's works also incorporate Japanese sources. Miller, p. 226, who disliked the Japanese heartily, nonetheless stresses how confused they seemed to have been throughout the Death March.

For an estimate of General Homma's character, deeds, and fate Cf. pp. 224-225, and John Toland, *Rising Sun*, pp. 317-330. Significantly, Homma's own American lawyers protested his death sentence and wrote him a personal letter of apology. Supreme Court Justice Frank Murphy publicly seconded them. Homma died with dignity and fortitude. Cf. Toland, *ibid* , p. 320.

For an excellent account of training, spirit, and life in the Japanese army during the campaigns in China in the 1930s, Cf. Hanama Tasaki, *Long The Imperial Way*, a novel by one who had served in that army. James Bertram regularly observed Japanese officers beating subordinates when he worked on the docks in Japan. Like me, he was incredulous. So was Colonel Miller. Cf. Bertram, pp. 169-170; and Miller, p. 340.

Yugi Aida, a well educated and perceptive Japanese soldier held by the British, was certain that they mistreated and humiliated him deliberately. Aida, *Prisoner Of The British*, pp. 30-89. For English translator Louis Allen's comments Cf. pp. 191-192.

The deficiencies of Japan's political and military leadership, particularly their failure to mobilize the nation's resources systematically, is dissected at length by Peter Calvocoressi and Guy Wint, *Total War: Causes And Courses Of The Second World War*, pp. 673-710, 721-722, 783-789, especially pp. 703-705.

Chapter Four
Prison Camp

Fʀᴏᴍ ᴛʜᴇ ᴍɪᴅᴅʟᴇ ᴏꜰ Aᴘʀɪʟ, 1942 I spent two months at Camp O'Donnell, followed by five months at Cabanatuan prison. Both places were originally envisioned as cantonments for the Philippine Army. Construction had been undertaken before the war but both were just collections of shacks in the middle of the central Luzon plain when I arrived there. O'Donnell was the more primitive of the two. Its barracks consisted of nipa or bamboo log frames over which were draped roofs of leaves. The floor was dirt. At Cabanatuan some of the barracks were wooden and had wood floors. In both places everybody slept on the floor. Each man had one army blanket and a mosquito net. This was enough warmth in the tropics and the net provided protection from the clouds of mosquitoes. Dirt was softer than boards but eventually I got used to sleeping on the latter. One gets used to anything. O'Donnell was an especially dismal place since the thousands who streamed through its gates were already in a dreadful condition from the long march up from south Bataan. It was indicative of our general state that Jack Donohoe, one of our maintenance men in the 21st Squadron, should have walked into O'Donnell with his socks stuck to his bloody feet. When we arrived, the Japanese did not yet have anything organized properly.

Many prisoners have recorded that one of the favorite exercises of certain Japanese officers was to puff out their chests, fold their arms, glare at their audiences, and then deliver stentorian orations on the greatness of their Emperor and the grandeur of the present historical epoch in which western influence in East Asia was being visibly supplanted by that of Japan. Colonel Miller thought the whole style had been copied from Mussolini, whom the Japanese admired. Whatever the accuracy of that conjecture, we had hardly gotten inside the gates of Camp O'Donnell when we were treated to one of these performances. The Japanese commandant, resplendent in shining black knee-high leather boots, shorts, and a white shirt open at the collar, got up on a box and informed us loudly and at length that we were captives, not prisoners of war, and would be so treated. We soon learned that this was a distinction to which the Japanese resorted whenever they wanted to justify some act of brutality towards us, much as the North Vietnamese were to do a generation later when they proclaimed captured U.S. personnel to be "air pirates" and thus not entitled to be treated as prisoners of war. The general Japanese attitude towards customary usages in war is indicated by the experiences of Agnes Keith, an American journalist held prisoner by the Japanese in Borneo for 44 months. She said she once pointed out to her camp commandant that certain of his actions were contrary to international law. He replied grandly that he decided what was international law in their corner of the world.

Our commandant embellished his oration with glowing descriptions of an array of Japanese conquests, and finished with a declaration that Nipponese forces had bombed Santa Barbara and Chicago. Most of us were skeptical of these latter claims but we knew that conquests in the Orient had taken place, and we had heard no war news for many days so we feared that the whole tale might be true.

When the commandant had finished, General King sensing our mood, acted with his customary bravery and good judgment. He got up and told us to hold our heads high; that we had nothing to be ashamed of; that he not we, had surrendered Bataan. This was not the least of General King's services to his country, in my opinion. Allied prisoners in other theaters testified that they often felt shame for their units and their country when they surrendered. We had no reason to feel ashamed since we had fought bravely in a hopeless cause. Nonetheless it boosted our morale crucially to be reassured by our commanding officer when our fortunes had fallen so low.

Facilities at O'Donnell were rude and inadequate. There were, for example, two water spigots for 6-7000 American prisoners. One had to stand in line for hours just to fill a canteen. There was no water in which to bathe or wash clothes. The first time I had a chance to take a bath came one night several weeks later when there was a hard rain. Few sensations in my life have been sweeter than standing under the eave of the barracks while cool, clean water poured into my mouth and over my parched, filthy body. How many water taps the 50,000 Filipino prisoners had, I have no idea. The Japanese were determined to prevent any contact between Americans and Filipinos and so separated us in the camp.

The casual way our overlords dealt with us on a day-to-day basis was through the American Headquarters in the camp. This "Headquarters" consisted of some of the American senior officers who were used to transmit Japanese orders to the rest of us and who could sometimes speak on our behalf to our mutual conquerors. How they were chosen I never knew. Jack Hawkins, who later escaped from Davao with me, says they were appointed by the Japanese. LIFE magazine said once that we prisoners chose the "most able" among our officers to fill these positions. If so, I don't remember the elections. At the time, I thought the "Headquarters" staff consisted of obvious people:

those who held the highest rank. Whatever the case these men had thankless, even dangerous, jobs. They had no real authority and their Japanese masters were fond of striking and humiliating them. The Headquarters staff did such things as pick the men to go on various work details, appoint American sentries to patrol inside the prison fences while Japanese patrolled the outside, supervise the preparation and distribution of our food, attempt to smooth relations between the prisoners and the Japanese, discipline malingerers, punish those who stole food from weaker men, and endeavor to maintain some vestige of military atmosphere in the camp. Nobody ever appealed a decision of this informal body to the Japanese.

Most days in camp were monotonously alike. We were awakened about 6:00 A.M. by the bugler, if we had not been already roused by the maniacal yelling of the Japanese taking early morning bayonet practice. Then we went to the mess hall for breakfast. This always consisted of about half a messkit of lugao, a soupy form of rice. Many men simply ate their meager breakfast, then lay down again and slept most of the day, a habit that became increasingly prevalent as we grew weaker from the lack of food. Those assigned to work details went off to do such things as cut wood, dig ditches, irrigate fields, repair roads, build airplane runways or, most commonly, to cut weeds and underbrush that harbored mosquitoes. Though the work was sometimes hard, those on details usually got a little more food and sometimes had a chance to buy food or get some on the sly from a friendly Filipino. For these reasons it was not hard to find volunteers for work. Still, I was on only two such details in the two months I was at O'Donnell. On one I chopped firewood to cook our rice. The other time I earned a bad beating, as I will describe later. Most men had nothing at all to do most days. Some of Lloyd Stinson's pals were inveterate card players who spent many hours at bridge and poker with an increasingly worn and greasy deck someone had managed to smuggle into camp. I played cribbage with Leo Golden a good deal.

The way we had to live in Japanese prison camps, virtually on top of one another, enabled a person to become better acquainted with his immediate neighbors in a week than in many years of ordinary civilian life. Experience soon showed that it was an excellent idea to try to become a fast friend of whoever slept a few inches away. If one man got sick the other could look after him and, most important, could go through the chow line for him. I was extremely fortunate to have two such close buddies in Ed Dyess and Leo Golden, though Leo and I were later separated when I was sent to Davao.

Though at some Japanese camps on the China coast prisoners were allowed to accept money from the Red Cross or, it was rumored, from the Vatican, and to use it to purchase musical instruments or sports equipment, at Camp O'Donnell no effort was made to provide any kind of recreation or instruction for us. A few people started quasi-academic classes on an informal basis. I recall one fellow who taught Russian to anyone interested. Little came of this for most of us were simply too weak and tired to try to think seriously. Eventually, when we were moved to Cabanatuan where both food and quarters were a little better, and where the Japanese had had time to organize things somewhat, the chaplains suggested to them that we prisoners would work better if we had a little time to play. Then we occasionally played softball, but it was hard to enjoy it because we were so weak. Though I was one of the stronger men, one day I fell down running to first base and was barely able to get up. Most of the time our "activities" were simplicity itself: thinking about food or gazing idly at fellow prisoners making their way to and from the latrines. Occasionally there was some grisly break in the dull routine, such as the day some Japanese soldiers came back from a skirmish with Filipino guerrillas bearing a severed Filipino head on a bamboo pole. They wished to remind us of the fate that awaited those who obstinately set their faces against the rising New Order in the East. It was existence of this sort that Steve Mellnick had in mind when he described the six months following his capture on Corregidor as ". . .so degrading as to suggest. . .the hallucinations of a diseased brain." And Steve was only in Cabanatuan; never in O'Donnell.

Nobody knows for sure how many Americans and Filipinos died in O'Donnell and Cabanatuan in 1942. Some American officers tried to keep track, but all figures then or later are mere estimates. Somewhere between 14,000 and 27,000 Filipinos perished in O'Donnell in the first three months after the fall of Bataan: somewhere between 1100 and 2200 Americans died. Mellnick was kept at Bilibid prison in Manila for a time after he was captured on Corregidor. While there he heard a story from an American sergeant who had a Japanese wife and who was, consequently, allowed to go into Manila to buy supplies. The sergeant told him that U.S. prisoners in O'Donnell were dying at the rate of one hundred per day. Steve thought the tale preposterous but found it to have been only exaggerated. The usual death rate was 20-30 per day; up to fifty some days. Mortality at Cabanatuan was comparable. At first, many of those who succumbed were men who were already grievously weakened by the Death March. The rest fell gradually to malnutrition, diseases, brutal treatment, and lack of medical care. By October roughly a quarter of the Americans who had surrendered on April 9 had died while another quarter were in what passed for hospitals, awaiting death. Mortality fell off sharply in October, partly because the weather cooled, partly because all the weaker prisoners had already expired.

Death rates were even higher among the hapless Filipinos. For me one of the most unnerving features of life in O'Donnell was the hideous yelling, screaming, and crying that came every night from the Filipino side of the camp. Perhaps the Filipinos were treated more savagely than we were; perhaps they were just less inhibited in their response to suffering. Whichever the case, they cried piteously and died so rapidly that the Japanese took to discharging them so they could die at home and free their captors from formal responsibility for their demise. I once counted 500 Filipino bodies wrapped in burlap bags, each slung on a pole carried on the shoulders of two men, presumably to be thrown into a mass grave.

When many of us who had been at O'Donnell were moved to Cabanatuan in June, Mellnick, who had gone directly to Cabanatuan from Bilibid, called us "The most woeful objects I have ever seen." Most of us were brought in trucks because only a few were strong enough to stand up and walk a few hundred yards. As on the Death March, heavy, robust men seemed less able to bear malnutrition than smaller, thinner men; heavy drinkers who had exercised little died rapidly; and many young men seemed to abandon all will to live amid the squalor of existence. In general, both in the fighting on Bataan and in the prison camps, farm boys seemed to make it better than city boys. It was not that they were tougher by nature but that they were more accustomed to the routine cuts, bruises, bumps, and privations that are part of an active outdoor life. Most of them were more self-reliant than those of us from cities. What they had learned in their past lives simply had greater application to our present situation than what we had learned. Whatever our backgrounds, those of us who had survived through the summer did so knowing that at present death rates we had only a few months to live even if we should be the last to go.

In normal times young men live variously for fame, glory, adventure, personal advancement, the acquisition of money, the pursuit of women, or some combination of these. In prison camp everybody lived from one meal to the next. "Food" was rice, three times a day, cooked a bit differently each time. The dreary monotony of the everlasting rice was such that we used to rub our messkits with garlic, red peppers, or anything else that might have been discovered in the jungle that would give the rice a slightly different flavor. The rice was supplemented by occasional half-rotten camotes (Phillipine sweet potatoes), a thin soup made from camote vines, a few mongo beans now and then, and a little flour periodically. It was a diet that barely kept one from starving to death. That we should have been fed thus in the Philippines, a rich area that produces abundant food, indicates that the Japanese starved us deliberately in order to make us weak and thereby easier to control. If we died it meant nothing to them. Another consideration supports the same assumption. Though the Japanese were clean people personally they made no effort to cope with dysentery among the prisoners. This compelled us to live in an atmosphere of filth and degradation in which diseases spread quickly and mortality was high.

The Japanese fed us in the simplest way possible. They allotted the American Headquarters staff a certain quantity of food and then let us cook and distribute it in any way we chose. Our people did a good job. Regular mess hall personnel cooked the rice in fifty five gallon drums, each barracks took its turn in the chow line, and if anything was left over for seconds it was parceled out to each barracks in turn. Though there were the inevitable complaints that this person or that group got more or less than they should, overall the system was as fair as could have been devised in the circumstances. The basic trouble was simply that there was not enough of anything. Consequently, everyone lost weight at an appalling rate. My normal weight was about 135, but I was once reduced to an 85 pound skeleton.

The main activity of everyone in camp who was not dead or wishing himself dead was trying to get more food. If someone was sick or about to die, others stayed close to him, less from compassion than from hope of getting his rice ration. Agnes Keith, who was interned with several hundred other women in Borneo, said that no matter how hungry she was she could not bear the sight of other women squabbling over bits of food: that she had learned that no meal was worth losing one's self respect. If this was true she must have possessed extraordinary self-control. Her fellow inmates apparently had much less. The Japanese allowed them to plant camotes but the women were so famished that they ate the tops off the plants before the tubers could mature. Most of the men I saw abandoned both pride and courtesy if they could just get a bit more to eat.

Sordid though such conduct may seem, it must be remembered that persistent starvation gradually alters one's mental state, in extreme cases inducing dementia. We did not all go crazy, but it is painful to recall how fiercely self-centered and primitive we became under the lash of hunger. Often the watery rice we got contained numerous swimming white worms. We ignored them and ate it anyway. To have sorted them out when we were famished would have taken too much time. Some prisoners would stand outside Japanese quarters and scramble like dogs for any scrap of food tossed out a window when our overlords were taking their meals. If something even vaguely edible was thrown into the garbage starved men would grub for it. We finally had to post sentries around garbage dumps to prevent such demoralizing sights. Prisoners who were responsible for feeding Japanese ducks often ate the food themselves, thereby causing the ducks to gradually develop the same vitamin deficiency ailments as their keepers. Anything that ran, swam, flew, or crawled was captured and eaten: monkeys, iguanas, dogs, cats, frogs, lizards, rats, snakes, worms, weevils, grasshoppers, and snails. So was much that was inanimate: animal entrails, fish heads, decaying vegetables, flowers, weeds, and any root that could be chewed. One of Lloyd Stinson's buddies was on a wood cutting detail where the Japanese guard allowed the prisoners to set traps for forest animals. Once he caught a wildcat. He brought it back to camp; Lloyd skinned and cleaned it, the kitchen crew cooked it, and Lloyd and his friends had a feast. Another prisoner trapped a dog. It was baked with rice and devoured ecstatically by the trapper and his cronies.

When men were this famished food and water were obviously the most valuable commodities in the camps. It was not uncommon for a can of pork and beans, fish, or corned beef to sell for as much as $100. If a man was sufficiently parched a canteen of water might command a similar sum. What a luxury was such a commonplace commodity as water in Camp O'Donnell! To have enough to drink; to be able to wash one's clothes; to be able to wash the sweat, dirt, and smell off one's body; just to stand in the rain; these were unimaginable pleasures. One of the main reasons life in Cabanatuan was somewhat less degrading and bestial than in O'Donnell was merely because we had all the drinking water we wanted in Cabanatuan. This difference alone pointed up sharply for me how little we appreciate life's simple necessities until fate takes them from us. How wonderful it would have seemed to any of us then merely to eat an ordinary civilian breakfast, to lie under a tree on a sunny afternoon, or to go for a stroll unmolested.

When we weren't actually scrounging for extra food we thought about food and talked about food obsessively. In our first days in O'Donnell we did talk about home, our loved ones, and the way the war seemed to be going. War talk picked up again months later in Davao when we were better fed and thinking about escape. In the intervening months, however, all subjects save food were virtually forgotten. I would wake up in the morning and in my mind make out menus for every meal of the day. I dreamed of clean plates and silverware; of hamburgers covered with ketchup, onions, and pickles; of rich milk shakes; of clean, cool water in clean glasses. The hot, dry, dusty taste that was always in my mouth and which was aggravated by fever blisters or scurvy made me dream endlessly of ice cream, cold fruit, lemonade, antiseptic gargle, toothbrushes, and toothpaste. We compared the menus we had composed, listened to lengthy descriptions of each other's favorite foods, and talked about all the steaks and salads, milk and eggs, vegetables and desserts we would consume one day when we got back to the U.S.A. . Colonel Miller even wrote a long poem about food.

If semi-starvation had any saving feature it was that it liberated us from what otherwise would have been a troublesome problem in our circumstances: sex. Though Japanese guards would go to town

71

on their days off and then regale us with tales of their erotic exploits, prolonged malnutrition so deadens the sex drive that few prisoners talked about women. The only time the subject even came up was after the arrival of Red Cross packages which would fill our bellies and stimulate normal appetites for a few days. Poorly fed American prisoners of the North Vietnamese a generation later were to undergo the same experience. The effect of malnutrition on women was even more dramatic. Agnes Keith said all the younger women incarcerated with her gradually ceased to menstruate.

While food was the main thing on our minds and in our conversations, the most disgusting features of existence in prison camps were diseases, filth, and insects. Though we were spared the three inch flying cockroaches which bedevilled Gwen Dew, an American newspaperwoman jailed at Fort Stanley in Hong Kong, clouds of mosquitoes and flies swarmed around us, making life especially hellish for those too weak or too sick to fend them off. Stinking bedbugs, seemingly in the millions, infested every barracks and everyone's meager bedding. All of us harbored colonies of lice in the seams of our clothing. One of the most heartening features of our passage from Camp O'Donnell to Cabanatuan was that as soon as we entered the latter all our clothes were thrown into vats of boiling water which killed the lice they contained.

Diseases were legion, and less easily dealt with than the lice. Malaria, dysentery, and beri beri were the worst in the sense that they caused the most deaths. Elephantiasis was the most horrifying. Various allergies, skin eruptions, tropical ulcers, pellegra, scurvy, and other vitamin deficiency disorders that sometimes produced night blindness, added to our collective misery, as they were to do to other American servicemen in the prison camps of North Vietnam after 1965. Malaria produced alternating spells of severe chills and fever that sometimes ran as high as 105 or 106 degrees. If one lived through it he emerged utterly exhausted. At one time or another I had twenty-six attacks of it. Beri beri, a vitamin deficiency disease, came in two types, wet and dry. The wet variety was not merely extremely painful but grotesque as well. The sufferer's body would swell unbelievably as his tissues filled with water. Men would balloon to 300 pounds and look as though their bodies would burst. Bert Bank, a native of Alabama who became one of my closest friends in prison camp, claimed that men who had bad cases of it would burst if they were dropped on the ground. I never saw such a thing happen, though I must add that Bert was better qualified to offer a judgment on the matter than I. I never contracted wet beri beri. Bert had a "mild" case of it once: his feet swelled so much he had to cut his shoes off.

The commoner dry beri beri produced agonizing pains in the joints and in the ends of the fingers and toes. Every day one saw men crying in pain for hours as they massaged the aching areas. Scurvy, likewise due to vitamin deficiency, produced sores in the mouth and terrible pains when one attempted to swallow. I got scurvy once at Cabanatuan. It was also one of the few occasions when our American Headquarters organization was able to persuade our captors to alleviate our condition a bit. They remonstrated with the Japanese about the prevalence of scurvy among the men. Each of us was then given two small limes. I carefully quartered mine and ate one quarter of a lime for eight successive days. The effect was astounding. The scurvy vanished at once. There could hardly have been a clearer demonstration that much of our suffering was unnecessary, that the Japanese did nothing for us because they did not care whether we lived or died.

Another common affliction was fungus between the toes, which produced a condition akin to athlete's foot. Worse was an extreme form of "jock itch," a rawness that developed in the genital area and itched maddeningly. The Japanese never gave us any medicines for such maladies. Many lost all control of themselves and scratched the affected areas till blood flowed. Some said the itching was so intolerable that scratching was more satisfying than sex. Tropical ulcers of several types abounded. Most of them oozed pus and blood, which attracted clouds of big green blowflies, if the latter were not already preoccupied about the anal area of exhausted sufferers from dysentery. One afternoon when he had nothing to do Colonel Miller decided to undertake an experiment that proved about equally useful and disgusting. He made himself a crude bamboo fly swatter and smote these huge, repulsive flies industriously for exactly ten minutes. Then he stopped and counted his victims. There were 520!

The incessant buzzing of mosquitoes drove some men nearly out of their minds, though they occasionally provided me with a primitive diversion that was satisfying psychologically. No matter how carefully a person put up his mosquito netting at bedtime now and then a mosquito or two would be trapped inside. When this happened I would put every other concern out of my mind and methodically pursue the mosquito, in the dark, inside my net, until I finally got it. The whole exercise provided something purposeful and rewarding to do, and used up time.

The most ghastly of all diseases in the camp was Elephantiasis, a horrible affliction caused by blockage of the lymph channels by minute parasites. The victim's body swelled until he looked like a zombie. A friend and classmate of mine whom I shall call Bill contracted Elephantiasis. It was aggravated by cerebral malaria, and by amoebic dysentery so severe that Bill stopped wearing clothes altogether since they were a nuisance during his dozens of daily trips to the latrine. Bill knew he would not live long. One morning I noticed that he had stopped eating. I spoke to him about it. He said food repelled him, that he could not eat. I told him he had to eat, no matter how bad the food tasted. He then turned to me and said, with utmost seriousness, "I pray to Almighty God every night before I go to bed that I won't wake up tomorrow morning." A few days later Bill collapsed on his way back from the latrine. He was naked, covered with filth, and swollen like a balloon. His deep religious faith and the composure with which he bore his awful afflictions made a deep impression on all of us who knew him and strengthened us to endure our lighter burdens. Sadly, it was true that no sooner was poor Bill dead than several men rushed to divide his pitiful possessions. Such is the degree of selfishness to which human beings can be driven by hunger and degradation.

Most of this dreadful loss of life and mass suffering could have been averted. Malaria, dysentery, and beri beri are not fatal diseases if elementary care is provided. Forty years before World War II the Japanese had carried through in their own army a revolution in sanitation and in the care and preparation of food which had cut their medical death rate in wartime more than 90% between the Sino-Japanese War of 1894 and the Russo-Japanese War of 1904-5. Thus they were not ignorant of medical conditions among the prisoners nor of what needed to be done about them. Moreover, there is much evidence that medicines and drugs must have been available to them in some quantities. When a diphtheria epidemic broke out among the prisoners in Cabanatuan, Japanese authorities immediately took preventive measures to protect their own troops. Even more significant, prisoners who were fortunate enough to have considerable money were able to buy medicines on the black market. James Bertram, a New Zealander interned at Shumshuipo on the China coast, avoided death twice when thiamine chloride was smuggled in to treat his beri beri and antitoxin to combat his diphtheria. Meanwhile, the Japanese there fed vegetables to pigs. In our own camp Steve Mellnick was able to secure 200 vitamin capsules and 100 quinine tablets from a Filipino doctor. Other supplies of quinine, sent by the Philippine Red Cross, were left unpacked for days on the pretext that they had to be inventoried. Only weeks later were small amounts of quinine doled out to the prisoners. There were many capable American doctors in the camps and hospitals but the Japanese never gave them essential equipment or medicines. The best they were able to do for us was to occasionally teach us some makeshift remedy. A few men learned to leach small quantities of vitamin C out of grass. They said it moderated scurvy and beri beri. Others, in Cabanatuan fermented rice until it formed a sort of yeast which presumably contained some vitamin B-1. Miller said it eased his beri beri somewhat. Still others undertook highly imaginative self-treatment. Once Jack Donohoe was able to make an advantageous trade with a fellow prisoner because Jack had a piece of moldy cheese from a Red Cross package. The other man wanted it badly for the penicillin on it. Most of us knew about improvised remedies like these, though I never tried any of them.

In a small way some of the American prisoners got back at the Japanese. Now and then a guard would acquire a venereal disease. He would then become anxious to trade all sorts of things to any prisoner who could manage to acquire sulfathiazole tablets on the black market. Some enterprising prisoners managed to secure Japanese tooth powder instead, from which they made up "sulfa tablets" for such barter.

To people who have lived their lives in American middle class comfort the squalor of existence in Japanese prison camps can scarcely be imagined. A horrid stench hung over the whole area day and night; from unburied corpses, unwashed bodies, the excrement of number-less dysentery victims smeared on men, bedding, and ground alike; and from the nightmarish latrines. The last were mere open trenches with half a dozen seats on either side. Due to the near universality of dysentery they seemed to fill up every few days. Anywhere in the tropics uncovered human excrement soon produces myriads of maggots. These open latrines were always covered with a boiling, frothing mass of maggots, to such a degree that they seemed to be actually *moving*. Many men never made it to the latrines at all, and so covered themselves or those packed near them in the barracks with filth. Others literally lived next to the latrines. Amoebic dysentery exhausts its victims utterly. Some men who suffered from it were unable to control their bowels or even make it, unaided, from their barracks to the the latrine and back perhaps twenty times a day. Very soon their clothes became soaked with feces. They then did the best they could: lie on the ground naked, close to a latrine, and wait for a seat to be vacated. Fortunately, most of them did not live long. Still others became so weakened or careless that they fell into the latrines. On one occasion at Camp O'Donnell the Japanese were going to shoot ten Americans because they thought one had escaped. Then someone found the missing man floating in the latrine. . . .

It indicates how rapidly one becomes acclimated to hunger, filth, and death that such squalor, which would ordinarily produce nausea, ceased even to penetrate our consciousness. We ate unconcernedly a few yards from the stinking latrines, close to men whose bodies were covered with lice, tropical ulcers, and feces from chronic dysentery. So inured did we become to such appalling conditions that I cannot recall what was used for toilet paper. Banana leaves, I suppose, or nothing. The Japanese never issued us any paper. Agnes Keith recorded that the women in her camp in Borneo became as insensitive to these matters as we did. She summed up the situation more succinctly than I: "Hunger outruns hygiene."

It was typical of the Japanese authorities that they made no effort to keep units together among the prisoners, but simply allowed each man to live wherever he could. It was typical of Ed Dyess, who never lost his composure or sense of military propriety, to want to get all the members of the 21st Pursuit Squadron together so we could look after each other and bolster each other's morale no matter how wretched our lives became. Ed and I had been separated ever since he had been beaten severely for wearing his helmet on the Death March. Despite the injuries, we had been in O'Donnell only a few days when he found some of us, counted heads to see who was missing, and then sent Leo Golden and I out to look for the absentees. What followed was one of the most sickening experiences of my life. We found a tech sergeant of ours lying on a rubbish heap, naked, covered with sores and filth, being eaten alive by myriads of blowflies. He was half-mad as well as half-dead. At first we tried to give him a drink of water. His only response was to plead with us piteously to take him away somewhere so the others would not see him die like a rat. We hurried to a nearby dispensary, got a litter and carried him to what was called a hospital.

Since World War II I have had many occasions to go to hospitals in the United States, not only to visit others but for treatment of a considerable array of my own ills. Each time I have been struck afresh by the sight of white uniforms, white sheets, light streaming through clear windows, antiseptic looking nurses bustling about, and a general air of cleanliness and order. It is impossible to exaggerate how sharply this contrasts with Philippine camp hospitals. The "hospital" at Camp O'Donnell was an old warehouse. It looked like a chicken pen that had not been cleaned for three or four months. It was not a hospital at all in the usual sense, but a place to die. The American prisoners in it looked much like the inmates of Nazi camps whose pictures everyone saw after the war. They were packed together hip-to-hip on the bare floor, virtually naked, their complexions a deathly gray, so starved that their protruding ribs reminded me at once of a venetian blinds, spattered with their own excrement, and covered with clouds of blowflies and mosquitoes. I have never been able to forget the looks of despair on their faces. It was here that we carried our sergeant for "treatment."

That this dreadful hovel was not untypical is indicated by the testimony of Ernest Gordon, a Scottish Highlander imprisoned along the River Kwai in Thailand. Gordon notes that when he was put in the hospital there he asked to be moved in with the corpses so he could at least sleep on dry ground. I used to wonder what it must have been like to undergo an operation in such a place, without anesthetics!

If the terrible inhumanity of the Japanese had any extenuating feature it was that they also tended to be brusque and unsympathetic about illnesses and complaints of their own troops. Japanese army surgeons considered their main task to be to keep soldiers ready for combat, while ordinary soldiers stayed away from dispensaries because they knew that repeated sick calls looked bad on their service records. What some of the latter thought of their own medical service is indicated by a talented Japanese novelist, Hanama Tasaki, who served in the Japanese army in China in the late 1930s and wrote a novel (*Long The Imperial Way*) about his experience. In his unit, he said, the men called their surgeon "Iodine" because that was his usual remedy for almost any ill.

Our jailers had no more respect for the dead than for the living. In the humid heat of the tropics bodies decompose quickly, and nothing stinks so badly as a decaying corpse. Though our captors took care to cremate their own dead and send the ashes back to Japan, they left it to us to dispose of our dead in any way we chose. The usual practice was for American Headquarters to appoint burial details. Though men tried to get other jobs in hope of getting additional food, nobody wanted on the burial detail. The work was hard, there was lots of it, sometimes there were too few men strong enough to undertake it, and it was depressing. Hence the grisly task had to be rotated. I was thankful I was never assigned to it. Burial itself consisted simply of digging pits a short distance from the perimeter of the camp, dumping in the dead bodies with no ceremony whatever, and covering them with dirt. There were so many to be buried that often only a foot or two of soil covered these mass graves. If there was a hard rain much of the dirt would wash away and rotting corpses would float up to the surface and saturate the vicinity with a paralyzing stench. The only thing to be said for such a "system" was that it got the dead bodies out of the camp.

If one excludes Russian captives, about 4% of the prisoners of war held by the Germans and Italians died. By contrast, 27% of those taken by the Japanese died. In O'Donnell, Cabanatuan, places in Borneo, and camps along the River Kwai the mortality was much higher than this. Conditions varied enormously from one Japanese camp to another all over the Orient, depending on whether the camp housed soldiers or civilians, who was commandant, what the Japanese expected to do with the prisoners, whether or not the Japanese were preoccupied with other problems, and much else. In all camps, though, there always existed the threat of punishment and torture. In many of them it was a deadly reality: certainly it was in O'Donnell and Cabanatuan.

Just why the Japanese should have been so unspeakably savage much of the time, yet maddeningly unpredictable in their responses and deeds, is not easily determined. Langdon Gilkey, an intellectual who was interned in a camp for civilians along the China coast, found the Japanese national character mysterious; a fascinating amalgam of cruelty, militarism, slavish obedience to superiors, and an inferiority complex, mixed with genuine love of beauty and culture. A Japanese medical sergeant, captured and interrogated on the point, was untroubled by subtleties like these. The Geneva Convention, he said, was all right in peacetime but when you fight a war you do everything you can to win. This reflected a common Japanese attitude in the camps I was in.

Some enemy cruelty was merely the casual barbarism of natural brutes. At Shumshuipo on the China coast, for instance, Formosan guards tortured and bayoneted children merely for sport and relief from boredom, while a camp official in the same place sometimes made the prisoners line up opposite each other and hit one another to amuse off-duty officers. Gwen Dew records that in Hong Kong she saw Japanese torture several Chinese and an Indian merely for amusement. Much of the torture that I saw was neither systematic and refined like that of the North Vietnamese twenty-five years later, nor was it inflicted carefully for the entertainment of sadists. Usually it consisted of a fusillade of blows, kicks, slaps, and stabs, delivered in reprisal for some minor breach of camp regulations, or else it reflected nothing more complex than the momentary rage or frustration of some guard.

Most bore it well. Pappy Boyington claimed he had heard many American prisoners moan when tortured but had never heard one cry out. Mrs. Keith, imprisoned on Borneo, witnessed torture many times. She said she never saw a victim lose courage or dignity. Rather, she said, the usual result of staged brutality was to increase everyone's hatred of and contempt for the torturers.

As on the Death March, there was no ideological or practical reason for much of the cruelty that I saw. Unlike the North Vietnamese who systematically inflicted fiendish tortures on captured American pilots in order to wring testimonials from them that could be used as propaganda, none of the Japanese I ever encountered showed any interest in brainwashing anyone. General Wainwright records that after having been beaten systematically for months by Japanese guards his captors turned around and tried to persuade him and other prisoners to testify that they had been well treated, but I never heard of anyone else who had a similar experience, and in General Wainwright's case the Nipponese change of heart came late in the war when Japan was clearly losing.

Sometimes brutality appeared to be designed to make us show fear or to break our spirits. Commander C.D. Smith, a riverboat captain in China before the war who was imprisoned by the Japanese in Shanghai, said he combated this not by hating his captors but by deliberately cultivating contempt and disdain for them, telling himself repeatedly that they were, after all, only inferior, silly little men playing at war but destined to be crushed ultimately. Maybe this course was both safe and wise for one who spent his time in solitary confinement, but anywhere I was an open expression of contempt for the Japanese immediately put one's life in danger.

On one occasion, in my experience, the motivation for cruelty was obvious and disgusting: perverted sexuality. One afternoon a sergeant in my outfit was on guard duty inside the camp fence. The Japanese guard on the outside ordered him to masturbate. The sergeant refused. The Japanese then came inside the fence and beat the sergeant so mercilessly that he went mad and died two or three days later. It was episodes like this that led many to claim that it was the worst Japanese soldiers, alcoholics, sadists, and the depraved, who were assigned to guard duty. Perhaps so, but that was not the whole story. Japanese officers must have known about such bestiality. They could have stopped it had they cared.

One major reason for Japanese cruelty was evident to all: the desire to humiliate us. Nothing delighted our conquerors more than to abase Americans in some ostentatious way. Perhaps their own concern to "save face" led them to think that to impose humiliation was the worst thing they could do to their enemies. Certainly they seemed anxious to repay occidentals for the racial arrogance white people had often displayed towards orientals. Probably they were also compensating for inferiority complexes. Yugi Aida, a well educated and thoughtful Japanese who was held by the British for two years after the war, wrote that Japanese knew that most westerners regarded them as ugly and that, at bottom, they regarded themselves as ugly. Interestingly, Aida, who hated the British, believed that the superiority complex of the British officer class, like that of the ancient Greeks, derived from their impressive physical appearance!

Whatever the explanation, the Japanese never missed a opportunity to rub it into us that they were the conquerors and that we had become mere Helots who must do their bidding. Everywhere in the Orient they loved to march either Allied prisoners of war, or western civilians encumbered with baggage, down roads and through city streets before crowds of Filipinos, Chinese, and other Asians. Often they would interrogate prisoners naked, or kneeling. They would lie to us to raise our spirits so that when the truth became known the let down would be worse. They would show us food and then not give it to us. They would administer beatings for failure to salute Japanese privates, or failure to salute guards before and after using the latrine. They beat up our officers in front of enlisted men and assigned high ranking officers to demeaning tasks or compelled them to flounder hip deep in mud to cultivate rice. With some men such treatment struck home painfully. Generals Wainright and Brougher repeatedly expressed their outrage and humiliation at having to perform "coolie labor," to herd goats, to address all Japanese with utmost politeness, salute privates, and arrange personal effects with meticulous care at inspections.

Lieutenant Jack Hawkins, who later escaped from Davao with me, was similarly outraged at such an inversion of normal military order.

The Japanese delighted in accusing prisoners of cowardice, lack of fortitude, and inability to endure suffering. Especially hard to take were calculated insults to the American Flag: using it as a dishrag or for other dirty vile purposes. Such treatment was designed, in words of one Japanese, to cure occidentals of "proudery and arrogance."

It must be admitted that the Japanese were not the sole practitioners of this sort of thing. Yugi Aida bitterly resented British arrogance in general, and in particular being given jobs such as cleaning excrement out of blocked toilets with his bare hands. But what galled him above all else was the way British nurses treated him unconcernedly as a mere beast. When he was assigned to clean their barracks they would walk around half-clad, even naked, give him their underwear to wash, order him about with motions of their feet or chins, and "reward" him by tossing cigarettes on the floor at his feet![1] After her release from prison Agnes Keith said she found it hard to listen to American G.I.s boasting of the indignities and beatings they had inflicted on the Japanese as it had been to endure what she had seen and suffered. For myself, the sight of what hatred and brutal training caused the Japanese to do made me appreciate as never before the humane atmosphere that had prevailed at home, in school, and in our community in my formative years.

One of the many peculiarities of the Japanese was their obsession with preventing escapes. Of course all people at war try to prevent prisoners from escaping. At the same time it is generally recognized that one of the duties of a prisoner of war is to escape if he can; and, like captives everywhere, war prisoners do think about escape a great deal. If a prisoner does manage to get away from a detention camp, authorities in most countries do not regard it as a major calamity. But the Japanese were different. While individual guards were vigilant to prevent escapes for an obvious reason: they would be blamed and punished if prisoners were missing; Japanese authorities seemed to be shocked by the very idea that a prisoner should attempt to escape. It angered them to think that anyone would want to run away from them. It seemed to them something of an insult, an act of personal disloyalty.

The Japanese devised elaborate techniques to prevent escapes. First of all, they used American sentries inside the barbed wire camp perimeter to supplement their own sentries on the outside. They also believed in mass punishment. Accordingly, they divided us into groups of ten. One's nine compatriots were usually those who slept nearby in one's barracks. These groups we called our "shooting squads." If one man escaped the other nine in his "shooting squad" were to be executed. When it came to the deed the Japanese often had mixed feelings about whether to actually shoot the nine helpless hostages or not. Sometimes they did, sometimes they didn't, but one could never feel any confidence about the matter. Bert Bank once thought he was scheduled to be shot so he decided he had nothing to lose by trying to escape. When he told this to his personal "shooting squad" they watched him carefully thereafter for fear they would all be executed if he tried. Months later in Davao when ten of us planned what proved to be a successful escape we agonized a long time about whether or not the Japanese would really kill ninety of our buddies after our departure.

The past had not been reassuring in this respect. Once at O'Donnell, Jack Donohoe was on a work detail along a river cutting timber and shaping it for piles. Someone brought a note from Filipino guerrillas, then operating in the mountains nearby, saying they were going to attack the camp that night and attempt to free the prisoners. They did attack as promised, but the Japanese beat them off and only one prisoner escaped. Camp authorities promptly called off the names of nine Americans and marched them off to a coconut grove to be executed. Jack, who was watching nearby, said the Japanese allowed one man, a Sergeant Mazurek, to make a statement. The sergeant stepped out and asked God to bless all those who were going to die and to bless America. The firing squad then mowed them down with a volley, and finished them off with more rifle shots at close range.

One attempt to escape, highly publicized in Life magazine afterward, had an especially gruesome ending. Three American officers were so desperate to get away that they tried to crawl through a ditch and get outside the camp in the daytime. Our guard on the inside tried to dissuade them. Maybe he was afraid he would be executed if the three got away? Maybe he thought of the hostages who might be killed? Maybe he thought the three had no chance and so tried to save their lives? Whatever his motive, he turned them in. The Japanese then tied them savagely. Then for three days any Filipino who came by was forced at bayonet point to smash the men's faces with a two-by-four. (The Japanese never missed a chance to try to drive wedges between Filipinos and Americans.) For three horrible days the men hung on their crosses, only 200 feet from my quarters, their faces and bodies beaten to mush, covered with dried blood and flies. Finally, a combination of starvation, dehydration, and their injuries mercifully carried them off. Afterwards the guards went out of their way to tell us that one of the men had been beheaded, another bayoneted to death, and the third buried alive, all to impress upon us the fate of those who tried to escape.

For all their brutality, the Japanese remained as puzzling in the camps as they had been on the battlefield and the Death March. On one occasion a Mexican corporal managed to escape. He passed himself off as a Filipino, and even got a job working for the Japanese in a nearby town. There he learned that nine men were to be executed because of his escape. Conscience-stricken, he returned to camp. The Japanese, for whatever reason, were content to assign him to clean latrines for a month.

Though most of the Japanese with whom I had any dealings were thugs, some were not bad fellows. Later, in Davao, one Japanese Catholic noticed my St. Christopher medal, smiled at me, and the next day brought me five scapular medals and a cross. Another, earlier, showed me an unexpected kindness after I had endured the worst beating I ever received in prison camp. A few days after we arrived at O'Donnell the Japanese put me in charge of a detail of twenty enlisted men to drive to Tarlac, some fifteen miles away, to bring back a truckload of rice. I was specifically instructed to have nothing to do with Filipinos and to pass these orders on to the enlisted men, which I did. We arrived, and the starved and weakened men went to work wrestling 158 pound bags of rice onto the truck. A Filipino boy of perhaps fifteen began to whistle "God Bless America" to get my attention. I looked in his direction. He made the "V for Victory" sign, pointedly dropped a bag in the street, and walked away. Oscar Wilde once said he could resist anything except temptation. He must have been thinking about people like me. I ignored what I had told my own men, walked over to the bag, picked it up, and was immediately observed by a Japanese guard who had also seen the Filipino boy. He ordered both of us to come to him. First, he beat the boy unconscious with his fists and rifle butt. Then he took me to a nearby warehouse alongside a railroad track. Some 500 fully outfitted Japanese were standing nearby, waiting for a train. The guard motioned for five of them to break ranks and join him in taking me into the warehouse. Once inside the place, which was filthy, the five soldiers set upon me methodically. They slugged me, kicked me in the groin, knocked me down at least twice, blackened both my eyes, knocked out two teeth, spat on me, and finished by laughing at me and mocking the American surrender of Bataan. The guard then took me back to the truck which, by now, was loaded. I ached from head to foot, and burned with humiliation in the bargain because I had been beaten for something I had ordered my own men not to do. Incredibly, the Japanese driver smiled at me and pointed to the back of the truck. There was the sack the Filipino boy had tried to give me! Back at camp the driver gave the sack to an enlisted man who eventually brought it to me. It was full of flat brown sugar cakes about the size of saucers. For a starving man it was a princely gift.

Afterward, when I ate some of the brown sugar, it affected me strangely. After having been starved for weeks the sugar jolted me far more than a big drink of whiskey on an empty stomach. The sensation was somewhat like an electric shock followed at once by a general glow and a feeling of renewed strength. The experience was common among prisoners who had been given sugar by Filipinos or who had managed to acquire it in some way. Leo Golden and others even claimed that sugar helped them control the jaundice which was common in the prison camps. I have never heard a medical explanation for this.

The sugar episode, which involved me, and another that took place on Mindanao but in which I was not involved, show how it was possible for both sides to have waged the war mush less inhumanely. Shortly after the war began, when the southern Philippines were still in American hands, six U.S. airmen were put in charge of an impromptu detention camp that held twenty-nine Japanese. Nominally, the prisoners were civilians, local businessmen. Actually, they were Engineering officers. Several of them spoke good English. They appointed a leader who got on well with the Americans. The Japanese worked faithfully, always wanted Americans to accompany them when they had to deal with Filipinos, for the latter regarded them with open hostility. The Americans appreciated the situation and were so confident of the trust-worthiness of the Japanese leader that they would let him sit in the front seat of a truck, driven by an American, and hold the driver's rifle. Needless to add, such camaraderie vanished as soon as reports of the savage and bestial fighting on Bataan began to circulate in the southern islands.

The morale of American prisoners in World War II has occasioned considerable discussion, though nothing like as much as that which followed the Korean and Vietnam Wars. James Bertram, who was a prisoner of the Japanese in China for forty-four months, remarked that two themes predominate in all prison camp literature: heroism, and man's inhumanity to man. I have to agree, and also to acknowledge that at camp O'Donnell selfishness and inhumanity were more in evidence than heroism. Nevertheless, the whole matter was complex and as a lawyer might put it, fraught with extenuating circumstances.

To start with, though the Japanese might have been intent on establishing a New Order in the Far East they were not above venality in the Old Order. Before long it became possible for prisoners who had managed to smuggle money into the camps or who had outside "contacts" to buy food and cigarettes, at inflated prices, in sufficient quantities to save their lives or even keep in tolerable health. In Santo Tomas Eve Hoyt managed to borrow more than $1000 to buy powdered milk for her daughter at $150 per can and brown sugar at $65 per pound. In Cabanatuan Mellnick and two others paid $75 for a box of tea, three pineapples, and 100 eight ounce cans of pilchards which Steve said "drew us back from the brink of death." Others traded cigarettes to the Japanese for food, stole various articles and bartered them for food, traded personal possessions for food, or simply bribed guards. Eventually the Japanese established canteens in most camps where prisoners could buy small quantities of food at extortionate prices.

Lloyd Stinson knew several prisoners who were energetic black marketeers. The Japanese employed them as truck drivers to haul supplies from Manila to camp. The men had managed to meet various Filipino civilians who, due to some snafu, had been thrown into the same camps as the military prisoners. Many of these Filipinos were former gamblers, bartenders, brothel keepers, and persons of comparably equivocal backgrounds who knew similar types still doing business in Manila. The truck drivers made contacts on both ends and brought money from the people in Manila to their friends in the camps. The truck drivers, certain Japanese guards, and peripheral figures received cuts from the whole operation.

Though I knew that such black marketeering, racketeering, smuggling, and bribery were commonplace I seldom actually saw such dealing and I had nothing at all to do with it personally. It was not that I had moral objections to buying food on the black market, much less stealing it from the Japanese. When a man is sufficiently hungry he will do almost anything for food. It was, rather, that like most of the prisoners, I never had the money or opportunity to deal or smuggle.

Some people of stricter training or more severe natural outlook regarded all such activity as extremely reprehensible. After the war, Yugi Aida, the Japanese prisoner of the British, complained bitterly that those who had been admired by their fellows in prison camps were not the daring, courageous, patriotic warriors but thieves and smugglers, connivers and word merchants, fixers and scroungers. On our side Marine Lieutenant Jack Hawkins, whom I knew, and Colonel Gaskill, whom I did not, had a similar views of similar types in our camps. They were dismayed by what seemed to them an erosion of morale that was little short of catastrophic.

I cannot say flatly that they were wrong, but I believe circumstances accounted for a good deal. When men are struggling just to keep alive they readily forget loved ones, concern for others, generosity, even common civility. They compete fiercely for scraps of food. They steal and refuse to share because they regard others as rivals for limited resources. When they are packed closely together they get on each others' nerves, become testy, quarrelsome, pessimistic, and insubordinate. Their conversation degenerates into an amalgam of oaths and curses. In O'Donnell most of us were so preoccupied with our personal misery that the plight of others meant little. Months later at Davao, where I worked in the kitchen and got occasional "extras" to eat, I used to smuggle food to Ed Dyess and two priests. I don't know if I could have made myself do it at O'Donnell. Almost anyone who has been in circumstances like these has thought, said, and done things he does not like to remember.

Our first few days in O'Donnell saw our morale sink to its lowest ebb. Many thought, "Here we are. We have surrendered. The U.S.A. can't help us. The Japs will let us die." There followed a phenomenon which seems to have been common in camps all over the Far East, and even in the Vietnam War a generation later: the prestige of officers declined dramatically. This took place, it seemed to me, partly because some officers did not honor the ideals they were supposed to exemplify, partly because normal military authority could no longer be exercised effectively, partly because of sheer insubordination. Many enlisted men blamed the officers for their plight, cursed them, and refused to show ordinary military courtesy.

Jack Hawkins thought this state of affairs, which he saw only at Cabanatuan and not at O'Donnell, was disgraceful. The prisoners seemed to him inexcusably soft, selfish, spiritless, and lacking in heroism, a condition which he attributed to the general softness, lack of discipline, and unconcern for high standards of conduct in American civilian life. Even in Davao, later, where morale was much higher, Jack did not admire or trust many.

Bert Bank put it more simply. He said many of us in the camps went insane and that all of us degenerated mentally to some degree. Bert was probably right on the latter point, though I would put it another way: that our harsh regimen brought into the open the dark side of the human character, which always exists, barely submerged, and warped our judgment. I particularly remember a case of the latter. One day I needled a former boxer who liked to boast about his pugilistic prowess. Admittedly, this was not an intelligent action on my part, though I was gentle about it. The ex-pug flew into a rage and flattened me with one punch. He was immediately and genuinely sorry and told me so profusely. He was just on edge. It is also indicative of Ed Dyess' concern for those whom he regarded as "his" men, even in prison camp, that he notified the chastiser pointedly that his fate would not be enviable if he ever again laid hands on anyone in the 21st Pursuit Squadron.

It is harder to judge the validity of Jack Hawkins' views on the shortcomings of the prisoners. I agree entirely with his contention that, as a group, the Marines stood up better than most others under the burdens, humiliations, deprivations and temptations of camp life; and that this was due to the quality of their training. It did seem to me, though, that not nearly as many men fell short of duty and civilized conduct as Jack and Colonel Gaskill thought. Doubtless the question cannot be answered satisfactorily, for what it really asks is how much heroism can reasonably be expected of ordinary men, and of trained men, under extraordinary pressure? I do not agree with the Japanese,

Aida, that camp "operators" were more respected than conventional "good soldiers."

One major generalization about morale is safe: collaboration with the enemy, on a significant basis, became a problem only later in the Korean and Vietnamese Wars. Of course collaboration was difficult in the Pacific in World War II. The Japanese made no effort to influence us ideologically so there was nothing to be gained by accepting their world view. It was nearly as pointless to try to curry favor with guards since none of them had access to appreciable quantities of food. Most prisoners had little contact with guards anyway. In Vietnam some Americans collaborated with their captors in varying degrees after being tortured, or threatened, or merely in response to offers of favored treatment; many more came to think resistance to the will of their captors was pointless when highly placed anti-war activists in the United States were being hailed as idealists and heroes instead of traitors. In the Korean War the question of morale among U.S. prisoners provoked much comment and some alarm. Many prisoners were treated as cruelly by the North Koreans and Chinese as we had been in World War II, and in many of the same ways. In addition, the Communists subjected great numbers of them to intensive interrogation, for which they were ill-prepared. Many G.I.s knew distressingly little about American history, traditions, or ideals, or why the war was being fought at all. Due to this, the hardships of prison camp life, and subjection to the techniques of brainwashing by skilled and tireless interrogators, somewhere between 10% and 70% of American prisoners eventually collaborated with their captors in varying degrees. The vast disparity in estimates is due mostly to different opinions about what should reasonably be considered "collaboration" in given circumstances.

No true crises of morale ever took place among American prisoners in World War II. Yet what went on in camps of all kinds was sufficiently disillusioning that it destroyed the whole liberal-humanist faith of Langdon Gilkey, a conventional "progressive" academician who was interned in Shantung. Though Gilkey was in a camp that contained only civilians, their greed, hypocrisy, and struggle for immediate personal advantage astounded him. What had happened to reason, fairness, justice, morality, compassion, learning, even common sense? He was shaken so profoundly that he rediscovered Original Sin and concluded that businessmen, ward heelers, politicians, lawyers, and policemen know a lot more about real human beings than do philosophers, natural scientists, social scientists, and humanitarians. I believe I would have to respond to Gilkey much as I have to my friend Jack Hawkins. In camps I saw people do things I had never heard of before. I was ashamed of myself occasionally for hiding food that my conscience told me should have been shared with others. Like the detainees in Shantung I hated to see more prisoners packed into our barracks when we were already overcrowded. Overall, life in prison camp sharpened my awareness of the unattractive side of human nature. Still, unlike Gilkey, I was not shocked to the depths of my soul because I had not harbored so many illusions about humanity to start with.

If men sometimes seem like devils, they are never entirely so. After an initial shakedown the mood of selfishness, gloom, disillusionment, and despair gradually lightened. After all, human beings can adjust to almost any regimen. As weeks, and then months, passed we began to fit into the routine of camp life better. Conditions improved some too. The Japanese got hold of things administratively, and life became more orderly and predictable. Simultaneously, our attitude began to change. A sense of proportion returned. From sad experience we learned how fruitless it was to snarl at each other and to try to take advantage of others when we were all in the same boat. After a few months there was a noticeable tendency to forget grudges, control speech, complain less, and work harder at trying to get along so life would be more bearable. Gradually, it became possible once more to appeal to men's honor, honesty, pride, and self-respect.

Finally, there had always been some individuals who had remained selfless and generous throughout our ordeal. Their example was an inspiration to others. One such case I will never forget because the men involved were close to me. One of them, whom I shall call Roger, had been a friend since the first days of the war. In Camp O'Donnell Roger was extremely ill with malaria, dysentery, and such a bad case of jaundice that he was deep yellow over his entire body. Somehow Roger had come to believe that Ed Dyess did not like him. I never knew the reason. Perhaps Ed had ridden him hard on the Death March or in our first days in camp in an effort to strengthen his will to survive. Anyway, Roger was a proud man and would not speak to Dyess. Ed knew that Roger might die. He also suffered from all Roger's illnesses himself. In various ways Ed had been able to accumulate a small stock of food, and he knew that Roger, who got only his daily rice ration, needed extra food desperately. He felt certain that Roger would never take anything from him so one day he gave me a can of sardines and asked me to give it to Roger without telling him where it came from lest he refuse it. That our squadron leader would give away such a rare and precious commodity when he needed food badly himself, and would trust me, also half-starved, to deliver the can intact, show what kind of man Ed Dyess was. Roger never learned where the sardines came from. The whole episode bolstered my own faith in humanity at a crucial time in my life.

Many prisoners of war have been asked what aspect of their existence was hardest to bear. Some have said solitary confinement is the worst punishment one human being can inflict on another; that if prolonged it drives one mad. Yugi Aida, the Japanese prisoner, said it was being treated cruelly with detachment; slighted, snubbed, insulted casually, regarded openly as a mere animal or "thing." He insists that he would have found it easier to bear intense cruelty at the hands of an enemy filled with rage or hatred, to which the Englishman who translated Aida's book retorted, "If you believe that you will believe anything." When he was not being tortured or thrust into solitary confinement Commander Richard Stratton, held six years and treated with great cruelty in Vietnam, thought mere boredom was the most onerous feature of being a prisoner. Carl Mydans, a LIFE photographer incarcerated in Santo Tomas, said lack of self-respect was the worst, though I am not sure exactly what he meant by that remark. General Brougher knew what he meant. He said he hated to be hungry since thinking about his stomach all the time diminished his self-respect. He added that the most maddening cruelty the Japanese inflicted on him was to deny him personal mail for eighteen months. Jack Donohoe, whom I still see occasionally (1994) agrees with Stratton that the dull routine of camp life was extremely wearing, but he thinks the feeling of sheer helplessness, of being powerless to improve one's situation, was worse. Nothing depressed him so much as to watch Japanese planes fly overhead. He found it hard to believe that the United States could overcome Japan and save him.

As for me, I never had the slightest doubt. I agree totally with Agnes Keith that loss of freedom and loss of privacy, which is a part of freedom, were harder to endure than anything else. To be packed closely into barracks with scores of others; to have to sleep for months only inches away from filthy, stinking, diseased men stained with their own refuse; to have to stand in line with hundreds of others, often for hours on end, to be fed, to get water, even to go to the latrine; to have to perform every bodily function before an audience only a few feet, or inches, away; to have no emotional privacy; this was my true crown of thorns in prison camp. A cynic might say, "Well, at least you weren't lonely. You might have been in solitary." I was never put in solitary so I don't know whether it would have been worse; but I do know that I detested the absence of privacy, longed for freedom above all else, and thought about escape every day. Lloyd Stinson stood it for forty-two months. I have never understood how. To this day I dislike lines and sizable gatherings of any sort.

Many people have asked me how I managed to survive the dreadful existence in the camps. For one thing, it is hard to kill a man by mere ill treatment if he is determined to live, and I was. I also thought I *would* live. Unlike some, I never thought our country had deserted us, or had lost the capacity to win the war eventually. I wanted to see my wife, family, and friends again. I wanted to let the American people know what we and the Filipinos had endured. At bottom I always believed that God would not desert me.

I am convinced now that faith and determination were crucial everywhere. For instance, the women who were imprisoned with Agnes Keith in Borneo brought with them a total of 34 children. Every one came through alive. Keith thought general determination to save the children probably enabled most of the women to survive too.

Be that as it may, individual responses to confinement varied enormously. Some decided to take advantage of all the free time to think carefully about every aspect of their lives, with an eye to eventual self-improvement. Some thought much about the postwar world, and made plans for it. Others thought systematically of all the fine places they had seen. General Brougher deliberately busied himself at everything from petty camp chores to writing poetry in hope of avoiding the mental and cultural degeneration he observed in others.

Such thoughts hardly crossed by mind. My concentration was not on self-analysis or a better world order. It was on food and escape, in that order. Had anyone suggested to me that those who remained in camps the longest would be the ones most likely to degenerate personally and that, therefore, they had a special need to think of their own lives and the future, I probably would have replied offhandedly that the reverse was nearer the mark: that only those who were strongest and best adjusted *already* could endure protracted captivity; but in truth I seldom thought of this side of life at all.

Unquestionably, many subsidiary factors bolstered our faith, courage, and capacity for survival. A certain stolid apathy, akin to oriental resignation, certainly helped. After one has been starved, beaten, and humiliated for a long time he no longer responds normally to stimuli of any kind. New beatings and insults touch him but lightly and briefly. More filth or degradation does not break him because he has already endured so much and gotten used to it. If he has a settled determination to survive, if only to outlast his tormentors, he may still die from some disease, or from having no food at all, or from a bullet in the head, but it is extremely difficult to wear him down further: to kill him indirectly or gradually.

Though it may seem odd to readers, agreement is remarkable among alumni of prison camps that survival owed much to unsubstantiated rumors for, on the intellectual level, the worst enemy of a prisoner of war is despair. The Japanese knew this, and in O'Donnell and Cabanatuan they tried hard to keep us from getting any news of how the war was going. In some places prisoners managed to get radios or to make their own out of scraps, even though the penalty for possession of a radio was death. Some of Lloyd Stinson's friends had one, but I never did or was close to anyone who did. Thus I got little real "news." Rumors, however, proliferated. Invariably, they were highly optimistic: pessimistic ones were disregarded and forgotten. Always some great American victory had been gained; or a secret weapon had been invented; or a major Allied landing somewhere was imminent; or in a month, or three months, or six months, the war was going to end; or the United States was going to do something that would improve our condition in some dramatic way. At one place on Mindanao nine U.S. airmen refused to surrender when Corregidor fell. They took to the jungle, became guerrillas and built themselves a radio. Even in those circumstances, which ought to have sobered the most confirmed optimist, they were so sure American forces would wind up the war in a couple of months that they squandered their batteries heedlessly and soon had only dead radios. Sometimes the rosy rumors had other bad side effects: they caused men to fail to save food, or to eat the contents of Red Cross packages too rapidly. Nonetheless, there is no question that glittering rumors broke the tedium of camp life and, when they were half-believable, kept up our morale by giving us hope. As one prisoner put it, "There is no more determined optimist than the convict on indefinite sentence." Jack Hawkins was convinced that our higher ranking officers had been wise to keep from us the full story of Pearl Harbor. The truth, he thought, would have destroyed our morale. Maybe the politicians are right when they think ordinary people need a steady diet of good news. . .

Significantly, the Japanese, displaying their customary blend of distorted insight and malice, would sometimes try to torture us by starting sensational rumors so they could puncture them later and thus let us down. This tactic eventually proved self-defeating for as soon as we got wise to the game we trusted our Japanese guards less, became tougher mentally, and began to pride ourselves on mastering our emotions.

Work helped keep us going too. Almost anyone's morale rose noticeably if he was on some regular detail. He was doing something purposeful, filling up his day, using up time that otherwise would have been given over to destructive self-pity or mere contemplation of his disconsolate fellow sufferers. To be on work details had tangible advantages too. A few berries pulled off a bush or some edible roots grubbed furtively and eaten were a marvelous tonic when one subsisted on a diet that was 90% rice. If the work was hard, as it was sometimes, Americans have never lacked skill in gold bricking.

Tobacco unquestionably buoyed up a good many. Non-smokers or light smokers like myself were amazed at the passion of some of our fellows for tobacco. The latter would trade their most precious possessions to get a few cigarettes, even though the smokes were often shredded banana or papaya leaves, or even dried grass, that tasted more like the paper in which they were rolled than anything else. But whether they were prisoners trying to bribe Japanese guards to smuggle them cigarettes, or the guards themselves angling to trade food or favors to prisoners in return for cigarettes, to all the smokers tobacco was life's premier luxury. For some, it deadened the appetite for food a bit, for others it provided a few minutes of pleasure in an otherwise sordid and dreary day. Cigarettes more truly than money constituted the currency of prison camps. Non-smokers and those of us who could control our appetite for nicotine naturally took advantage of this. We traded any cigarettes we might obtain from Red Cross packages, or in more devious ways, for medicine or extra food that might save our lives. Jack Donohoe, always an enterprising sort, even figured out a way to steam the mold out of cigarettes that had gotten wet in the Red Cross packages, and so restore their marketability.

Alcohol would have sent the morale of many soaring, had there been any chance to get it. In fact the opposite occurred. Several heavy drinkers whom I knew said their health improved in the camps because they were cut off liquor entirely.

My own greatest solace in camp, by far, was religious faith. This was also true of many others, in different ways and varying degrees; of still others not at all. Edgar Whitcomb said he envied men who could attend religious services and pray but felt that for him , a non-believer, to get "foxhole religion" and resort to prayer when he had malaria would be cowardly. The Scot, Ernest Gordon, who was not a religious man when the war began, said he could not attend services for a long time because he knew that most of those who had turned to religion were merely scared: they hoped the Bible would prove to have magic properties and they prayed to God to get them out of a tight spot. Subsequently, he changed his mind entirely, grew religious, and became convinced that developing religious faith was all that saved many of the prisoners who toiled with him in the dreadful Kwai valley. After the war he became a Methodist minister. Pappy Boyington said he prayed properly for the first time in his life when he was floating, wounded, on a raft in the ocean after having been shot down by a Japanese pilot. He did not try to bargain with God, he said, but merely expressed his willingness to accept whatever a Higher Power had in store for him. He thought this helped him a good deal in the next two months. Ed Dyess had been taught the doctrine of predestination in his Presbyterian youth. He said he was confirmed in this belief when he leaned to one side in the cockpit of his plane and thereby missed being killed by a Japanese bullet. It simply had not been his time to go, and the thought fortified him thereafter. Several pilots captured in the Vietnam War turned to prayer and religion though they had not been religious before. Afterward, they considered that they had been strengthened crucially. Even Japanese soldiers reported finding the doctrines of Buddha immensely fortifying when they were plunged into despair at the end of World War II. In the Korean War no United Nations troops stood up so well in captivity as the Turks: simple, stolid, devout Moslems, impervious to the doctrines of Marxism or the pressure of their North Korean captors. It seemed to me that those who endured life in the camps most successfully were men of this general temperament: uncomplicated, straightforward, religious, patriotic, and tenacious.

Some non-believers found it impossible to become Christians themselves but were generous in their praise of religious fellow captives. Sidney Stewart was one of many who spoke admiringly of a Father Cummings, who became an almost legendary figure for his kindness and expertise in keeping up the spirits of suffering men. Agnes Keith wrote warmly of the serenity, unselfishness, and obvious goodness of many nuns who were imprisoned with her. Because they were better disciplined than lay people and lived for God they bore hardships with better grace than anyone else, thereby giving invaluable example and encouragement to everyone. She added that they were not blind to the worldly side of life either: they were the most skilled smugglers in her camp! Langdon Gilkey, interned with civilians in China, thought some of the many clergymen in his camp were lazy and that a fair number of the Protestants were narrow, unsympathetic, righteous types, but he acknowledged that, as a group, the clergy were more honest and cooperative than any category of lay people. All admired the Catholic clergy, he said, because they mixed with everyone, bore burdens without complaint, worked at anything willingly, and were also black marketeers whose activities ultimately added to the food supply of everyone. Ernest Miller spoke well of all chaplains. He thought the treatment they provided for the spiritual hunger of men did more good in the camps than even food.

My own reliance on religion was less complex than this. I had been born, raised, and educated in Catholicism. My grandmother had always lived with us. She was a profoundly religious woman who prayed several hours every day. In addition, every day, whatever the weather, she walked to church to hear two or three Masses. I went to Saint Aloysius Grade School, which was run by the Holy Names Nuns, and later to Gonzaga High School and University, where I was taught by the Jesuits. I liked and respected my teachers at both places. While there has never been any public clamor for my canonization, and I took part in more than my share of adolescent pranks and adventures entirely devoid of any religious dimension, the influence of my family and teachers did make me totally Catholic in the sense that I accepted the doctrines of that Church without question and prayed and attended Mass regularly all my life. Consequently, when I faced hardship, danger, or death in the war I turned to faith and prayer at once, reflexively. It seemed to me close to impossible to be immersed in human suffering and inhumanity, to see dozens of men dying around me every day, and still keep my sanity and will to survive without having strong religious faith. I did not attend Mass at O'Donnell because it was not available. The priests who had been on the Death March were like the rest of us, still recovering, and the Japanese had not yet granted them facilities. When we got to Cabanatuan some sort of contact had obviously been made with religious authorities in Manila for host and sacramental wine had been secured, and Mass was said periodically. Thereafter I attended when I could.

Like so many others in prison camp, I found the chaplains immensely inspiring. They were unselfish when most of the rest of us assuredly were not. They got up at four or five o'clock in the morning to say Mass for their fellow prisoners. They worked hard both to comfort the dying and to make the lot of the living a bit easier. Overall, their conduct more than measured up to the ideal they were supposed to personify. This strengthened my own faith in God and my conviction that, somehow, God would not let me die in a Japanese prison. Like Gilkey, I was more impressed by priests than by the Protestant clergy, but in my case little can be concluded from this since most of my contacts were with priests. Those Protestant chaplains whom I saw performed their duties faithfully and earned general respect.

NOTE: Starving their unhappy captives was standard Japanese policy all over the Far East. Bert Bank, who was in the same camps as I, went from a normal weight of 185 down to 130 in Cabanatuan in June, 1942. A year later, he weighed only 102, and had also gone temporarily blind from malnutrition. Bank, p. 36. General Wainwright, a lean man already, was starved from his normal 170 down to 132 in six months and 125 in eight months. Considine, pp. 180-181. Pappy Boyington, imprisoned in Japan, went down from 190 to 110 in nine months, gained it all back when he got a job in the camp kitchen, and was then worked back down to 110 near the end of the war. Boyington, pp. 298-301, 325-326. Agnes Keith lost thirty pounds in a camp in Borneo, watched fat women lose more than a hundred pounds, and saw her six foot husband starved to a skeletal eighty pounds. Keith, p. 112. Eve Hoyt, a woman of average size, spent three years in Santo Tomas, widely regarded as one of the "easier" camps. She weighed sixty-five pounds when she was rescued in February, 1945.

Colonel Miller in *Bataan Uncensored*, and Colonel Gaskill, in *Guests Of The Son Of Heaven*, relate many gruesome tales about the exotic and disgusting things men were driven to eat in their desperate anxiety to stay alive. Cf. especially Gaskill, pp. 41-43, 47, 53-55, 71. Pappy Boyington records that he ate great handfuls of stinking lard when he got into a camp kitchen, and that once in the course of two days he gradually gnawed to bits and swallowed a large soupbone. Boyington, pp.298-301. A Marine who worked as a stevedore on the docks in Japan once made soup of the Japanese commandant's pet cat. Martin Boyle, *Yanks Don't Cry*, pp. 192-193.

In most ways, though, prisoner stevedores like Boyle had an easier time of it than men in the Philippine prison camps. Their Japanese custodians were usually less harsh. More important, they could often steal food from the cargoes they unloaded.

Like myself, General Brougher was surprised that lean men endured starvation diets better than those who were overweight (D. Clayton James, South To Bataan, pp. 63-64). Steve Mellnick, *Philippine Diary*, p. 170, was struck, as I was, at the low resistance of alcoholics.

One of the few happenings in the camps that provided a little humor occasionally was the effort of some Japanese to speak "impressively" in English when they had only half-learned the language. The officer who wanted to cure occidentals of "proudery and arrogance" served in a women's detention camp. Keith, p. 44. Captain Imamura, the commandant of Camp Karenko on Formosa, expressed the same thought in comparable colorful phraseology. He forbade American prisoners there "to have the haughty attitude over the people of Asia or to look them down, which have been their common sense for a long time." James ed., p. 47.

Gwen Dew's experiences with Japanese caprice resembled mine. Though she despised the Japanese in general, she also recorded that various Nipponese guards and journalists had brought her extra food, lent her money, and shown her other kindnesses. One even took her for a walk on Lincoln's birthday! Dew, pp. 139, 160-161, 179-181, 184-185, 193-196, 198, 203. Mrs. Keith found the Japanese even more inscrutable than Dew and I. With us, at least it was different individuals who were cruel or kind. With her, the *same persons* would treat her brutally and then give her presents or do her favors, Keith, pp. 164, 200-206. Carlyle Townswick, *Too Young to Die*, pp. 24-30, describes the camaraderie between Americans and their Japanese prisoners on Mindanao in the first days of the war.

The conduct of American prisoners in the Korean War is depicted in a highly unfavorable light by Philip Knightley, *The First Casualty*, pp. 351-352. Most American newspapers and magazines during and after the war were more lenient in their estimates and judgments. John G. Hubbell, *P.O.W.: Definitive History of the American Prisoner-Of-War Experience in Vietnam, 1964-1973*, pp. 478ff. provides a more extended discussion of the subject in the later war.

Langdon Gilkey's disillusionment with his fellow prisoners is described vividly and at length in *Shantung Compound*, pp. 18-20, 71-96, 101-161.

The phase of pessimism, greed, and despair, followed by a general mellowing and gradual return to more civilized habits, also took place in other camps. Cf. Keith, pp. 104, 111, 235-236; and Gordon, *Through The Valley Of The Kwai*, pp. 113-214.

Many of the American prisoners in the Vietnam War displayed great personal courage and exceptional devotion to each other. Probably it was easier to respond thus when the most hideous aspect of their existence was torture rather than the threat of starvation. Cf. Hubbell, pp. 85-88, 411-412, especially.

---

[1] Aida, *Prisoner of the British: A Japanese Soldier's Experiences in Burma*, pp. 30-40. European aristocratic ladies in the Old Regime sometimes acted similarly around peasants and male house servants, as though they were animals rather than men.

Chapter Five
The Voyage to Davao

IN OCTOBER, 1942, the Japanese offered 1000 "literate laborers," as they engagingly phrased it, a chance to volunteer for regular work somewhere other than Cabanatuan. Those taken would be sent to Japan, to Mindanao, or to any of several other places. All ten of us who would eventually escape into the jungles of Mindanao five months later came from Cabanatuan. Though we did not all know each other yet, all of us wanted to leave because we had become convinced that to stay would mean eventual death. Still, we did not all volunteer in the same spirit. Ed Dyess feared that the destination of the "literate laborers" might be Japan. If so, we would probably be put to work in factories and would never have a chance to escape. He pondered the matter at length, and finally dealt out two poker hands: one to stay, one to go. The "go" hand was the better one. My own choice was simpler. When Ed told me he had signed up, I did too. Three Marines, Lieutenant Jack Hawkins, Lieutenant Mike Dobervich, and Captain A.C. Shofner, volunteered together, not knowing where they were going but figuring it had to be better than Cabanatuan. Major Steve Mellnick, a more cautious man, waited until he became convinced from the rumor mill that Mindanao rather than Japan was where we would go. All of us had heard that there was much fruit in Mindanao. We hoped that there would be more of other kinds of food too. We knew it was 600 miles closer to New Guinea and Australia than where we were now. Presumably, Americans were operating somewhere in the South Pacific. To go to Mindanao would at least move us nearer to our countrymen and reduce our problems should we ever have an opportunity to escape.

About October 25, the thousand of us who had volunteered to be transferred were fed before dawn, assembled in groups of 100 with full packs, and marched off towards the town of Cabanatuan, a few miles away. Many of those who stayed behind waved to us from inside the barbed wire fence. We thought it a bad omen that Lieutenant Hozumi should be in command of the operation. Hozumi was taller, stronger, and better looking than most Japanese but he was a self-conscious Bushido type. Unlike most Japanese soldiers, whose clothing usually looked slept in, Hozumi's well cut uniform was sharply creased and spotless. He wore shiny leather boots and a samurai sword in a gleaming silver scabbard. He was cruel by nature and regarded all prisoners of war with undisguised contempt. We all hated and feared him but, of course, had to hide it. His second-in-command, by contrast, was Lieutenant Yuki, a small, mild, reasonable man; one of the few Japanese I ever saw who was a Christian.

In the town of Cabanatuan we were loaded into the same sort of small boxcars that had taken us from San Fernando to Capas a few months before. This time things were better. A sudden rainstorm soaked our clothing and packs but refreshed us and, even better, cooled the metal cars. Moreover, only eighty men were packed into a car instead of 100-115, and the doors were left open for ventilation. After several hours travel we reached Manila. The Japanese marched us through empty streets to Old Bilibid prison where we were to spend the night. A classmate of mine, "Ship" Daniels, collapsed on the March from a combination of disease, malnutrition, and exhaustion. The guards promptly beat him up and then carried him to Bilibid where he died that night.

Bilibid was not a camp but a real prison with stone walls and cells. To our surprise, we were fed soon after our arrival: more rice than usual, augmented by greenish soup that contained stringy vines and some fragments of meat of undetermined classification. We slept on a concrete floor. The next day, the Japanese, concerned as usual to humiliate us, turned out Filipino crowds and marched us through the city streets to the waterfront. The people were silent save for some who whistled "God Bless America." Filipino women wept openly, and an occasional brave soul would flash the "V for Victory" sign to us. The exhibition was hardly a Japanese triumph.

We were put aboard a ship that the Japanese used to haul both cargo and prisoners. Though the old tub was filthy my spirits were high, momentarily. It seemed wonderfully refreshing just to be out of camp and on a ship of any kind. I should have known better. Anything connected with the Japanese that was half-pleasant or promising always had a catch in it somewhere. We soon discovered several catches. For one thing, the ship was not marked. American submarines would have no way of knowing we were aboard and might torpedo us. To add to our disquiet, scores of barrels of gasoline were loaded. One hit from a torpedo would kill us all for sure in the ensuing explosion and fire. Immediately worse were the sleeping quarters: decks three feet high partitioned into compartments five feet wide and ten feet deep. Their floors were covered with filthy mats populated by thriving colonies of lice and bedbugs. The guards crammed twelve men into each of these revolting sweat boxes. Troopships, of course, have always been crowded but, as Bert Bank put it, the Japanese were undisputed world champions when it came to packing soldiers into railroad cars and the holds of ships.

Steve Mellnick described our ten day voyage to Davao on the southern shore of Mindanao as a luxurious interlude on our existence as prisoners. He wrote of filling our bellies with squash, dried fish, and even some corned beef, along with the inevitable rice; of salt water baths, of his health improving dramatically; even of hearing men talk about girls for the first time in months. Even Dyess commented on the markedly improved food.

All I can say is that their memories were remarkably selective. The only pleasant feature of the trip I can recall is that when we got out to sea some enterprising soul managed to open a hole into the ship's hold. The hold contained large stocks of such canned commodities as sardines, pork and beans, and corned beef. From that moment, whenever we thought we would evade the Japanese guards who came down to our sleeping quarters periodically, we would send a man from each "sleeping group" to steal what he could as quickly as possible. I took a chance for my group once and managed to get half a dozen cans of Ritter's pork and beans, a brand I never heard of before and have never seen since. No matter! They tasted like filet mignon. We had a feast. Predictably, some men could not restrain themselves and stuffed their shrunken stomachs with far too much rich food. I saw one poor fellow drink a whole can of sweetened condensed milk. It produced alternating convulsions and vomiting that nearly killed him. At least as surprising as our discovery of this marvelous larder, was that somehow the Japanese never found out that we had raided it.

Far more memorable than the stolen food was some that we were given by our captors: a generous issue of salt pork. Most of us ate all we received, with relish. The aftermath was catastrophic. We were soon beset with atrocious stomach cramps, followed immediately by attacks of diarrhea. Cramped into our tiny sleeping quarters, we were usually unable to get out of them soon enough to make it up to the top deck where the latrines were located. Even if we did get there the latrines were usually occupied, and we could not wait. In short order the ship was covered with excrement throughout the sleeping quarters, on the floors in the hold, and all over the deck. Though the Japanese would clean the deck with fire hoses a couple of times a day this basic condition lasted for the entire voyage. Every hour I dreamed how good it would be to get off that foul, stinking ship and onto the ground again.

Moreover, as always, I thought about trying to escape. Chances were virtually nil, though since the ship was well out to sea most of the time and even the strongest of us were too weak to swim more than a few hundred yards. Besides, within two or three days my persistent dysentery, aggravated by pork-induced diarrhea, left me exhausted, dazed, and apathetic. Perhaps it was for the best for then, like so many others, I lapsed into a stuporous sleep much of the time. Thus the voyage passed faster.

The trip did have a few redeeming features. The food *was* somewhat better than what we had been used to and, periodically, the Japanese began to act more like human beings. Now and then the guards would rotate us up to the top deck so we could get some fresh air and exercise. More noteworthy, when two Americans died aboard ship their bodies were not merely chucked overboard to the sharks, but were buried at sea with proper courtesy and ceremonial.

A few prisoners, whose luck was running, got to live on deck instead of down in the stinking, suffocating hold. This happy occurrence was not due to any sudden outburst of Japanese humanitarianism but to the mundane fact that it was physically impossible to cram everyone aboard into the hold. Ed Dyess and the three marines who would one day comprise part of our escape group, Hawkins, Dobervich, and Shofner, stayed on deck throughout the trip. Though they were rained on every night their clothes dried quickly next morning and they were spared the infernal existence below deck.

One day there was a lot of excitement. A fight broke out among the Japanese crewmen, probably from somebody getting drunk. For perhaps twenty minutes Japanese chased one another all over the ship, yelling, cursing, and swinging at each other. The whole ruckus came to a climax in a general battle on the bridge. In the course of it one man was thrown down onto a lower deck where he lay unconscious for many minutes. The few Japanese officers on board showed no interest in the brawl. They merely stood by idly and watched it subside of its own accord.

There were many rumors of mutiny during the voyage. Since the American prisoners and two companies of Philippine Constabulary troops aboard together outnumbered the Japanese overwhelmingly, there is little doubt that had we made up our minds to disregard casualties the ship could have been seized. But what would we have done next? There was much furtive talk about how a mutiny should be carried out, and much speculation about whether an American submarine would be able to recognize Americans on deck and so refrain from torpedoing us if we should seize the ship. I had nothing to do with planning a mutiny though I would have joined one energetically had it begun. Dyess said afterward that he wished we had tried; that Filipinos would have joined us eagerly, and that he thought there were plenty of places we could have taken the ship. I have little doubt that had an American submarine surfaced while all the talk was going on it would have triggered a mutiny. But this never happened. Instead, some of the ringleaders talked to Navy men on board, especially to Commander Melvyn McCoy. The sailors were not sanguine. They pointed out that we lacked weapons and that even if we should manage to overcome the Japanese, which was problematical in itself, they would almost certainly get off a radio message before they were subdued. We would then be attacked by Japanese planes or ships. So the projected mutiny, like the Japanese free-for-all, gradually faded away.

On November 7, most of us were put off at the dock of a lumber company about fifty miles from the port of Davao City on the southern island of Mindanao. With his habitual cruelty, Lieutenant Hozumi made us sit in the sun for several hours before he set us marching towards Davao prison camp some twenty miles away. We followed a dirt road through a dense jungle. Gigantic Philippine mahogany trees hundreds of feet tall rose on each side. They supported vast tangles of vines filled with chattering monkeys and screaming parrots. There were swamps everywhere and the smell of decaying vegetation filled the air. The March was difficult in daylight. It grew terrible when darkness fell and a rainstorm broke. Then the road became a sea of mud, filled with holes we could not see but often stumbled into. During the rest period I fell asleep at once from utter exhaustion. When the March resumed many prisoners collapsed in the mud. On the Death March they would have been bayoneted but now our bodies were wanted for labor so trucks picked up the straggling and the helpless. Long after midnight those of us still on our feet staggered into camp.

Chapter Six
Davao

Our new home was situated on a slight rise in what had formerly been an impenetrable jungle. It was a penal colony, established by the Philippine government in 1933 for long-term convicts. When we arrived its native population consisted of some 100-150 Filipino murderers. From the first the Philippine government had wanted to clear the jungle. This would keep the inmates busy and promote their rehabilitation. Equally important, Manila wanted to make Davao a large scale model farm. By 1942, several thousand acres had been cleared and brought under cultivation. The land was fertile and produced a variety of crops: rice, avocados, sugar cane, cassava, peanuts, camotes, corn, mongo beans, coffee, and a great array of fruit. There was also much fine mahogany timber near the camp so the colony had a lumber mill. Cinchona and rubber plantations, and a chicken farm, completed the layout. When we were there Davao fed and supplied the convicts, its own agricultural staff, and 2000 prisoners of war with what they needed to sustain life, and provided a considerable surplus for military posts and government hospitals as well. The whole colony was surrounded on three sides by what seemed an impassable barrier of jungle and swamp.

Our living quarters consisted of nine barracks about 150 feet long and sixteen feet wide, located parallel to each other about fifty-to-sixty feet apart. They were bare, with wooden floors, and wooden walls a few feet high. Above these sideboards was closely meshed barbed wire which reached to the tin roofs. Inside, the barracks were lighted by a few dim electric bulbs. Outside there was a kitchen and mess hall, latrine buildings, a chapel where religious services were permitted, and primitive hospital with some medicines that had been brought in on the GRIPSHOLM, the last ship from the western world that the Japanese allowed to bring Red Cross supplies to prisoners and to evacuate civilian internees. The whole living quadrangle was perhaps 100 yards square, surrounded by a barbed wire fence, and guarded by elevated watch towers at the corners. Outside the compound were some modest frame houses where the Filipino agricultural staff lived with their families, and the barracks of the Japanese guards.

Nobody was glad to see us. The morning after our arrival Major Maeda, the Commandant, delivered one of those ornate orations which always seemed to delight the Japanese. He expressed disappointment that we seemed so weak and unhealthy, but promised that we would be able to overcome our degeneracy by regular outdoor work.

Some one thousand fellow prisoners who were already on hand did not put out welcome mats either. There had been little fighting on Mindanao. Most of them had surrendered at Del Monte when Corregidor fell. The Japanese had then moved them to various prison camps, letting them take along their footlockers, canvas cots, books, and Army Rations. Since the Japanese did not like G.I. food they let the prisoners eat their own rations. Due to this regular, nutritious diet the men had remained healthy and strong. They also had their own administrative organization in the camp; even a finance officer. To them, we seemed like poor relations. Indeed, they found it hard to believe what we told them had happened to the survivors of Bataan and Corregidor. Soon enough, their own food ran out and they got a chance to discover, first hand, what we had endured for the preceding six months.

The Japanese did not treat us badly at the outset. They gave us blankets, mosquito nets, and shelter halves; assigned us to barracks according to rank; expanded the American camp administrative staff; and, on our first morning, gave us a filling breakfast of cassava root fried in coconut oil with our standard rice. It was not Hollywood, nor home, but much less dismal than Cabanatuan. Though Davao had its ugly features, the fact that only fifteen Americans died in the five months I was there indicates the difference between it and Cabanatuan or O'Donnell.

Davao had ten Philippine agronomists. Their function, and that of the convicts, was to teach us to farm and to make sure that the colony throve. They began, quite sensibly, by leaving all the men who were sick or over forty-five years old in the hospital to convalesce, or in the barracks to weave baskets. Everyone else went out to work in the fields or forest. Overall, the regular work was good for us in several ways. It gave the stronger men something to do and so kept up their morale. Many outside jobs also provided opportunities to pilfer food and thereby maintain strength and health. Nonetheless, some tasks were tough. Planting rice was the worst. Not only was there no chance to steal extra food when one was hip deep in the mud in a rice paddy; the work itself was unhealthy and fatiguing. Filipinos usually covered their feet and legs with wrappings when working in rice paddies to protect themselves against sticks, sharp stones, leeches, and other hazards in the mud. Americans had to work barefooted, which meant that their feet and legs were soon cut, bruised, and covered with the infected sores that develop so rapidly in the tropics. Moreover, most of the work had to be done stooping. Men whose stomach muscles had been weakened by starvation and inactivity often developed hernias.

102

Cutting and sawing timber was also arduous, wearing toil since the mahogany trees were huge and hard as iron. Other jobs were less onerous. Harvesting rice, picking fruit, digging ditches, repairing roads, plowing fields, hauling gravel, and cutting grass on the malarial control details were not easy tasks but not man killing either. Ed Dyess eventually got one of the better jobs: chauffeur of the camp bull cart. Because Ed had demonstrated unusual capacity for handling cattle he had been assigned to haul poles, coffee, and other commodities from place to place. The knowledge of every part of the camp which he acquired while making his rounds, and the fact that Japanese guards got used to seeing him and his bulls, were to be important factors in our eventual escape.

One of the redeeming features of Davao as compared to Cabanatuan was that Japanese supervision was less close. Our keepers did not think anyone could survive in the swamp and jungle. Thus it seemed to them that there was little possibility that anyone would try to escape in any direction other than along the single road out of the camp that went westward and then south to Davao City. Consequently, they did not watch the eastern and northern sides of the camp with much care, and did not assign guards to every work detail as had been done in Cabanatuan. Instead, they relied considerably on roving patrols to check the details periodically. Since the patrols usually came at the same time every day the American field workers could often goldbrick, look for extra food, or plan for the future.

On our first day in Davao the Japanese lined us up and selected certain men for various jobs. My luck was running. A Japanese mess sergeant whom we came to call Abes-san picked me to work in his kitchen. I never knew why. Perhaps because I was near to the front of the formation? Maybe because I was smaller than most Americans? Anyway, it was a great break. Kitchen jobs were among those most sought after in all camps. It was in this kitchen that I first met Mario Tonelli, the Notre Dame football player, a cool, fearless man who soon became a fast friend, and another congenial American, Sergeant Smith.

Abes-san was in his forties. He had been a tailor in Tokyo in civilian life. For some reason, he liked me from the first and treated me well. He would defend me against other Japanese, let me eat food Japanese officers left on their plates, and pay no attention if I occasionally snitched stray morsels around the kitchen. I am sure he would have favored me and the others in the kitchen crew even more had there been no other Japanese around. Still, he did not allow himself to be imposed upon. Once he caught a famished American major trying to steal some onion trimmings and gave him a severe beating.

My tasks in the kitchen were to start fires under the rice cauldrons in the morning, haul wood, prepare bath water, and do odd jobs.

Some prisoners thought the Japanese were dirty but I agree with Pappy Boyington, who also worked in a Japanese kitchen, that they were clean people both in their persons and when handling food. They had a particular love for hot baths, and preparing their bath water was one of my more interesting duties. Every afternoon I had to fill fifty-five gallon retired oil drums, start fires under them to heat the water, and then transfer it into corrugated iron community bathtubs that would hold four or five people. Japanese guards coming off duty delighted to soak in those tubs. They were never empty.

Once Abes-san took me fishing at a small local lake filled with sunfish. He angled in country club style. He had me bait his hook with a bit of banana, seemingly the No. 1 lure in that part of the world. Then he would cast. The sunfish must have been starved or suicidal for they bit immediately. Hooking a fish drove Abes-san into paroxysms of joyous excitement. He would land his fish amid loud shouts of sheer delight. I would then take it off the hook, put on more bait, and the process would be repeated. In about forty-five minutes he caught a whole bucketful of fish. No child on Christmas morning was ever more elated.

Another time Abes-san was comparably overjoyed because I was able to do him a different kind of service. He had heard that a certain American major had a seventeen jewel Bulova watch. Though he did not know it, it was the same major whom he had previously pummeled for trying to steal onion tops. Now he wanted the major's watch and was willing to trade food for it, food, incidentally, which he would steal from his own larder. He asked me to make the contact. I sought out the major and inquired how many cans of and what kind of food he would expect for his watch. He indicated that five of almost anything would be splendid. I told Abes-san that the major was willing to barter but had not been explicit about the price. Abes-san then suggested five cans of fish and five of corned beef, mangos, and pork and beans. Since I could not carry twenty cans of food past the guards at the gate I took a few each day. Abes-san, who outranked the guards, would walk with me to the gate to make sure I got through safely. In a few days I brought him the watch. He pried it open, counted the jewels, and fell into transports of joy comparable to those he displayed the day he caught all the sunfish. He congratulated me repeatedly for my good work on his behalf. Sadly, the major who traded the watch later went mad in the camp, attacked a Japanese, and was killed.

Incidents like the last reminded us regularly of the grim reality of war and captivity. One day a Japanese guard whom we were used to seeing come through the mess line stole a wristwatch from another American major. On the Death March and at Camp O'Donnell guards had plundered prisoners at will but by now Japanese authorities had things better organized. Now theft from prisoners was strictly forbidden. The major complained to American authorities, who relayed the protest to their Japanese superiors. The thief, whom everyone knew, was taken into a small banana grove only fifty yards from the kitchen, where I could see everything clearly. He was made to stand at attention and absorb a merciless beating from two fellow guards.

The culprit was so mortified by this experience, and so fearful that news of his deed would follow him home and disgrace his family, that soon afterward he shot himself while on guard duty. Such drastically different ideas about what constituted honor and dishonor constantly bedevilled our relations with the Japanese and must have caused some of their seemingly senseless brutality towards us.

One much happier day in the kitchen I still recall with relish. One morning someone brought in a big tuna. Abes-san's chief assistant was Toka, a short, stocky, powerful, industrious, three-star private with wide gaps between his front teeth. On this occasion Toka attacked the huge fish with a sharp knife and assigned me to wave a banana leaf to keep the flies away. He filleted the fish expertly, cutting it into small chunks about an inch square. Before he had gone to work Toka had thoughtfully provided himself a mixture of ginger root and soy sauce. Every few minutes he would dip a square of tuna into this mixture and toss it into his mouth with a loud grunt of satisfaction. Occasionally he would pop a piece into my mouth. It was delicious, and my enjoyment of it was evident. Toka would then grunt and give me a huge toothy smile. Unfortunately, we had tuna only once.

My good relations with Abes-san proved extremely useful when we began to make serious preparations to escape. Because I was known as his friend I was able to wander all over camp without alarming guards or being molested by them. This made it easier for me than for any others in our party to gradually smuggle supplies out the gate and hide them in the jungle. I had been caching supplies for many days before I was transferred to the plow detail, some two weeks or so before we tried to escape.

Afterward, Ed Dyess wrote that I gave up my job in the kitchen because I hated the Japanese so much I could no longer trust myself around butcher knives. Ed's memory must have failed him because reality was more prosaic. I came down with one of my many attacks of malaria and could not work at all for four or five days.

When I lay ill Abes-san came to see me. He told me he was being transferred to a war area hundreds of miles to the south and that he had come to say goodbye. He gave me an egg, a can of mangos, and an atabrine tablet for my malaria. The only place I can think of where he might have gotten such a rare commodity as an atabrine tablet was from a Japanese soldier who had taken it off a dead American in New Guinea. Wherever he got it, it was a rare gift at that time. It left me with a warm memory of one of the best Japanese I ever encountered.

There was lots of food in Mindanao. The problem was how to get it. Our captors allowed us some, but to get anything like what we needed to maintain health or comfort we had to purchase it at high prices, when few of us had much money, or resort to theft. As always, Filipinos would be beaten if apprehended giving food to Americans. At first the Japanese fed us reasonably well, certainly much better than they had in Cabanatuan. For breakfast we got rice with either cassava or camotes; for noon and evening meals more rice with some mongo beans or vegetable soup. Maybe twice a week a couple of bites of cara-bao meat would be added. At Davao too, for the first time, the Japa-nese taught us how to cook rice so its full food value was preserved and it turned out to be something other than mere rice soup. They employed a steaming process which required much less water than we had been using. It left the individual rice grains separate and the bot-tom layer in the cooker almost crisp. Sometimes we were given pieces of dried fish too. Fastidious men objected to the worms that frequently resided in it; others, more concerned for their health, ate the fish, worms and all, in order to get sorely needed protein. Those who worked in the fields could usually improve this diet considerably by "liberating" fruit, vegetables, and even an occasional egg or chicken. They also frequently smuggled food back into the camp compound and gave it to old or sick prisoners. I, of course, had opportunities to get extras in the kitchen. A few others were even more fortunate. Mike Dobervich, for instance, was assigned to a detail where he could steal all the food he wanted. Eventually he developed a thirty-nine inch waistline. Of course many people become pot-bellied when they are chronically half-starved, and some did so in both Cabanatuan and Davao, but Mike's equato-rial bulge derived from eating much culinary contraband, particularly banana.

Such luck was highly exceptional: most men had little chance to supplement their regular diets. Hundreds suffered terribly from beri beri and other vitamin deficiency diseases. In April, 1943, when we escaped only about 1,100 of the 2,000 prisoners were still able to work. Most of the remaining 900 were partially or totally blind from diet deficiencies, unable to walk due to beri beri, or disabled by severe her-nias. Many were not expected to live long.

What just a little extra food would have meant to most of them became apparent when some of the sick prisoners, heretofore con-fined to camp, were put on light work on the coffee plantation without guards. Many of them were near death from semi-starvation. Within two weeks the addition of fruit, camotes, and an occasional stolen chicken to their rice restored them amazingly.

In the absence of most medicines, the line between life and death for chronically undernourished men was narrow. Ed Dyess said he survived scurvy only because friends who worked in the fields stole melons and fruit for him, and that he kept up his strength during an attack of malaria only because I was able to smuggle food out of the kitchen to him. The Japanese issued just enough quinine tablets to keep malaria sufferers alive. We never got enough to really combat the disease until Red Cross packages arrived around Christmas of 1942. Much is indicated by the fact that I, who got to work in the kitchen for about three and a half months out of the five I was in Davao, was once reduced to eighty-five pounds by repeated attacks of malaria and weighed only ninety pounds when we made our escape in April, 1943. Even then I had to be one of the stronger men or I could not have attempted to escape: the others could not have risked taking someone who might quickly prove to be a burden to them.

Outside of actually escaping from the Japanese the best thing that ever happened to me in captivity was the arrival of the Red Cross packages noted above. We subsequently discovered that the boxes had been sent in June. Why it took six months for them to reach us, when American prisoners in German camps got Red Cross supplies EVERY WEEK, nobody ever knew; though the most likely explanation is mere Japanese callousness and vindictiveness. That we received them at all may have indicated that the Japanese authorities thought it desirable to appear to be making amends. Whatever the case, nothing could have meant more to famished prisoners. Men cried unashamedly when they opened the packages.

The boxes were about a foot square and perhaps eight inches high. The contents varied considerably, depending on whether they had been packed by the American, British, Canadian, or South African Red Cross, but all of them had been put together with real intelligence. They contained an array of foods and useful articles: cheese, butter, jam, canned meat, canned fish, canned fruit, biscuits, prepared puddings, condensed milk, corned beef, vegetable stew, tea, rice, coffee substitute, cocoa, soap, combs, razors, and cigarettes. A few even contained sweaters and hats. Even more valuable were the medicines in them: quinine for malaria, sulfa pills to combat the curse of dysentery, Vitamin B concentrate to reduce beri beri, iodine, and various anesthetics.

The packages were a boon in several ways. The food and medicines undoubtedly saved many lives. The mere arrival of something from the outside world was immensely heartening for it assured us that we had not been forgotten. Most important to several of us, we could now begin to stockpile the foods and drugs that would be essential if we were ever to have any realistic chance to escape. We could save some commodities from the packages, and barter others for things we had to have in greater quantities, especially medicines.

The Japanese, with their customary meanness, confiscated most of the cigarettes, chocolate, and cane sugar, and some of the medicines, before giving us the remainder. They said they would give us brown sugar in exchange for the white sugar, but they never did. They also cut vegetables out of our diet on the ground that we no longer needed them, though when all the food from the packages had been consumed the vegetables were not restored.

As usual, some of the prisoners lost control of themselves, gorged on rich food, and got sick; but for most of us the packages were the proverbial manna from heaven. I used some of my Red Cross foods to vary the daily rice ration. The rest I stashed away for the day when I might try to escape.

Better food at Davao and the addition of the Red Cross boxes wrought a marked improvement in our habits and dispositions. Just a little more to eat greatly moderated the wolf-like selfishness so much in evidence at O'Donnell and Cabanatuan. No longer did we fear to leave our food and other possessions unguarded where we slept because men no longer stole from each other. In fact, we even gave each other a few things. For instance, Lieutenant Gordon Benson gave me some clean underwear. This would have been an unheard of act of generosity in O'Donnell. Most of us were more friendly now too. Banter became more common, card playing increased, and many read such books as were available. Civilization gradually made a comeback.

Our Japanese overlords remained as capricious as ever. Everyone hated Lieutenant Hozumi, the handsome sadist, who slapped around his own guards if they failed to salute him with sufficient smartness and who regarded us with open disdain. Still, we seldom saw Hozumi or any other Japanese officer since the chore of handling prisoners was largely given over to the enlisted men. Most of the latter were third rate troops who dealt with us according to their individual temperaments and momentary feelings.

Some of them were as savagely cruel as the worst guards in O'Donnell and Cabanatuan. One day an American working just outside the barbed wire fence called to someone inside to throw a canteen of water over the fence to him. A guard in a nearby tower saw the canteen go over and raised a shout. The American unscrewed the top of the canteen and poured out some of the water to show the guard that nothing was amiss. The Japanese replied by shooting him down in his tracks and firing two more rounds into his back as he lay in the dirt. One nasty little Japanese guard used to swing his gun butt at the heads of men, stupefied with fatigue, as they strained to push overloaded railroad cars along the track. When we were trying to learn how to handle brahma bulls and carabao, as will be described later, we did a lot of crude and inefficient plowing. For that the Japanese made many men do minor jobs in swamps during the rainy months, insuring that they would thereby acquire more colds, infections, and malaria than usual. And the Japanese still beat prisoners with their fists on occasion.

Still this was the worst side. In most ways relations with our conquerors improved somewhat. Japanese guards were usually young, seventeen to twenty-two. Most of them wanted to learn as much English as they could. A few Americans also learned Japanese though most were like myself, content to master a few phrases. In my case, Abes-san taught me two Japanese phrases: Happy New Year and I like you very much. He urged me to employ them whenever I could. I did so, with salutary results. The Phrase for Happy New Year was particularly productive since the Japanese customarily give presents on the New Year. Now and then I reaped a small gift for my studied politeness. This would never have happened in the earlier camps. There, more likely any Japanese would have beaten me for presuming to address him at all. Some of the guards were decent fellows too, at least part of the time. Now and then they would do such things as exchange food on details, give an American a few cigarettes, look the other way while some prisoner sequestered forbidden fruit or vegetables, trade looks at pictures of wives or girlfriends, compare notes about different kinds of training in our respective armies, or even express the wish that someday America and Japan might be friends.

Occasionally the goodwill gestures were more important. Now and then an English language news sheet was passed out. It contained information about the war, from a decided Japanese point of view, of course, but we welcomed it as better than nothing. Once the Japanese gave Sidney Stewart and his friends a violin, which they enjoyed immensely. They also gave the rest of us some other instruments and allowed the Filipinos to donate a few more. With them we formed a band. Soon after, our captors played a baseball game against us. We never tried harder in our lives to win but our opponents were so much stronger physically that they eventually beat us 14-10. They never invited us to play again, perhaps because we acted undiplomatically. Marine Captain Shofner slid hard into the Japanese second baseman, upending him. The American viewers responded with loud cheers, and our band struck up "Stars and Stripes Forever." The Japanese were miffed, of course, but what was remarkable was not their reaction but that they had allowed us to form a band and play a ball game with them in the first place.

Their most civilized act was to give us a five day holiday at Christmas. To celebrate the occasion properly a variety show was planned for Christmas Eve. All communities in the camps were to take part. The production certainly approached the ultimate in variety. The American band played Christmas carols, which we prisoners sang. Some young Filipino girls, mostly daughters of agricultural staff people at the camp, performed native dances and managed to look so touchingly beautiful in the process that for the first time in many months the thoughts of most of us turned to something other than food. The Japanese then finished off with some hair-raising war songs, sword dances, a mock demonstration of hari-kari, and a Japanese version of the Charleston performed by the chief interpreter. Though we could not say so openly, most of the Americans agreed with Dyess who said of the war songs that he had never heard such abominable caterwauling in his life.

Not the least indication that some of the Japanese had taken a turn for the better was their failure to punish us on an occasion which Colonel Mori, the commandant at Cabanatuan, surely would not have missed. A savage little Igorot tribesman had been caught selling tobacco to the Americans and had been whipped for it. Seething with rage, he bided his time. One day at noon break, a Japanese guard was seated on a log between Marine Captain Bill Prickett and a classmate of mine, Lieutenant Chuck O'Neil of Ames Iowa. The Igorot was chopping wood a short distance away. Stealthily he slipped up behind the Japanese and nearly decapitated him with one blow from the axe. Within seconds he took the dead man's shoes, rifle, and parts of his uniform, and disappeared into the jungle. We were all extremely fearful that the Japanese would inflict some awful mass punishment on us in retaliation, but they recognized that no American had been involved and did nothing.

My personal relations with the Japanese were equivocal. On one occasion a guard found me alone, grabbed his crotch, and made unmistakable gestures indicating pain. It was not hard to guess what troubled him since venereal diseases were common among the guards. I gave him a couple of sulfa tablets that had come in a Red Cross package. He expressed his gratitude by slipping me a can of fish a day or two afterward. Another time I got into trouble that might easily have become more serious than it did, due partly to my mentor Abes-san and partly to my own ill-advised optimism. One of the Japanese guards was a cocky little fellow named Moliama. Abes-san disliked him. One day after I had been in camp a few weeks and had gained some weight and strength Abes-san suggested a wrestling match between Moliama, who happened to be on K.P. that day, and myself. I was not enthused since Moliama was heavier and stronger than I, but I had no choice. As soon as the "contest" commenced I grabbed Moliama around the waist, jerked him upward, threw him down as hard as I could, and landed on top of him. Since I did not like the little peacock any better than Abes-san did, and was sure Abes-san would defend me, I was as rough as possible. I am convinced that the Lord has favored me on numerous occasions. He must have done so then by giving me more strength than I normally possessed. Abes-san was overjoyed and applauded. Moliama, understandably, was mortified. Like the Igorot tribesman, he did not forget.

Some time later Abes-san gave me some flour, eggs, and sugar. My kitchen compatriots, Smith and Tonelli, suggested that we make some donuts. We did so and set them aside to cool. Moliama happened to come in and tried to filch a few. Without thinking, I rapped his hand and reported him to Abes-san, who then gave him a public slapping. Humiliated once more, Moliama hated me thereafter. Weeks later I was out on a detail with Father Albert Braun, the Chief of Chaplains in the camp. Dressed only in G-strings, knee deep in mud, and beset by mosquitoes, we were supposed to be packing dirt around rice shoots to shore them up. I pursued the task resentfully and nonchalantly, merely kicking or slapping mud carelessly towards the plants. Father Braun warned me repeatedly that the Japanese would never be content with what resulted; that I should do the job right and stay out of trouble. I ignored him. We came to the end of the row. There, on guard, was Moliama, bayonet fixed and a malevolent gleam in his eye. He motioned at what I had done, barked at me, shook his bayonet, and made me do it all over.

Less impetuous men among us were careful to treat the Japanese with discretion. On one occasion Commander Melvyn McCoy, whose mind was much on escape, gave a band of Americans on a work detail a memorable dressing down for not responding properly to Japanese orders. He emphasized in words not easily forgotten the necessity of getting along with our overlords if existence was to remain tolerable within the camp.

Sometimes I have been asked if we ever played jokes on the Japanese. Not exactly, though we did manage to make fun of them in various ways. There was no merriment of any kind in Camp O'Donnell. Everybody there was exhausted physically and "down" psychologically. In Cabanatuan, though, and later in Davao when health and spirits had improved we mocked the Japanese in several ways. We gave nicknames, usually derogatory, to most of the Japanese officers and guards. One we nicknamed Stepin Fetchit because he had the same mournful look and shambling gait as the black comedian of that name. Among ourselves we mimicked the way the Japanese talked, walked, and comported themselves. Nothing like this could be done openly, of course, but we enjoyed a good many laughs privately. Now and then at Davao our rulers would make us line up to salute the rising sun, usually contriving to get a Japanese Flag somewhere near the sun. We rose to the occasion by thumbing our noses as we saluted. Sometimes an American would salute a Japanese guard, bow to him, smile, and then call him a whole string of unprintable names, a practice that had to be abandoned in Davao when English classes were instituted. The guards learned too many English words.

Men on work details sometimes figured out ways to kid the Japanese a little and ease their own lot at the same time. The guards feared the Moros, the fierce little Moslems who inhabit much of Mindanao. They also disliked going into the jungle, where many of the Moros lived. Sometimes on a detail somebody would slip into the jungle a short way and pound on a hollow log or make some other ominous noise. Someone else would then raise a cry of "Moros!" This invariably panicked the guards. For a few minutes they would go through the motions of searching the underbrush. Then they would find an excuse to move the detail away from the jungle, usually to some easier job. American ingenuity was likewise displayed when prisoners were put to work fortifying the camp. The prisoners built log embankments out of porous banana and papaya logs and covered them with a thin layer of dirt. Such "defensive positions" would not have stopped any missile more lethal than a baseball. In the same spirit prisoners strung barbed wire in such a way that a jerk on one strand would collapse the whole lot. The Japanese must not have had any military engineers in the camp since neither their officers nor their guards seemed to know one kind of timber from another. This was the nearest we ever came to sabotaging our conquerors. Most of the time there was no opportunity to sabotage anything for there was almost no complicated machinery or military equipment in any of the camps. We could have set fire to camp buildings, of course, but that would have punished ourselves rather than the enemy.

On one occasion Shofner and Hawkins humiliated a Japanese guard by accident. A Filipino had shown them how to dig, camouflage, and bait a pit to catch a wild pig. Their objective was to add some pork to their diet. Instead of a pig falling into the pit, however, a Japanese guard did! It happened right after a rainstorm and the man nearly drowned in the muddy water. Luckily for us, nothing was ever done about it, and we all had a good laugh.

Many Americans in the Pacific Theater, both in prison camp and outside, regarded the Japanese as ignorant, stupid, and inferior to western peoples in all significant ways. The indictment was long and detailed. Japanese were good at set pieces militarily but could not improvise because they were products of an authoritarian society and so lacked intellectual flexibility. They also lacked mechanical understanding and aptitude; hence they did such silly things as beat on the engines of stalled vehicles and leave airplanes grounded when they had only minor mechanical defects. They tried to work prisoners productively but refused to give them enough to eat to enable them to work harder even when the food they needed, fruit especially, simply rotted on trees or on the ground. They habitually asked prisoners ridiculous questions, and seemed incapable of coordinating details. Some of them were such blockheads that they couldn't even get either prisoners or their own troops to count off correctly. Their building techniques were a generation behind those of the United States, and they were blind to the utility of labor-saving devices. Many thought a nation of such thickheaded robots was bound to succumb to America in the long run.

Of course there was some truth in this conception of the enemy but it never seemed to me to be fundamentally correct. To be sure, the Japanese did tend to repeat their tactics. They would do such things as bomb a certain target at the same time every day, to such a degree that one could almost set his watch by them. Junior officers and enlisted men would carry out orders faithfully after they had become obviously inapplicable, even absurd. It was true that Japanese were better at set pieces than at free-lancing. Their refusal to feed us properly is more equivocal. I am convinced that it was due to malevolence rather than stupidity, though I suppose it can be argued that malevolence is a form of stupidity. Refusing to feed men well when they were worked was certainly counterproductive, as current jargon has it. The brainless cruelty of the Japanese also continued well past the time when they had any reasonable prospect of winning the war and thereby escaping punishment for their shameful deeds. They never marked prison ships, and thereby lured U.S. planes and submarines to torpedo and bomb ships loaded with American prisoners. As late as October, 1944, they still machine gunned prisoners struggling in the water after a prison ship had been bombed. In this particular case, my friend Jack Donohoe was one of the eighty-three men out of 750 who were neither killed by the explosion nor by Japanese shooting those in the water. He managed to hide amid some debris. Eventually he floated ashore and was rescued by guerrillas.

Even granting these indisputable demonstrations of imbecility, the other side of the case seems more impressive. Japanese soldiers, after all, were well trained, remarkably disciplined, enthusiastic for war to the point of fanaticism, and usually supplied adequately. It is hard to fault military leaders capable of planning, coordinating, and executing the attack on Pearl Harbor, the Singapore campaign, the conquest of the East Indies, and several lesser campaigns almost simultaneously, even though Japan's grand strategic design to conquer and hold all East Asia and the western Pacific was probably beyond the nation's intrinsic strength.

If all the Japanese sometimes did foolish things during the war we must not forget what other peoples, governments, and armies did. We Americans were caught napping at both Pearl Harbor and Clark Field. Several times during the war we bombed our own troops. The

British suffered ignominious debacles in Norway, at Dunkirk, at Singapore, in Hong Kong, and in Burma. The wretched incompetence of both the French and Italian armies has passed into legend. We need to recall that Stalin ignored more than ninety specific warnings that Germany would invade Russia, many of them so accurate that they named the day the attack would begin; and that the Russians clung to the notion that the tank was an infantry support weapon long after the German blitzkrieg had shown conclusively that tanks should be massed. We need, above all, to remember some of the things done by the Germans, the supposed masters of war in our century. They never mobilized women for war work with anything like the efficiency of the British or Americans. They tied up a million troops all over Europe and north Africa murdering Jews and enslaving conquered peoples when those troops might have conquered Russia. They allowed continuous friction and rivalry between regular army and Nazi Party outfits to undermine their overall war effort from the beginning to end. When General von Paulus' army was trapped at Stalingrad in the depths of a Russian winter at the end of 1942 his men were freezing, starving, and short of ammunition. What did the Luftwaffe airdrop them? Cellophane covers for hand grenades (but no grenades), four tons of marjoram, and millions of contraceptives. In the Orient, General "Vinegar Joe" Stilwell found the all-purpose inefficiency of Chiang Kai Shek's Chinese army maddening. If the Japanese were stupid in some ways, they had no monopoly on that characteristic.

If one thinks of the history of Japan since about 1850 it is hard to maintain that her people are unintelligent. Alone among the non-white peoples of the world, the Japanese responded to the threat of imperialism by modernizing their whole nation within forty years. They sent missions to the leading western nations a century ago, studied the governmental, educational, industrial, scientific, and military systems of all of them, and then tried to adopt the best of each for themselves. Since 1945 the Japanese have adjusted with amazing speed to the whole new constitutional and social system imposed by the Americans and implemented by General MacArthur. They rebuilt their shattered economy and are now (1982) among the world's foremost nations in almost all phases of industrial and scientific development. Japanese scientists have won their share of Nobel Prizes; Japanese technicians are second to none in the manufacture of automobiles, radios, television sets, optical equipment, and similar products. Japanese children show up well in schools in competition with those of other nationalities. If many Japanese soldiers were overbearing, cruel, and unreasoning during the war, that does not make it realistic to malign, much less underestimate, a whole people. Differences in language, culture, and national traditions are the commonest causes of the grotesque misjudgments peoples sometimes make of one another. Japanese soldiers in 1942 thought the Dutch, British, and Americans were soft, decadent, and cowardly; much inferior to themselves. Events soon showed this estimate to have been both exaggerated and premature. At times Japanese misunderstanding of American psychology approached the comic. On Guadalcanal Japanese infantrymen launched attacks on U.S. positions amid shouts of "To hell with Babe Ruth."

But to point out things like this is, as usual, to be wise after the event. *At that time* what could we prisoners be reasonably expected to think of Japanese who had behaved towards us with such brutishness? To my friend Bert Bank the matter was simple. The Japanese were a pack of savages who deserved to be wiped off the face of the earth for their cruelties. Ed Dyess agreed. He hoped one day to come back to the western Pacific and fight them again. General Wainwright concurred, though he did concede that the Japanese might be induced to moderate their cruelty by changing their educational system. Edgar Whitcomb, who became a conservative Republican in politics; and Ernest Gordon, the Scottish Highlander who endured a horrible existence in Thailand and turned permanently to a religious life, held that Japanese cruelties must be balanced against American employment of the Atomic Bomb, a weapon which they regarded as uniquely inhuman.

Philip Knightley, an English journalist of the Left, considers wartime atrocities in the Pacific to have been about even. He ascribes them, on both sides, to the "racist" character of war, a view which unquestionably contains some truth since cruelty always comes more easily when its objects are perceived as a lower branch of humanity. Pappy Boyington, the Marine air ace who was beaten savagely and repeatedly by the Japanese, reacted with magnanimity, perhaps because he was a naturally tough man who took brutality in life for granted. The only Japanese he hated, he said, were the guards who had clubbed and slapped him. As for the rest of the Japanese, they seemed to him to be composed of good and bad individuals in about the same proportion as other peoples. He thought they needed only some re-education to become as pro-American as the Filipinos had grown after 1904. He looked forward to the day when they would become America's allies, for they were more industrious and cooperative than the Filipinos! C.D. Smith, the China riverboat captain, thought the brutishness of the Japanese was confined mostly to their army; that the Nipponese navy was composed of gentlemen like their counterparts in America. I have to agree with Smith to some extent. On the voyage from Manila to Davao it seemed to me that the Japanese naval officers were, on the average, more reasonable and civilized than most of their Army counterparts. Perhaps the difference was due to the psychology of Japanese soldiers deriving from the age of the Samurai, centuries before Japan was influenced appreciably by Occidentals. By contrast, the Japanese

Navy was built after 1870, in a modern technical and scientific age, and in deliberate imitation of Western navies. Consequently, Japanese naval officers were more westernized in outlook and manners than most Army officers.

James Bertram, an ideological Leftist, attributed most of the atrocities to the Kempetai, the Japanese "thought police," who were the oriental equivalent of the German SS. He also blamed the whole fascist military-social system of pre-war Japan for brutalizing Japanese youth. Agnes Keith was sometimes angered sufficiently by the Japanese to call them "apes" but, basically, she was a pacifist who saw the Japanese as victims of their environment and war itself as the true source of all the brutalities. her remedies were the conventional liberal injunctions to work hard in peacetime to make the world a better place, and for the rich countries to remove the "causes" of war by sharing their wealth with the world's poor. Sidney Stewart, who survived several Japanese prison camps, and Stanley Falk, an academic historian, are typical of many who have contended that Japanese cruelty and indifference to human life in the 1940s was due mainly to that nation's past history, national traditions, and Bushido Code, and to the general hardness of life on a poor, crowded island. Consequently, in their view, the Japanese had reached only a sixteenth century European level of social development and humanitarian concern in a society that was twentieth century in its scientific and technological sectors.

When I was in the camps I often hated the Japanese, and I still did in the latter stages of the war. I will say for myself, though, that at no time, not even when everything was darkest in O'Donnell, did I hate *all* Japanese *fixedly* and *remorselessly* to the depths of my soul. Both the religious training of my youth and the fact that I had grown up with people of several different nationalities made it impossible for me to hate whole categories of humanity without reservation. Besides, even during the worst days in the camps some of our captors and overseers had behaved decently. As years have passed since World War II, I have come increasingly to agree with those who see wartime Japanese primarily as products of pernicious traditions and an unfortunate national history, both of which contemporary Japan appears to be surmounting.

It is also foolish to bear fixed, sweeping animosities for quite another reason. There is much in human affairs that is always transitory. Nowhere is this more evident than in international relations. Before 1948 Americans regarded the Chinese as friends; from 1948 to 1970 as enemies; since 1970 as at least potential friends once more. The Russians were our allies in World War II and our enemy at the end of that war. Today they are our friends once more. The Germans were enemies in that same war: now they are among our most valuable allies. Japan and America were enemies in World War II, but they have been political friends and quasi-allies ever since. Germany and Russia cooperated clandestinely in the 1920s, were fierce ideological enemies from 1933 to 1939, then became allies 1939-1941, then enemies once more after 1941. Italy was allied with Germany and Austria-Hungary in 1914, remained neutral when World War I broke out, and joined the Allies in 1915. In World War II she changed sides after the fall of Mussolini in 1943. When nobody knows what the next turn of the international kaleidoscope will produce it is wise to maintain reservations about all peoples.

If our relations with the Japanese improved somewhat in Davao, those with the Filipinos remained as heartening as ever. The Filipino convicts might have been murderers of some of their own countrymen but they were friends to us. The Japanese tried to win their support by promising them periodically that they would be pardoned since Japan had no interest in crimes allegedly committed in the Philippines before the war began. Since no action ever followed such words the convicts were unimpressed.

They were supposed to show us how to farm. One of the first things they taught us was how to appear busy while doing little. Various Filipino overseers were helpful to us in more positive ways. They taught us how to make pig traps. They listened clandestinely to radio broadcasts and then relayed the war news to us. They told us about the location and activities of Filipino guerrilla groups. They gave us invaluable information about possible escape routes, and even secured us some bolo knives for hacking through jungle vines and swamp grass. If some of us asked to be assigned to particularly desirable work details where we could secure extra food, build up our health, and store supplies for the future, they would arrange it if they could. Ultimately, two Filipinos acted as our guides in the actual escape. Without the aid of these friendly and courageous people we never would have survived.

People have often asked me if I ever despaired during my long months of captivity, if I ever concluded that the struggle for life was pointless because Japan would win the war? I never did, though I came close. On the Death March and in Camp O'Donnell it often seemed possible to me, even likely, that the Allies would lose the war. No doubt this was due mostly to my misery and consequent depressed state of mind. In Cabanatuan my natural faith and buoyancy began to return. That I took part in an attempt to escape from Davao indicates that the earlier mood of pessimism had passed entirely, for escape would have been meaningless had Japan eventually won the war.

On April 4, 1943, ten of us and two Filipino convicts walked out of Davao into an uncharted jungle. More than three months of careful planning preceded the event. Many of us had thought about escape and talked idly about it ever since our days in O'Donnell. The spirit quickened in Ed Dyess in January when he became a bull cart driver. Within a short time he became acquainted with the whole camp. The guards got used to seeing him and paid less and less attention to him. His natural optimism then grew rapidly. By February he had outlined a plan in his mind with sufficient vividness that when he was allowed to send a postcard home he added to it the words, "I will be home." One day Ed asked me quite suddenly if I would like to attempt an escape with him. I answered "yes" immediately. I had more confidence in Ed than in anyone I have ever known. If he proposed to me to try to escape I was sure things must be well prepared.

It was an easy decision for me to make on other grounds too. Even though conditions in Davao were better than in Cabanatuan they were by no means good in any objective sense. Nearly all the prisoners in the camp were by now underweight and undernourished. Men died regularly, albeit at a much slower rate than on Luzon. If I stayed on in the camp it would be just a matter of time until I died of malaria, some vitamin deficiency disorder, or the cumulative effects of chronic malnutrition. If we tried to escape and were caught and executed, so what? It would only be faster than staying on to expire of disease or starvation. If the escape was successful, I would save my life. Thus my initial response reflected quiet desperation.

After our plans were considerably advanced I came to believe that we had a good chance to succeed. When I got to know all the members of our eventual escape group my confidence grew, for all of them were impressive men. After we had definitely decided to make the attempt we began to think of all the subsidiary benefits that would flow from a successful escape: we would see our loved ones again, we could publicize Japanese atrocities to the world, and we might thereby aid our fellow prisoners whom we were leaving behind. But all these thoughts developed gradually later. At the outset, all I thought about was that a successful escape would mean that I would save my life and regain my freedom. I believe the same was true of the others as well.

Ed and I would have liked to have had Bert Bank join us had he been healthy. Bert was high spirited, energetic, daring, and liked by everyone. He was the source of more laughs than anyone I knew in Davao. He would have been a great asset to any escape group in normal circumstances, but we could not take him because he was nearly blind from malnutrition. Dyess then suggested that we approach Leo Boelens. I agreed at once. Leo was flattered to be asked, and immediately agreed to come.

While Dyess was hatching plans and pumping up his own optimism three Marine officers were scheming too. They were Lieutenant Jack Hawkins, Captain Austin Shofner, and

Lieutenant Mike Dobervich. All were strong men, in different ways. Hawkins was always quiet and cool; a bright, clear headed man who never lost his composure. He had graduated from Annapolis. Dobervich had come from the tough mining country of northern Minnesota. His nickname was "Beaver," a tribute to his strength, determination, industry, and reliability. Shofner, called "Shifty" because he had once been a football player at the University of Tennessee, was the archetypical U.S. Marine. The Marines, whom he regarded as the greatest organization in the world, were his whole life. To Shifty nothing was impossible. No matter how tough the situation he was always sure there had to be some way out of it. He was also a big, powerful man, in better physical condition than any of the rest of us. This last quality was to prove crucial at least once during our escape. All three men had seen combat: Dobervich on Bataan, which for him had been followed by the Death March; both Shofner and Hawkins on Corregidor. I did not know any of the three until we were thrown together in the same barracks in Davao, but I came to admire all of them.

Their escape plans were born in the aftermath of the Christmas party of 1942 when Hawkins told Dobervich that he was determined not to spend the next Christmas in captivity. The two talked at length the next night, and Hawkins studied a map of the Pacific he had gotten from a friend who had hidden it from the Japanese guards. From the English language 'newspaper' in the camp and from scuttlebutt purveyed by Filipinos, Jack had a fair idea of how the war was going, though he did not know how many, if any, of the islands north of Australia were controlled by Americans. Australia itself was about 1,200 miles away. Scores of islands lay along the most direct route there from Mindanao but at the southern end there was a 250 mile stretch of open sea between Timor and the north coast of Australia. Jack and Mike speculated about whether Filipino outrigger sailing ships could make such a trip. Some days later Shofner joined them, confessing that he had been harboring similar thoughts. After more conversation they decided that before they set out they had to have more information about such matters as the geography of Mindanao, where Japanese troops were stationed on it, and the location of guerrilla bands.

Memories differ about whether Dyess sought out Shofner or the reverse. Whichever the case, one night in February the two talked for an hour about escaping. Both were convinced that more men were needed to make an escape attempt practicable. Ed was willing to take Shofner's two Marine buddies. Both were in good physical condition; and Hawkins knew Spanish, as well as something about navigation. The Marines were more wary of us. According to both Hawkins and Dyess, they were willing to take me. I slept close to all three Marines in our barracks and they knew me well. At first they balked at Boelens because they did not know him. Actually, Leo proved to be an invaluable asset. An Air Corps Engineering officer from Basin, Wyoming, he was a wizard with anything mechanical. He had repaired the last plane to leave Bataan, the one that carried Carlos Romulo, MacArthur's Chief Information Officer, to Corregidor. It was so overloaded that those on it had had to throw all their luggage overboard to keep the plane above water. Leo had escaped from Bataan but had never made it to Australia. The Marine's mistrust of him may seem excessive to readers now, but in 1943 many prisoners were depressed, unstable, and untrustworthy. If only one wrong man learned that an escape was under consideration, he might succumb to temptation to curry favor with the Japanese by turning in the plotters; or he might do so from fear that he would be executed in reprisal for the escape of others. Moreover, the Japanese remained unpredictable. If they learned that some prisoner knew of a plan to escape, even though it did not include himself, they might torture him until he revealed what he knew. All of us remembered the fate of other men who had tried to escape from O'Donnell and Cabanatuan. Invariably, much discussion preceded any approach to a new man. In Leo's case, the Marines took him at once when they had a chance to talk to him for an evening.

As soon as the six of us began to talk seriously about the details we agreed that to get to Australia we had to have a navigator. Hawkins remembered some of his training in the subject but was frank about his limitations. After much discussion and with many misgivings about expanding our numbers beyond six, it was decided to approach a Navy man. Shofner suggested Lieutenant Commander Melvyn McCoy, whom he had met on our trip from Manila to Davao when the possible mutiny had been discussed. He had also played poker with McCoy. He emphasized to us that McCoy had a keen mind, good judgment, and exceptional self-descipline. Dyess had also met McCoy at Cabanatuan, and seconded Shifty's estimate. Unknown to us, McCoy and three others had already made more elaborate plans than ourselves.

Every single person in the escape group eventually contributed to the venture in some significant way. The three leaders at the outset were Dyess, Shifty, and Melvyn McCoy. McCoy had the most complex character and personality of the three. A 1927 graduate of Annapolis, he was a brilliant man: sharp eyed, intense, with an excellent memory and great self-confidence. McCoy was determined to escape. He remarked once that all prisoners think a good deal about escape, mostly because they have little else to do. Hundreds make some plans, but only a few ever make an effort. That is because the most important factor in an escape attempt is the will to try. One has to want freedom more than anything else in the world. Only then will he calculate all the risks and still be willing to accept them. Yet McCoy had a cool side too. Much as he wished to escape he had opposed the incipient mutiny aboard the ship that transported us to Davao because he had been convinced that that particular venture would fail.

In Davao, McCoy had been put to harvesting rice with Major Steve Mellnick, a thin, balding West Pointer from the Coast Artillery who was also an alumnus of Corregidor, Bilibid, and Cabanatuan. The two became fast friends. Mellnick was a more careful, systematic man than McCoy. They began to talk furtively about escaping but were unable to figure out a way to negotiate the miles of jungle and swamp around the camp.

The agricultural advisor on their particular detail was a fat old Filipino named Candido Abrina; "Pop" to all his associates. I never knew Pop though I heard a great deal about him and eventually realized that all of us owed our lives to his good will, wit, and courage. With sound instinct, McCoy and Mellnick set about making friends with Pop. He relayed to them much news of events inside and outside the camp, and eventually got them transferred to a detail to harvest corn. Some of the corn was to be fed to chickens to increase egg production.

One day after starting the corn harvest two enlisted men, Sergeant Robert Spielman and Corporal Paul Marshall, paid a call on Mellnick. They were tough, resourceful men who Steve knew well from extended association on Corregidor. They too had been in Cabanatuan. More recently, they had spent a month on the coast near Davao City evaporating sea water to make salt for the camp. Once that task was completed they had been sent to the camp. As soon as they found out Mellnick was there they looked up their old boss. They now asked if they could be assigned to the same corn detail with him. With Pop's aid this was arranged. Spielman, a self-confessed ladies' man of considerable renown before the war, was an expert scrounger. At once Mellnick and McCoy began to develop the potential latent in this whole situation. Pop was an amiable egoist and natural actor who enjoyed nothing so much as regaling audiences with improbable tales of his many and amazing exploits, mostly erotic. The Japanese guards were callow youths whose imaginations ran strongly to girls. During noon breaks Pop, who could speak Japanese passably, would embark on long, lurid descriptions of his innumerable sexual adventures, in minute anatomical detail, for the delectation of all and sundry. When his imagination ran dry occasionally, McCoy would pinch hit with comparably colorful accounts of his own imaginary conquests in seaports all over the world. These, Pop would translate into Japanese. The guards were enthralled and never noticed that Spielman and Marshall were always absent. They were busy gathering fruit from vines, trees, and bushes for the fifty men on the detail. The health and spirits of all the men soared.

After about a month nearly all the corn was harvested. The

sanguine McCoy and Spielman, both in good health by now, wanted to escape, no matter what the risk. They proposed to break out of the prison farm, elude the guards, make their way through the jungle to the coast, steal a sailboat, and head for Australia. It was always assumed that a boat had to be secured. Merely to escape into the jungle would be pointless. There death would be certain within a week or two. Mellnick and Marshall, whose health was less good, were less enthused. They emphasized how much food, equipment, and medicine would be required to maintain life in the jungle, even for a few days. They also reminded their partners of their obligations to Pop and the other men on the corn detail. Marshall said flatly that he was willing to try but only when there was a fair chance of success: that he did not intend to throw his life away on some 50-1 shot, no matter how slim chances of survival in camp might be ultimately.

By now the four plotters and Pop were fast friends. When the corn harvest was over Pop got them and sixteen other men assigned to a detail to pick coffee. The coffee plantation was close to the chicken farm. Soon Pop was beguiling a new set of guards with accounts of his youthful adventures in Moslem harems while Spielman and Marshall were devising ways to steal eggs, and then chickens. Since those on the coffee detail prepared their own lunch in the field, and the guards paid no attention to what they cooked, it was possible to boil chickens with rice for lunch. Other members of the detail who were not in on the plot were told that the chickens arrived because Pop had certain "connections," but that if word got out there would be no more of them. Everyone was grateful for the extra food and said nothing.

Pop was scared half out of his wits that Spielman and Marshall would get caught. They *did* have a few narrow escapes, but persevered. In the course of three months they stole 133 chickens and thousands of eggs. Not less important, they roamed extensively and familiarized themselves with the whole camp. All four of the plotters got stronger physically; some of the stolen chickens were traded for sulfa, quinine, and canned commodities that might be useful in the jungle someday; and the health of many other prisoners, especially some of the older officers, improved. McCoy said later that he thought only the addition of chicken to his diet had made him strong enough to escape. And, of course, with the improvement in their health the plotters' confidence grew.

As the four refined their plans McCoy gradually changed his mind about going with Spielman. He now convinced himself that more than four men were essential if there was to be any chance of success. He eventually concluded that ten would be an ideal number: three watches of three each to take turns handling the boat, plus a captain. One day Mellnick told Pop of their half-developed plans, impressing upon him that a successful escape might change the whole course of history: that if the world was told what the Japanese were doing to war prisoners there would be such a surge of patriotic feeling in the United States, combined with passionate hatred of Japanese, that America would intensify her war effort and turn what seemed an uncertain outcome into a speedy Allied victory. Pop was aghast and would not speak to Steve for days. McCoy then offered to take Pop along, but the old man said they were crazy: either the swamp or the headhunters on the other side of it would get them for sure.

McCoy's group now began to look for extra men, quite as apprehensively as ourselves and for the same reasons. They approached a young captain, Maurice Shoss, who had performed well on Corregidor, but he was too weak. They put out vague feelers to others who had talked of escaping. Nothing happened. Then one day McCoy met Dyess and Shofner. Soon after, all six of us had a talk with McCoy. He proposed to add the other three from his own party. He stressed that more men were needed for mutual protection from headhunters in the jungle and to handle a ship, especially in rough weather. He also said he couldn't desert his own men to join us. Finally, he reminded us that if either party left by itself it would spoil the chances of the other. Most of us were unconvinced. Ten persons seemed too many. The risk of discovery would be increased. We were also skeptical about including Mellnick and the two enlisted men because none of us knew them. McCoy assured us that all of them were sound, brave men who would be assets; as, indeed, events proved them to be. At length, he served us with an ultimatum: if we wanted him we must take his companions. We sweated, but eventually concluded that anyone as intelligent as McCoy seemed to be would not tie himself to a pack of incompetents. We caved in. It was a splendid decision.

Many times afterward the rest of us talked about McCoy. He was a remarkably self-confident man who thought, talked, and did everything swiftly. For considerable time most of us were wary of his rapid judgments and assured air, but since his anticipations and predictions nearly always came true our confidence in him grew. I have never known anyone who could predict the future with such persistent accuracy as Melvyn McCoy. He was not infallible though, as will be described later.

It was one thing to decide to escape, quite another to determine when, where, and how. Where should we try to go? The whole area was bounded by swamps and dense jungle, portions of which appeared on maps as "unexplored." The only easy way out was towards Davao City, but it was full of Japanese civilians, not to speak of the Nipponese troops stationed there. We toyed with the notion of dashing for one of the airfields around Davao City and seizing a plane, which Ed or I would then fly out, but nobody thought it likely that we would find a plane full of gas and ready to go. Besides, we would be immediately pursued by Japanese fighters.

Even to decide *when* to try to get away was perplexing. Nighttime would be virtually impossible. In the daytime we could overpower or kill guards on some remote detail and break away, but such action would certainly bring down bloody reprisals on other members of the detail or other prisoners in the camp. One of the first things we agreed upon was that, come what may, we were not going to kill any Japanese. Camp authorities could not ignore such acts, and their vengeance was likely to be terrible. The whole issue of retaliation against other prisoners worried us, and produced many discussions which delayed our escape for some time. Everyone agreed that Colonel Mori, the Commandant at Cabanatuan, would have punished the escape of ten men with mass murder of hostages. Nobody doubted that Lieutenant Hozumi would do the same if he was in command. But the Davao Commandant, Major Maeda, seemed more humane. All of us were extremely anxious to get away, not only to gain personal freedom but to tell the world what was going on in Japanese prison camps and thereby pressure the Japanese into treating the remaining prisoners more humanely. Though we all remembered the horrible fate of the three caught trying to escape from Cabanatuan, and recalled the hostages shot at Cabanatuan in reprisals for the escape of one other man, we eventually convinced ourselves that Major Maeda would not shoot nine or ten hostages for each of us who got away.

It was also difficult to figure out how to get all ten of us out of the camp at the same time. If we could all be assigned to the same detail that hurdle could be surmounted, but in February we were scattered in several parts of the camp.

Sunday seemed the most promising day of the week to try to escape. It was a day off for most of the Japanese guards. Guards were in short supply at the moment anyway because 200 of them had recently been transferred to combat areas. The three Marines had told Pop they liked to work on Sunday both because it was dreary in the camp compound and because the Japanese let them go without guards. Thus they could eat better. No objection had been raised, and the guards had gotten accustomed to seeing Mike, Jack, and Shifty, with their bulls, head for the fields on Sundays. To leave camp on Sunday would also have the advantage of not implicating Pop or the other men on the plow detail who worked the rest of the week.

When I had to leave the kitchen for a few days with malaria, Shofner arranged to have me transferred to the plow detail to replace one of the regular plowmen who was also ill. The objective was to get as many of us as possible on the same details, thus improving the chance of all of us to escape. This transfer proved quite an experience for me. I was raised in a city. I knew nothing about plowing with either tractors or horses, much less with the brahma bulls and carabao that served as Philippine draft animals. The plows were ancient one-handled relics like those used in India and other underdeveloped countries. The driver held the handle with one hand. With the other he held a cord attached to a ring in the nose of the animal who pulled the plow. A slight tug on the cord signaled the bull to turn left while a flick of it on his flank indicated that he should turn right. I was unaware of these subtleties at the outset, not to speak of being none too confident about handling mean looking bulls in any case. I was also unaware that Shifty, a great joker and needler, intended to play a trick on me. He gave me Mike Dobervich's bull, which was more skittish than most. He and Mike began by assuring me that the beast was gentle as a lamb, but added, unhelpfully, that I should look out for his huge curved horns since he was playful. I approached my prospective partner in agriculture with some apprehension. He, vastly more assured, turned almost eagerly and started towards me. Later I was told that Mike usually began the day by giving him a little salt, which he relished. I did not know that; only that the bull's interest in me seemed excessive. I took off like the proverbial ring-tailed baboon, amid uproarious laughter from a motley crowd of onlookers. Afterward the jokesters reassured me, and with some practice I soon became an acceptable bull skinner.

Once I became a fledgling plowman, that made four of us on the same unguarded Sunday detail. But what of the other six? McCoy, with his customary ingenuity, eventually devised a way out. He suggested to Pop that it would be a great convenience for the coffee pickers if they had a rain shelter. They would have a place to go during downpours and would be less susceptible to colds. He added that he thought he could get six volunteers who would build it on their own time on Sundays. This would avoid taking time away from the regular coffee harvest. Pop passed on the suggestion to camp authorities. Major Maeda, impressed by the improved attitude and diligence of the detail, consented. The six volunteers, of course, were the remaining six in the plot. Now all ten of us routinely checked in and out with guards on Sundays. Now, for the first time, our plans could become definite. We could gradually cache needed supplies outside the camp; then one Sunday check in for work as usual, pick up our stashed supplies instead, and go into the jungle. If we were lucky nobody would miss us until the details failed to return at 5:00 P.M. . That late in the day the Japanese who feared the jungle, would probably conclude that there was no use setting out after us until the next morning. We would have almost a whole day head start.

If we were to live for a week or more in the jungle all sorts of supplies were essential: canned or dried food, quinine for malaria, as many other medicines as we could secure, good shoes and leggings to reduce scratches and insect bites to a minimum, antiseptics to treat infections that could not be avoided, blankets, shelter halves, mosquito nets, matches, small knives for protection and various personal uses, and bolos to make our way through the jungle. Whenever we got to the coast and got a boat we would need an array of navigational devices and charts. Some of this one or another of us had: much of it nobody had.

The canned food in the Red Cross packages was invaluable as a start. Some of the other commodities in those blessed parcels could be traded to other prisoners for additional canned food or medicines. The addition of McCoy and associates to our ranks was crucial for building up our food supply for the chickens and fruit sequestered by Spielman and Marshall were often bartered for canned meat, blankets, dried fish, hard biscuits, mosquito nets, shoes and leggings. Ed Dyess got some sorely needed medical supplies by taking fruit to the American doctor who was in charge of Red Cross medical supplies in the hospital storeroom. No doubt Ed could have simply offered to trade the fruit for medicine but that would have involved revealing the escape plan to another person. He got a break and did not have to do this. One day the doctor was away for a few minutes while Ed was in the storeroom. He loaded up. Leo Boelens made all sorts of useful things in the machine shop, a workable sextant being the most vital. He also stole field glasses, a file, a hammer, and a pair of pliers from the shop. McCoy had stuffed some navigational tables and a Nautical Almanac into his musette bag when he left Corregidor, and still had them. Boelens had a chart of the South Pacific. A protractor and dividers needed for navigation were borrowed from an Army Engineering officer. The Japanese around the kitchen were used to seeing me there so I had no difficulty pilfering some matches. Every day McCoy passed by a storehouse where rice was kept. Most days he could manage to fill a couple of stockings full. Pop got some bolos for us and Leo managed to save out a few more that came to his shop to be sharpened. Watches and compasses essential for navigation were secured somewhere, but whether some of our people already had them or they were stolen from the Japanese, I no longer remember.

As has been noted earlier in this narrative, many times during the war Filipinos risked not only their own lives but those of their families to aid Americans. Two did so for us at Davao. Without them we could not have escaped. One, of course, was Pop. The other was his superior, Juan Acenas, the assistant superintendent of the colony.

Acenas was particularly interested in the coffee plantation, which had been neglected in recent years but which McCoy's detail was endeavoring to restore. He visited it many times. McCoy, who could be charming and persuasive when he chose, soon made friends with him. Eventually, McCoy asked Acenas for aid. Acenas accepted the terrible risk involved. He told McCoy that we should try to link up with the nearest Filipino guerrillas who were operating in the mountains about twenty miles north of the camp on the opposite side of the enormous unexplored swamp. They would welcome us, he felt sure, and would take us the fifty miles or so to the east coast of Mindanao where we hoped to secure a boat. He added that there were two possible ways to reach the guerrillas. Before the war a narrow gauge railroad had been built across the eastern edge of the swamp in order to haul out mahogany logs. This would be the quickest and easiest way through the swamp but it would also be the obvious route the Japanese would take in pursuit of us. There was also a trail that ran for many miles through the jungle west of the swamp, then turned north and east on the other side. It had never been used much and was probably badly overgrown by now.

Somehow we acquired two Filipino guides. Once more, memories are hazy many years after events. Hawkins, Mellnick, and Dyess each relate a different version of how we got our guides. My own memory of it is clean in some respects, vague in others. It is possible that Pop first suggested the idea, located two likely prospects, and then arranged for me to contact one of them. I do recall meeting a handsome, intelligent young Filipino who knew a great deal about pharmacy and first aid. In the camp he was a medical corpsman. His name was Benigno de la Cruz. He was in for murder. As he told it, when he was very young he courted a girl whose brother objected to his attentions. The brother told Ben that if he ever came near his sister again he would be killed. Ben ignored him and went to see the girl again. The brother caught them, chased Ben down an alley to a dead end, and threw a knife at him, but missed. Ben grabbed the knife out of a tree and told the brother to stay away. The brother charged instead, and Ben killed him in self-defense. Whatever the truth of this story, Ben was obviously a bright fellow. He spoke English and seemed much above the level of most of the other Filipino prisoners. I think I first met Ben when I worked in the kitchen, though it may have been later when I was employed briefly in a camote field. Either way, I mentioned to him that I was thinking of trying to escape but would like to be accompanied by a Filipino who knew local languages and something about negotiating jungles. He said he would go only if his friend, Victor Jumarong was included because Victor knew a great deal about the jungle while he, a Manila boy, did not. Victor was a different sort entirely. He was an Illocano: short, stocky, inarticulate, semi-literate woodsman and fisherman who had killed two men. Despite his dubious background and unpromising exterior Victor was potentially an invaluable asset. Before the war, Ben said, Victor had helped to clear the trail around the western edge of the swamp and therefore knew exactly where it was. Both Ben and Victor were anxious to try to escape. I said nothing to Ben about my nine companions but arranged to have him and Victor walk by the coffee detail so Mellnick, McCoy, and Spielman, and Marshall could get a look at them without the Filipinos knowing they were being evaluated. All four were impressed with Ben. McCoy then contacted him. Ben assured McCoy, and later everyone else, that Victor was reliable. McCoy then told him when we planned to make our attempt, and where to meet us.

Once this was settled we agreed that we would not approach any more Filipinos. Trusting them was even more precarious than trusting fellow Americans for a Filipino convict had only to turn in his fellow conspirators to the Japanese to quite possibly win a pardon for the act. We did not *guarantee* Ben and Victor anything in return for joining us but we all promised to do whatever we could for them if we made it to freedom. These were not empty assurances. McCoy had some influence in the Navy. Mellnick had worked for both General MacArthur and Philippine President Manuel Quezon. Eventually the two Filipinos accepted a gamble with us just as we did with them. Unlike most gambles, this time everybody won.

Preliminary preparations were completed in early March. McCoy was edgy, anxious to start, keenly aware that every day of delay increased the danger of discovery. Mellnick, more restrained and methodical, refused to set a date until all hands were in better health and everything was ready. A major problem was how to get the bulk of our supplies out of the camp and into caches in the jungle. We could not possibly have ten men, packs bulging, walk past the sentries. Yet most of what we proposed to take was scattered all over inside the camp. Much of it was hidden near where McCoy, Mellnick, Marshall, and Spielman worked. One day Dyess drove his bull car there, put the supplies in the bed of it, loaded some poles on top, and had Mellnick sit on the load, ostensibly to keep the poles from falling off. He then drove his bulls across camp and past several guards without incident, since they had long since gotten used to seeing him, only to encounter a new guard on the outside where we had planned to secrete the supplies. There was no way to refuse to unload the poles in front of the guard but, fortunately, he did not watch closely so the poles came off on his side of the road and our supplies disappeared into the tall jungle grass on the other side. Even though the supplies were bound to suffer from the daily rains, it was a vast relief to all of us to learn that this hurdle had been cleared. Meantime, beginning March 17, we four plowmen took as much as we dared with us every day. I had stolen some five gallon cans from the mess hall in which to store our supplies. We put banana leaves on top of them to keep out the rain. Mellnick said afterward that he found the tension involved in smuggling nearly every day so excruciating that he was often tempted to junk it all and return to picking coffee.

On March 27, we had an appallingly close escape. Everyone was on edge. Then, of all times, our determined enemy Lieutenant Hozumi pulled a snap inspection of the plowing detail. He found Shofner and others eating bananas. He reached into Shifty's musette bag and found more bananas. He flew into a rage, cuffed all the miscreants vigorously, and beat Shofner with special enthusiasm because he was the senior officer involved. Luckily for me, I was some distance away, though I was close enough to see it all. I waited as long as I dared before coming forward unobtrusively. For whatever reason, Hozumi did not hit me. For punishment he ordered that next day, March 28, a normal day off, everyone must work in the rice paddies. He also kicked Shofner's musette bag in anger. Providentially, his hand had not reached far enough into the bag to find a quart of quinine tablets, nor did his foot break the bottle. Had either occurred he surely would have become suspicious and would have launched a general investigation that might have ended anywhere; or at least he would have punished Shifty in some way that would have upset our plans drastically.

Next day everyone had to work all day, hip deep in the rice paddies, in a driving rain. We emerged exhausted and unstrung, thought perhaps the postponement had been good luck in disguise since the hard rain would have made the going in the jungle slow and miserable. Probably it was a break in another way too. During the week that followed we measured distances, time movements, and watched the guard towers and patrols more closely. We also learned that the following Sunday would be our last chance. Since at least half the prisoners were too weak to escape, even if not guarded at all, the Japanese had allowed the number of guards to dwindle to 250, but reinforcements were due to arrive soon. When they did Sunday details without guards would be ended.

My companions all said, then or afterward, that the tension of that last week was close to unbearable. I do not doubt them, but it was not my predominant mood. I was nervous, to be sure; only a corpse would not have been; but mainly I was enthused, impatient, anxious to start.

Looking back, I must admit that the attitude of the others was more logical. All our cached supplies would now sit a week in the rain. How much would still be usable April 4? With every day that passed the danger of discovery grew. We even had another close escape. Lieutenant Gene Dale, whom I had replaced as a bull driver, had recovered from his illness and wanted his old job back. Once more quick wits come to the rescue. This time they belonged to Hawkins. Jack asked Gene if he would let me go one more Sunday. He said I had used my connections in the camp kitchen to steal some chickens. These

129

could not be cooked in the kitchen, if they were not cooked promptly out in the field they would spoil. Gene, who died tragically soon after the war, was an understanding fellow and agreed to let me go once more in return for the promise of a piece of chicken. April 3 Pop told those on his detail that he and his wife had prayed for their success. McCoy was so jumpy that he feared that, even at this eleventh hour, something disastrous would happen merely because Pop had told his wife of our plans. Pop himself was so tense that he went home after lunch, saying he had an upset stomach. None of us slept much that night. I could hardly contain my eagerness to start. Next morning when we approached the last sentry we had to pass, one of Mellnick's friends shouted to Steve that his toothbrush was sticking out of his musette bag. He added jovially, "Are you planning to escape?" Steve nearly collapsed.

NOTE: This account of the origins of the various plans to escape, the merger of the three groups, and our subsequent preparations, is based on what I have been able to recall thirty-nine years after the event; what Steve Mellnick wrote in *Philippine Diary*, 1939-1945, twenty six years later; what Jack Hawkins remembered(*Never Say Die*) eighteen years afterward; what Charles Leavelle wrote for Ed Dyess (*The Dyess Story*); and what McCoy and Mellnick told Welbourn Kelly (*Ten Escape From Tojo*). Since the last two books were published in 1944, only a year after the events described, one might suppose that they would be much the most trustworthy sources. This is not the case, for several reasons: the war was still in progress then, censorship still prevailed, and both accounts were deliberately brief and sketchy about the circumstances of our escape so as not to jeopardize the chances of other prisoners to get away.

Of Dyess' initial plan to escape, I know what he told me. Hawkins describes (*Never Say Die*, pp. 55-58) the scheming of Dobervich, Shofner, and himself. Hawkins' account, pp. 62-63, of the merger between the Marines and our group differs in some details from Dyess' recollections (*The Dyess Story*, pp. 166-167). The activities and planning of McCoy's contingent is described in detail by Mellnick (*Philippine Diary*, pp. 181-226. Memories differ about whether McCoy sought out Shofner and Dyess, or they first contacted him. McCoy says in *Ten Escape From Tojo*, pp. 85, that he was first approached by Shofner, who asked him to take charge of the whole combined escape effort. Mellnick (*Philippine Diary*, pp. 212-215); Dyess, p. 167, and Hawkins, pp. 65-71, differ somewhat on details of this and the subsequent agreement of all three groups to merge. I cannot remember the precise details so long after the event, but I have preferred Hawkins' recollections to Mellnick's because Steve's memory failed him on a related matter. He says in *Philippine Diary*, p. 215, that I worked in the camp repair shop and he attributes to me a promise to make a sextant there. I never worked in the repair shop and I could not have made such a promise since I lack mechanical aptitude. Leo Boelens worked in the repair shop and made the sextant.

Mellnick says McCoy suggested to Pop that the rain shelter be built for coffee pickers. Hawkins says Shofner proposed it to Major Maeda. I was not involved in these negotiations so I cannot be sure who is correct. Here I have followed Mellnick.

Likewise, there is no general agreement about exactly how we acquired Ben and Victor as guides.

I have followed Hawkins' account of Lieutenant Hozumi punishing Shofner and kicking his musette bag. Mellnick and McCoy in *Ten Escape From Tojo*, p. 89, says Hozumi actually saw the bottle of quinine tablets in the bag. They assume he did nothing about it because they attribute to him a one-track mind and think he was so blinded at finding the contraband bananas that he missed the implication of the bottle of pills.

Thus the overall account of our plans to escape that is given is accurate in all important respects, but human memories are so fallible that it is impossible to be certain about every detail so long after the events. It is a salutary reminder that the writing of history has never been one of the exact sciences.

On a much complex matter—how thin was the line between life and death for so many is illustrated by what happened to Gordon Benson, the pilot who gave me some clean underwear. Gordon was shot down off the Mindanao coast. He tried to swim ashore, became exhausted, gave up and started to sink. His feet hit a coral reef and he walked ashore!

For a sampling of the many different views of the character and motivation of the Japanese Cf. Bert Bank, *Back From The Living Dead*, pp. 52-53; Robert Considine ed., *General Wainwright's Story*, pp. 203-204, 257; Philip Knightley, *The First Casualty*, pp. 292-294; Gregory Boyington, *Baa! Baa! Black Sheep*, pp. 361-362; Quentin Reynolds ed., *Officially Dead: The Story Of Commander C.D. Smith*, pp. 15, 35; James Bertram, *Beneath The Shadow*, pp.104-105; Agnes Keith, *Three Came Home*, pp. 3-13, 231-233, 294, 306-314, 317; Sidney Stewart, *Give Us This Day*, pp. 82-83, 97, 104-105, 173-174; Stanley Falk, *Bataan: The March Of Death*, pp. 227- 230 especially; Clark Lee, *They Call It Pacific*, pp. 280-282; Ernest Miller, *Bataan Uncensored*, pp. 366-371; Edgar Whitcomb, *Escape From Corregidor*, p. 267; and Ernest Gordon, *Through The Valley Of The Kwai*, p. 53.

Stewart hated the Japanese during the war but afterward came to see their savagery as deriving mostly from their environment, an evolution similar to my own. Falk holds that much Japanese cruelty derived merely from red tape, inefficiency, and foulups of the sort that plague all armies.

The view I have found most difficult to appreciate are those of Whitcomb and Gordon. Whitcomb, who described himself as an "unbeliever" during the war and who went into politics afterward, thought it "inconceivable" that our country would resort to something as "inhumane" as the A-Bomb. Gordon, likewise an unbeliever when the war began, but who became a minister afterward, expressed shock that millions in the western world still refused to accept moral responsibility for the destruction of Hiroshima and Nagasaki.

I have never understood this obsession with Atomic Bombs. American firebombing caused more destruction and killed more people in Japan in the spring of 1945 than did either the Hiroshima or Nagasaki bombs. The British and American obliteration of Dresden in February, 1945, was also more costly in human lives. The Germans and Russians inflicted dozens of times as many casualties on each other as the Japanese lost from the two A-Bombs. If you are dead you are dead. What difference does it make if the deed is done by a sword, a rifle, an incendiary bomb, an explosive shell, or an Atomic Bomb?

Chapter Seven
The Escape

IN THE COURSE OF PLANNING OUR ESCAPE I had suggested that it might be helpful to take along a Catholic priest. Since most Filipinos are Catholics a priest who could say Mass for them would probably be warmly received. He might be able to open many doors for us and secure us invaluable aid. Everyone accepted the idea as sound and also agreed that I had the right man in mind. He was Father Richard Carberry, a courageous and personable man who was also young, strong, and athletic. I knew Father Carberry well; indeed, I had often purloined food from the kitchen for him. When I approached him he was willing to join us. He also gave us considerable useful information and advice.

On the morning we were to leave, April 4, we assembled inside the camp. Father Carberry was nowhere in sight. I made inquires. Someone said he was in the hospital with malaria. I went there at once and found him lying in bed. He told me he had hoped to go with us but that he was far too weak to make the attempt now; that we should go without him. Long afterward, back in the States, I found out from Father (Colonel) Albert Braun, the senior chaplain in Davao, that he had *ordered* Father Carberry not to go with us. Father Braun feared that if a chaplain escaped, or even tried to escape, the Japanese would employ the act as a pretext to forbid any religious services in camp. He told Father Carberry that his duty was not to try to save his own life but to stay in the camp and minister to the spiritual needs of the prisoners. Father Carberry could not bring himself to tell us the truth of the matter so he feigned an attack of malaria in order to stay behind. Like so many brave men in the Philippines, his life ended tragically. He obeyed his superior with good will and stayed on to endure many additional months of diseases and malnutrition which gradually complicated an old chest wound that had never healed properly. On a freezing day in January, 1945, aboard a prison ship headed for Japan, the combination finally killed him.

After telling Father Carberry goodbye I ran into a classmate, Chuck O'Neil. Chuck had been sitting on the log next to the guard who had been nearly decapitated by the Igorot. Now he was suffering from malaria, but was not in the hospital. Knowing him to be entirely "safe," I told him I was leaving and said goodbye. He said I was crazy.

I then asked him to tell my wife and family what had become of me if it should happen that he got back to the United States some day and I did not. These brief conversations with Father Carberry and Chuck delayed us perhaps twenty minutes.

We went out the main gate in two different parties. All the other participants who have written about our escape say they felt that the Japanese were scrutinizing us with unusual care even though they knew in their minds that there was no reason to suppose this. I cannot say I was not nervous, but I felt exhilarated too. Save for a few terrible occasions later in the middle of a swamp I never really doubted that we would make it. We soon found our stashed gear. Most of it was soaked and some of it had begun to mold but all of it was usable. We rolled it, heavy and sodden, into packs, and waited for our Filipino guides.

The Japanese did not watch Filipino convicts as closely as they did prisoners of war but the Filipinos still could not move around the camp at their pleasure. Ben and Victor did not arrive. Minutes passed, seeming like hours. We began to worry, then to grow suspicious. Perhaps the two of them had decided to try for pardons by turning us in to the Japanese after all! If so, we would soon be ambushed. We decided to scatter out along our anticipated route to assure that , at worst, we would not all be caught in the same trap. After what seemed like ages, but was probably something like forty-five minutes or an hour, Ben and Victor appeared. They said they had had to attend a roll call and then had met some friends who could not be shaken off quickly. Meanwhile a torrential downpour had soaked us thoroughly and added pounds to packs that were already heavy.

We soon found the entrance to the trail and began moving briskly along it. Somebody, trying to be optimistic, remarked that even though the path was muddy and slick the rain would cover our tracks. A more realistic soul observed wryly that we had not made many tracks yet. Soon the trail became dim and the going more difficult. The ground was slippery, paths had to be slashed through the undergrowth, and we slid into gullies filled with water. Stream after stream had to be waded or bridged. Brambles tore at our clothes and flesh, mosquitoes badgered us ceaselessly, and huge leeches fastened onto our arms and legs. The leeches were disgusting creatures. They could not simply be pulled off for that left the head in the wound. If they were touched with a lighted cigarette, fortunately, however, or rubbed with tobacco they would let go and fall to the ground. Unfortunately, the wound left behind often became infected.

As hours passed a feeling of uneasiness grew over us. What sort of trail were we following that was as difficult as this? Were we really on the trail at all? Skepticism increased. Anxious remarks were exchanged. Then we saw footprints in the mud. After a brief flurry of excitement the awful truth dawned: they were our own! We had been thrashing through the jungle in a circle! After a hurried conversation between Ben and Victor in a Philippine dialect, Ben acknowledged to us that Victor had lost the way and now thought we should go back to camp and start over. The impact upon us of Ben's words would be impossible to exaggerate. Our spirits simply collapsed. We were shattered, stunned. This immediate shock was followed almost at once by a surge of blind rage at Victor, then as quickly by cold, sickening fear. We had wasted many hours in the jungle. We had cut a path which the Japanese could follow in a small fraction of the time we had taken, and it led directly to us, somewhere still close to camp! All because Victor had been ashamed to admit his mistake and had wasted hours trying to find the path he had lost! In retrospect, it is clear that we had expected too much of both Ben and Victor. We never knew for certain the extent of Victor's acquaintance with the trail. He probably knew considerably less about it than Ben had represented to us for Ben was a good salesman.

In semi-panic we huddled. To return to the camp was vetoed at once. We studied a map Juan Acenas had given us. McCoy thought he knew about where we were, and recommended that we head for the railway that ran around the southeast side of the swamp. It was a measure of our current desperation that this was the route we had originally rejected on the ground that it was too obvious and dangerous. We started off northeast, with McCoy holding a compass while Ben and Victor chopped away at the dense jungle undergrowth with their bolos. Swarms of insects buzzed about us, got into our eyes, crawled up our noses, and bit every exposed patch of skin. The humid heat beat down on us with the same merciless intensity that we had experienced during "sun treatments" on the Death March. Still we plunged on doggedly, desperate to get as much distance as possible between ourselves and our presumed Japanese pursuers. It seemed to me that there were jungle streams every few hundred yards, all of them swollen by the heavy rain. Several times we had to fall trees to cross them. On one occasion the tree trunk was slippery. I was last in line. Everyone else got across but I was so exhausted that I lost my footing and fell into the muddy torrent. Shifty Shofner, still a strong man despite our generally weakened physical condition, grabbed my arm and hauled me out. He immediately named me "Surefoot," and added some pointed remarks about what kind of a pilot I must have been if I had insufficient sense of balance to walk on a log. Momentarily, I didn't know whether to be grateful or angry. Shifty was a great needler, in the best sense of that term. To force a comparison, he was the Eddie Rickenbacker of our group. Elsewhere in the war Captain Eddie saved his own life and the lives of others with him in an open boat in the South Pacific by prodding, driving, and insulting the others so mercilessly that some said afterward that they had resolved to live mostly because they wanted to outlast such a tyrant. Shofner never acted in such an overbearing fashion among us, but he played a similar role. His judgment was remarkable about who could profit from a few words of encouragement, who needed a few minutes relief from carrying his pack, and what kind of half-joking, half-jarring remark would pick us up a bit. Most of the time, though not always, we had more confidence in McCoy than in anyone else. Dyess' persistent courage and determination buoyed us up steadily. But Shifty's jibes were vital too. He without question was the principal motivating force in the ultimate success of our escape. Shofner knew what had to be done, how to do it and possessed the dynamic leadership to get it done. We were indeed fortunate to have him as one of the key members of our escape. I felt confident when Shifty was calling the shots.

By early evening we were wading in ankle deep water. Then we came to a stream too big to cross quickly. We were exhausted and had not eaten since morning. Night falls rapidly in the tropics, especially in a dense jungle where sunlight penetrates only fleetingly in the middle of the day. We decided to pitch camp, eat, sleep, and get up early next morning so we could cross the stream in daylight and put more distance between ourselves and the Japanese. Victor redeemed himself somewhat by showing us how to get clear, sweet water in sufficient quantities for drinking and cooking. He cut into certain hollow vines that were entwined profusely among the trees. Water, purified by some vegetable process, poured out in a small stream. He and Ben also showed us how to build sleeping platforms above the swamp water by driving piles into the mud and tying poles onto them with rope-like rattan bark. When I lay down I was utterly exhausted and beset by the usual cloud of mosquitoes.

Even so, the jungle had caught me in its spell. It may seem strange to say this since most Americans hated the jungle as much as the Japanese did. Father Edward Haggerty, whom I later came to know well with the Filipino guerrillas, described the jungle as a terrifying place full of mud, slime, thorns that ripped clothing and skin, poisonous vines that caused itching, loathsome leeches, maddening myriads of malarial mosquitoes, noisy, insolent monkeys, hordes of rats and, hanging over all, a deep gloom that weighed heavily on the spirit. His description is not inaccurate, but I simply never *felt* the same way about the jungle. No doubt this was due to our circumstances, and therefore our states of mind, being different. To him the jungle was a miserable, foreboding place into which he had to retreat periodically to escape Japanese patrols. To me it was a refuge, an avenue of escape, the potential path to freedom. Thus I did not think of the mud and the leeches and the mosquitoes alone. I was also entranced by the brightly colored birds that had flitted through the tall trees all day, emitting a variety of strange sounds; and by the innumerable frogs and other jungle creatures who maintained a cacophonous yet somehow attractive din throughout the day and into darkness. In some parts of the earth the night is still as a tomb. In the jungle it was noisy, even raucous. Tired as I was, the racket rather soothed me, until a different kind of noise suddenly profaned the night. The sleeping platform built by the three Marines had collapsed, spilling them into the water amid many colorful expletives.

The next day was one of the worst of my life. It had rained heavily during the night. We awoke with our sodden shelter halves flattened on top of us. They were hard to roll, heavy and burdensome to carry. We ate a cold breakfast of half a can of corned beef, crossed the stream, and found ourselves in a swamp. Due to all the recent rain the water was up to our knees, and the mud beneath it was soft and yielding. It was an effort to pull one's foot out of the clinging ooze and take a step. Only an occasional grassy hillock provided firm ground.

Ben and Victor continued to hack a path with their bolos. In mid-morning the short bushes gave way to sword grass, a plant which must have been invented by Satan personally. Sword grass was seven-to-ten feet tall, about four inches wide, and perhaps half an inch thick in the middle. It was covered with sharp spines that ripped clothing and flesh impartially, and it grew in thickets dense as hair on a dog's back. Our Filipino guides wrapped their forearms with burlap to protect them as they wielded their bolos, but they were soon bleeding from the razor edges and points of the terrible grass. Soon water was halfway up our thighs, then to our buttocks, then waist deep, an especially sinister progression for me since I was the shortest of the whole group. We could not see more than two or three feet on either side; over the grass not at all. We felt imprisoned in ever deepening water and hellish spiked grass while the fearsome heat and remorseless insects rapidly depleted our scanty physical resources. There wasn't even any place to sit down for the water and grass were the same everywhere. Worse, if anything, the Marines had become convinced that McCoy was leading us in a circle just as Victor had done the day before. Never had death seemed so close, so inevitable.

The Marines called a halt. A general consultation followed. McCoy admitted that his extensive navigational training had never included anything about traveling in swamps. Everyone agreed that if we were to have any chance at all to survive we must proceed in a straight line. We decided that henceforth Hawkins would navigate with our compass and would stay right behind the grass cutters to keep them going in a straight line. If we came to an obstacle we would either go over it or hack our way through it: we would not risk getting ourselves lost by trying to detour around it. It was further agreed that grass cutting must be rotated. We would form six pairs of cutters. Each pair would hack for ten minutes and rest fifty.

Our forces reorganized, we plunged on. The water deepened. Victor predicted that it would become deeper still since we were going with the general flow in the swamp. By now it was difficult for the shorter of us to put our feet down solidly enough to maintain our balance. Mike Dobervich suggested that we change course slightly to the north so we could cross the flow of water rather than go with it. Early in the afternoon the end seemed near. We had been hacking the dreadful grass for hours but had advanced only a few hundred yards. Ed Dyess was staggering. He said he would have to abandon his pack if he was to go on. Mike insisted that this would be suicidal, and took Ed's pack onto his own shoulders. McCoy was so exhausted that he collapsed onto an underwater obstacle and just sat there, in water up to his lips, his mustache full of mud, not caring if he ever moved again. Only after a rest was he able to get up and continue. Somebody offered the ludicrous proposal that we try to return to the Davao Penal Colony. Steve Mellnick, my grass chopping partner, says I was so exhausted by the cutting that I told him to tell McCoy to go on without me; that he, Steve, urged me on; and that he and Spielman then stayed close to me to see that I did not slip under the water. This may be entirely true; indeed it probably is, for I have no reason to think Steve made up the story. All I can say is that I don't remember the incident clearly. What sticks in my mind is that Mellnick himself, and McCoy, the two oldest of us, seemed utterly spent, and that Shofner did more prodding than anyone else. My inability to recall any of this distinctly doubtless indicates how near to collapse I must have been.

When human beings are sufficiently determined or scared they are capable of prodigious feats. Even so, there are absolute limits to human endeavor and endurance. About 3:00 P.M. it was clear to all of us that we had to quit or we would fall, exhausted, and drown. By now only Victor and Ben could cut grass. Whatever had been their failings as guides, all of us would have died without them for they had always been the best grass cutters and they had cut by far the most, both because they were more skilled at it and because they were in better physical condition than the rest of us. Nonetheless, it was clear that they too were close to their limits. We halted. Paul Marshall managed to climb atop Spielman's shoulders so he could see over the devilish grass. He spotted a huge fallen tree, perhaps eight feet in diameter, lying half submerged no more than a hundred yards away. We summoned our last reserves and hacked our way over to it.

Once we managed by a sheer act of will to clamber atop the log we lay there for what must have been two or three hours, utterly motionless, as thoroughly spent as if we were corpses. But man is hard to kill and human recuperative powers are marvelous. At length thought began to return, then movement. We decided that the best we could do was to cook as nourishing a meal as our slender resources permitted, cut some nearby saplings to make a sleeping platform, and sleep. Hopefully, next morning we would be rested and capable of planning rationally.

There is a Country and Western song that contains the line, "If it wasn't for bad luck, I wouldn't have no luck at all." We had little but bad luck since leaving camp, and it was not over yet. Victor and Ben were busy building sleeping quarters out of small poles and vines the rest of us cut for them when somebody inadvertently cut into a nest of yellow jackets. We had seen some of them before, around camp. They were much larger than ordinary American yellow jackets, and more pugnacious. Now they were on us before we realized what was happening. Their stings were like stabs with a hot dagger. Agonized yelps filled the air, followed by loud splashes as we plunged into the water. We stayed submerged as much as possible for the next half hour until the winged hellions calmed down and returned to their nest. After the war, Mike Dobervich told me once that he thought this episode was the real turning point in our fortunes. We had allowed Victor's original errors to unsettle us. We had succumbed to fatigue and discouragement. Then the terrible stings shocked us, awakened us, got our adrenalin flowing again, and thereby saved us. Mike had a point, though I believe the decisive factor was something else.

Once we recovered from the yellow jackets we secured some dry vines, built a fire atop the log, made some tea, and boiled a good meal of rice and canned meat. Everyone ate voraciously. We agreed not to skip meals henceforth merely to save food. We still had enough food for a few days and if we did not keep up our strength we would never make it out of the swamp.

Shortly after supper we heard several sudden violent splashes in the water that surrounded us. Fearing that the Japanese had discovered us at last, we grabbed our bolos. It was only mildly reassuring to discover that the noise had been caused not by Japanese but by crocodiles. Nobody had even thought about *them* when we were struggling waist deep in the water and sword grass. With our luck so far, we should have stepped on a couple. No sooner had this alarm faded when an outburst of gunfire replaced it. By now we were so jumpy that the shooting shook us to the marrow in our bones. Some of it was rifle fire. Some was clearly the chattering of machine guns. Now and then we could distinguish the unmistakable grrruuummpffff of Stokes mortar shells. To top it off, all these sounds were coming from different directions. Some sort of battle must be going on. Were some of the participants shooting at us, or would they soon do so? Yet what could we do about it? We could hardly join the battle, if that was what it was, even if we knew where it was taking place and who were the combatants.

Eventually McCoy calmed us somewhat with the backhanded observation that the gunfire could hardly be coming from Japanese who had discovered us since we didn't know where we were ourselves.

At this juncture, when we had eaten but were otherwise still frightened, uncertain, and worn out, with night coming on, Shifty suggested that we pray. Ed then said he believed I was the most religious member of the group; therefore it would be appropriate for me to lead the prayer, if I wished. I knelt on the log and said the *Memorare*, one sentence at a time, with the others responding. The *Memorare* is a prayer to the Blessed Virgin. It had been taught to me by the nuns in Saint Aloysius' grade school. I had been devoted to the Blessed Virgin ever since. After this prayer we said others, formal prayers and improvised ones, together and individually. All those who have written about our escape have remarked how much more calm, secure, and hopeful we all felt almost immediately. I thought a miracle had occurred. I felt now that God would save us.

Aside from the Marines falling in the water again, the rest of the night was uneventful. We slept eleven hours and had a hot breakfast of tea, rice, and canned corned beef. Despite our stiff, aching joints the sword grass looked less dreadful than the day before. This was illusory. It was just the same! We hacked at it for hours. The going was dispiritingly slow; but whether it was from the yellow-jackets, a good night's sleep, the breakfast or, in my opinion, the prayers, we did not grow despondent again. And there was one mildly encouraging material development: the waist deep water did not get deeper. In fact, by 2:00 P.M. it was visibly receding; down to our buttocks now. By 2:30 it reached only to our knees. Now the cutters could go faster. Before long the water was only ankle deep and we were moving briskly. Abruptly the swamp ended. We were back in the jungle with leeches! We immediately flopped on firm ground to rest, leeches or no. Mellnick says I was especially grateful and exclaimed, "Thank God! Us little guys can't take this high-water walking." Needless to say, four decades afterward, I can't remember if those were my exact words but they certainly represented my sentiments. Nobody can know how welcome and comforting is mere solid ground unless he has struggled and foundered in marshes and swamps.

Our joy at deliverance from the swamp was soon tempered by caution. After all, we did not know for sure where we were or who else might be in the vicinity. Victor went off into the underbrush to scout. He soon returned, saying he had found a path. We went along it a short way until we reached a place where several trails branched off. We looked at them, puzzled at what course to take, when Shofner remarked that Marine doctrine in such cases was to split up and reconnoiter all the paths just in case an ambush might have been laid. Then we wouldn't all be killed. We did so, but soon the paths converged and we followed a single trail a short distance to a railroad track. Scattered about were expended .25 calibre cartridges, Japanese rations, Japanese G-strings, other bloody clothing, Japanese cigarette butts, and numerous footprints pointing in all directions. The footprints had been made by the split-toed tennis shoes Japanese soldiers wore because they gave a better tochold when climbing than regular western tennis shoes. It seemed obvious now that the gunfire we had heard the night before had come from a skirmish between the Japanese and Filipino guerrillas. From the look of things, the Japanese had not come off too well. We now stopped and used the ready made fire to boil some rice and brew some tea.

Afterward, we learned that there had been a great hullabaloo back in the Penal Colony when our escape was discovered. Next morning the Japanese had sent out a patrol of eighty-five men to find us. They stumbled onto some luckless Filipinos instead and shot them. Back in camp the Japanese authorities seized the "shooting squads" of two or three of us, beat them up, and interrogated them extensively for several days, but did not execute anyone. They also reduced everyone's rations, and their guards became more strict and cautious. This general punishment was capped by one of those oriental actions that western psychology could never fathom: they sentenced many prisoners to either fifteen or thirty days of "meditation," during which they were supposed to ponder the sins and crimes of the escapees!

Thirty years later Colonel Gaskill said in his memoirs that the men who came back to Cabanatuan from Davao in mid-1944 told him that our escape had been resented bitterly by those left behind in Davao because they believed that by our action we had jeopardized the lives of all of them. Of course all of us had thought much about this aspect of the matter, and it weighed oppressively on my conscience until the war was over, but I am convinced that Gaskill was mistaken. After the war I talked with several prisoners who had been in Davao when we had slipped away. Every one of them said there had been no such resentment: indeed, quite the opposite; everyone had been glad we had made it. All ten of us would have been consoled immensely had it been possible for us to know this, and to know that we had estimated Major Maeda's character correctly: that he would not slaughter others for what we had done; but we were not to learn anything about it until after the war.

After having our tea and rice we retired into the jungle for the night. Next morning we moved cautiously down the railroad track. Soon two figures appeared in the distance, coming our way. All of us dashed into the bushes save Dyess who continued to walk on, much like the sheriff in *High Noon*. He made the "V for Victory" sign. One of the oncoming figures raised his rifle, then lowered it. Both then turned and ran. Convinced that they were Filipinos, we all ran after them, but they were too fast for us and disappeared.

We followed, at a walk, down the trail they had taken until we came to some cleared ground where a Filipino hunchback was working in a field. Ben went up to the man, told him who we were, and said we wanted to meet guerrillas. The Filipino replied that he could not take us to them but would go himself and relay our message. Meantime we should wait until his wife fixed us something to eat. We saw a well behind the house and began to haul up buckets full of water for impromptu baths. The sensation was nearly as delightful as feeling solid ground underfoot had been the day before. While we were still bathing a sharp whistle rent the air. Suddenly we were surrounded, in the best theatrical style, by several dozen ominous looking characters brandishing a variety of weapons. They were led by a tall, husky man, much larger than most Filipinos, who carried a .45 revolver at his waist and a Browning automatic rifle in his hand. This was our introduction to the guerrillas of the Philippines.

Back in Davao Penal Colony no Americans had any actual contact with Filipino guerrillas. We knew only what some of the Filipino employees there had once told us about them. Now, our first meeting with the real article was awkward and cautious. After assuring themselves that we were really Americans and not Germans or Italian allies of the Japanese, the guerrillas unbent. Their leader said his name was Casiano de Juan, Commander of all the guerrillas in that locality. He and his followers were amazed to learn that we had crossed the swamp. Local people regarded it as impenetrable, and never ventured into it.

Some of our new friends told us some interesting things. They had ambushed the Japanese patrol that had been sent to hunt us down and had killed ten or fifteen of the enemy, at no cost to themselves. The gunfire we had heard two nights before had come from that clash. The bloody garments, expended ammunition, and smoldering embers we had found a day later had been all that was left after the brief battle. The guerrillas said also that they had been watching the Davao Penal Colony for months and were familiar with what went on in it. They were sure they could overcome its Japanese garrison at any time, but they had not made the attempt because they had never been able to think of a way to save the prisoners. To have taken them down the road towards the port of Davao City would have been suicidal for prisoners and rescuers alike since the guerrillas were not strong enough to engage the Japanese garrison there. To have tried to move 2,000 sick, starved, and weakened men through jungle and swamp had seemed equally hopeless. So they had done nothing but observe.

Ordinary Filipino people were overjoyed to see us. They regarded us as heroes for having escaped the enemy, and were greatly honored when some of us consented to be godfathers to several village children. One guerrilla youth confided to Dyess, somewhat disconcertingly, that God had been with us for the guerrillas had first mistaken us for Japanese and had set another ambush. He, personally, was one of the two men who had walked towards us along the railroad track. It was he who had raised his gun and pointed it at Dyess. He had even pulled the trigger, but the cartridge was bad and it had not fired. Little wonder Ed believed in predestination!

Casiano de Juan told us there were other guerrilla bands in this part of Mindanao, all of them under the ultimate control of a Philippine Constabulary officer named Claro Laureta, who lived several days' march distant. Laureta, de Juan assured us, would be able to help us get to Australia. Mike Dobervich was sick with malaria by now so we started for Laureta's headquarters at a leisurely pace, loaded with food and gear that were carried for us by porters supplied by de Juan. Every time we stopped at a village the local people fed us, treated us kindly, and if possible staged a fiesta in our honor. (Filipinos are the most enthusiastically friendly and hospitable people I have ever known. They love fiestas and will arrange one on the slightest pretext.) After twelve months of brutality, starvation, and degradation, an abrupt change to such hospitality left us midway between tears of gratitude and utter bewilderment. After about three days of mingled feasting and travel we reached the town of Kapungagen where we met Senor Eligio David, a well educated businessman who spoke English and who had fled from Davao City to this remote area when the Japanese had landed. Senor David had become the mayor of Kapungagen. He fed us sumptuously, had local medical people treat our numerous cuts, sores, and other ills, and staged what seemed by now the inevitable fiesta in our honor. It was held in a sort of community hall, where we were also billeted. We consumed impressive quantities of chicken, roast pig, and varied fruits and vegetables, washed down with generous amounts of tuba, a Philippine wine fermented from the juice of coconut palm buds and collected in hollow tubes. When most of us had been strengthened by this memorable liquid, a dance began. My comrades rose to the occasion and danced energetically with the Filipino girls. As a dancer I was no Arthur Murray so I drank tuba and regaled an admiring audience of teenagers and children with my exploits as a P-40 pilot perpetually engaged in mortal combat with squadrons of villainous Japanese. Ed kidded me about it good naturedly for many days afterward.

The end of the evening was profoundly touching. Our host

suggested that we all sing "God Bless America." This typified the spirit of most Filipinos throughout the war. They would feed us, give us money, inundate us with hospitality, even risk their lives for us. Unquestionably, the stupid barbarity of the Japanese gave them much incentive to act thus. Still, they were not mere fair weather friends. They stayed on our side when we were down and beaten, when it really *did* look like a Japanese New Order was the wave of the future. All of us were deeply moved during the singing. I recalled how many times I had heard Kate Smith sing that song so beautifully. When it ended Melvyn McCoy rose and immediately suggested that we all sing it again but change the words to God Bless the Philippines. There were no dry eyes afterward.

We did not spend all our time in Kapungagen going to fiestas nor did we forget that the earnest prayers we had said on the log in the swamp had been answered. One morning Mass was said at 6:00 A.M. All ten of us were there. McCoy, who told this to newsmen later, added that since coming back to the United States he had gone to his own church much more frequently than had been his wont before the war.

Our otherwise delightful stay was marred by a tragedy. Inigen, the fierce little Igorot who had nearly cut off the head of a guard in the camp and had then fled into the jungle, had fallen on bad times. The Japanese garb he had stolen made him look all too much like a Japanese soldier. Guerrillas soon mistook him for one and shot him. He now lay, mortally stricken, in Kapungagen. Ben powdered some sulfa pills and packed his infected wounds, but it was too late. He died the next day.

One day three big, strange looking men arrived armed with Browning automatic rifles. They viewed us with suspicion, questioned all of us at length, and insisted upon searching our persons and baggage. We complied with some reluctance and much wonder. They turned out to be scouts for Laureta. They had been dispatched to make doubly certain that we were really Americans and not Germans or Italians. Soon after, Laureta himself arrived. He was still not entirely convinced of our identity. He wanted to know, for instance, how someone with my name, Grashio, could be an American rather than an Italian. He was finally satisfied only when he asked us numerous detailed questions about American military regulations and received accurate answers. He also questioned us at length about our escape and intentions. He agreed that the world should be told what went on in Japanese prison camps but he did not think it likely that we could ever make it to Australia in an open sailboat. He advised us to abandon our plans to go fifty or sixty miles east to the port of Cateel and to go instead 125 miles to the north coast of Mindanao. There we could contact more numerous and better organized guerrilla groups led by American officers. He added that by now U.S. submarines appeared off the coast there occasionally. Our chance of getting to Australia, he thought, would be much better in a submarine than in an open boat on the high seas. Laureta was equally confident that we could make the north coast in about three weeks even though the intervening jungle and mountains were marked "unexplored" on maps. The only people who lived in this wilderness were primitive Atas and, on its northern edge, Manobos. Both tribes were headhunters who killed for the sport of it. While we did not find this information exactly heartening, Laureta assured us expansively that not only would the unsociable Atas not harm us but they would make excellent cargadores (porters). His guerrillas had assured their good behavior long before by taking their old people hostage! When one lives in isolated parts of the world he learns a good deal about politics and human relations that is seldom encountered in American textbooks.

He also learns medical treatments that are not standard in the Mayo Clinic. One day one of these half-wild Ata tribesmen saw me scratching my groin, for the itchy fungus that had plagued me for months had not abated. He grabbed some leaves off a nearby bush, crushed them in his hands, gave them to me, and motioned for me to rub myself with the mess. I did so, and in couple of days the vexatious malady disappeared.

We discussed the advice Laureta had given us and decided to take it. He then began to outfit us extensively. We would need about twenty armed men as guards, he thought, to deal with potential troublemakers of whatever sort, a couple of Philippine Army guides who had some knowledge of this part of Mindanao, and eighteen Ata cargadores. We were given several hundred pounds of rice, maybe 100 live chickens, and a carabao which the guerrillas promptly turned into jerky by slaughtering the beast, cutting the meat into strips, soaking it in vinegar and brine, and putting it out in the tropical sun. Though legions of insects tried to carry it off bodily, within two days it became so hard and tough that is was impervious to them and nearly so to human teeth as well. Laureta assured us that is would keep indefinitely and that is was quite nutritious, if one could manage to chew it.

Our Ata porters were strange creatures. Most of them were about four feet tall. They weighed perhaps ninety pounds but were strong, wiry, and agile as cats. They could carry seventy-five pound packs all day while scrambling up and down mountainsides, through jungle, and across rivers. Their teeth were black and filed to sharp points. This must have been done for cosmetic reasons since they ate remarkably little. Instead, they chewed betel nut, a strong narcotic, all day long. So did all their fellow tribesmen, young or old, male or female. Their mouths and lips were bright red from the betel nut, and most of them had a half-dazed anthropoid look which probably derived from that drug. They did not live in villages. Each family stayed by itself in a tree house in the jungle. The houses were built just higher than spear points could reach. At night the Atas would pull up their ladders, mere notched logs, and be safe till morning.

For our personal comfort and convenience we were provided with an incredibly efficient handyman named Magdaleno Duenas. Magdaleno was a great little fellow whom I still recall fondly. Hardly bigger than the Atas, he had no peer when it came to packing, unpacking, scrubbing, and otherwise looking after the personal gear of each of us. Finally, Laureta himself agreed to accompany us during the early stages of our trip.

Our journey northward through the interior was varied. The first three days were fairly easy. We went up a small river in dugout canoes. Now and then we had to pull the canoes through shallow water and sometimes we walked in the stream instead of riding. Central Mindanao was remarkably empty and incredibly wild. Once we saw a few Ata tribesmen pass us going downstream; to fish, our guide said. They gave no sign of recognition. Occasionally we would see an abandoned tree house of the Atas. One night some of us slept in one. The only other people we saw in the interior were an ancient white man clad in a white sheet like Mahatma Gandhi and three old, nearly toothless Filipino women who were with him. He said he was a veteran of the Spanish-American War who had fled from Davao City to escape the Japanese. Here he subsisted on camotes with his antiquated harem as his only companions. They lived in an open ended shed roofed with leaves. Such were the sole indications that human beings had ever come into this portion of the world. At the end of the third day we had to leave the river since we had come to a mountain range. Laureta and a few of his men left us, to return down the stream we had just ascended.

In the "unexplored" interior we went up mountains and down them again, across rivers, through swamps, across plateaus where the closely packed high trees had choked out all the underbrush until the area resembled a well kept German forest, through mountain passes above the clouds, back down into the clouds, below them once more where it seemed to rain constantly, up again into still, high areas where there were neither animals nor snakes, back into stinking, molding jungles filled with strange birds and other creatures who kept up a constant cacophony of unfamiliar grunts, cries, and squawks. Wherever we were we could never see much because all the mountains were heavily forested to their tops. Sometimes we waded in clear, cool mountain streams, but, strangely, we never saw a lake. Always we were wet, muddy, slipping and sliding on some greasy mountain trail, hanging onto vines as we let ourselves down steep hillsides, or clutching at other vines and bushes as we tried to clamber up some new mountainside. Our hands and faces swelled from myriad scratches and insect bites. Ulcers developed on our legs from the noxious leeches. Our wet clothing rubbed sores on our bodies. Our shoes fell to pieces and we had to walk barefoot. But no human agency ever troubled us.

After crossing what seemed to me to have been our fiftieth mountain range, but was probably only the fifth or sixth we reached Libertad, a village on the lower reaches of the Augusan River. Here our porters left us to return to their own country. We needed them no longer, both because we were stronger now and because much of the remainder of the trip would consist merely of floating down the river. At Libertad we were ushered into a guerrilla shack to meet Lieutenant Antonio, the leader of a local band of fifty men. He had American and Filipino flags on the bamboo wall behind his desk. Seldom in my life have I been so shaken emotionally as I was at the sight of our flag. This may seem maudlin in our time when national patriotism is discounted by so many. But the last time I had seen an American Flag flying had been thirteen months before when Bataan had fallen. Since then I had seen the detested "flaming meatball" of Japan on numberless occasions but had glimpsed our own national emblem only when our conquerors were deliberately using it for some ignoble purpose. People may talk of the brotherhood of man and work for greater realization of the commonality of all humanity. It is a worthy ideal, and the future may belong to those who espouse it, but in our epoch the world is still organized in nation states. Ours had been locked in deadly combat with a cruel and powerful enemy state for a year and a half. For thirteen months we had gone through hell for our nation or, to be more accurate, we had been put through hell by the enemy. We had seen many despair and die along the way. We had been near death ourselves on many occasions. Now, suddenly, we saw our national flag in the most unexpected place. For the first time since April, 1942, I felt like an American again rather than a prisoner of the Japanese perpetually on the run.

Such strong emotions were not mine alone. Colonel Miller recorded that when news of Japan's surrender came to the camp where he was incarcerated, a Naval Lieutenant brought out a U.S. Flag he had managed to hide for years. When it was hung up it became an object of virtual adoration. The same thing happened a few days later when the Rising Sun of Nippon came down from the camp flagpole and Old Glory went up. A U.S. newspaperman recorded that 1,500 civilian internees being repatriated aboard the *GRIPSHOLM* cried, applauded, cheered, and whistled when the Stars and Stripes appeared on the movie screen, and the Star Spangled Banner and "God Bless America" were played. He thought nobody who had not experienced Japanese domination could fully understand and appreciate what it meant to be a free American once more.

147

An even more dramatic and memorable episode than these had occurred when Corregidor fell. There Colonel Paul Bunker was ordered to take down the U.S. Flag and burn it. He did so, but ripped off a small piece and later sewed it under a false patch on his khaki shirt. Weeks later, in Bilibid prison in Manila, he thought he would die from blood poisoning so he gave half the bit of the flag to a friend, Colonel Delbert Ausmus. Ausmus sewed it under a false patch on his shirt, just as Bunker had done. Bunker died in a Japanese prison camp on Formosa but Ausmus survived the war to present the fragment of the Corregidor Flag to the Secretary of War, Robert Patterson, and relate the story behind it.

The next five days were a welcome respite from the toil and hardship of the previous week. We simply floated down the Augusan River on bamboo rafts. It was restful and we regained some strength. On the fifth day we stopped. Inquiries at villages along the river had elicited the information that the Japanese occasionally sent patrols as far as thirty-five miles up the river, approximately where we were now, and that a sizable enemy garrison was located near the river's mouth. A local guerrilla leader told us we should make for Medina, a coast town which was the headquarters for American guerrilla activity in North Mindanao. We were advised further that it would be safer to approach our destination indirectly, by going over the mountains to Buena Vista, a smaller place to the east where we could be picked up by boats and taken to Medina. At this juncture Ed Dyess suggested that the only two who still had shoes, Shofner and McCoy, should go on ahead, try to make contact with guerrillas in Medina, and then send word back when the rest of us might follow. All agreed. Four days later a messenger, Lieutenant Santiago, returned with a letter from McCoy saying they had arrived safely and that Santiago would now lead us to him and Shifty.

It has often been maintained that the historical process can be likened to the swinging of a pendulum: an alternation between extremes modified by a tendency to settle in the middle. Our fortunes resembled the first part of this conception, but not the tendency to settle in the middle. After a week of the most arduous toil up and down mountain ranges we had then enjoyed five days of peaceful drifting down the Augusan River. But now the pendulum swung back violently. We decided that we must travel at night since we might be intercepted by Japanese patrols in the daytime. The next three nights were nightmarish. We clambered barefoot up and down mountains again, cutting our feet on stones and thorns, battling the tenacious leeches, and agonizingly retracing our steps as we repeatedly got lost in the darkness. As soon as daylight came we stopped, but in a short time it grew too hot to sleep much. All that was left to eat was fruit. After three days of this we staggered into Buena Vista.

Here everything took a comparably dramatic turn for the better. A boat was supposed to come from Madina to pick us up, but it did not arrive for several days. We spent the time eating, treating our varied wounds and infections, getting Mike through an attack of malaria, and resting on the beach. Once more we had been abruptly restored after having been driven to the brink of collapse.

Our boat eventually arrived. It was a forty foot banca, powered by a diesel motor, with auxiliary sails and outriggers. Its skipper, a boisterous Filipino named Vincente Zapanta, said we had to keep close to the coast so we could make a run for it if we were intercepted by any of the Japanese gunboats that frequented the area. For two hair-raising days we sailed inshore, dodging shoals and reefs, trying to avoid the Japanese, and wondering if we would survive shore-based gunfire from guerrillas who repeatedly mistook us for the enemy. Finally we reach Medina.

NOTE: As with planning our escape, memories differ about the details of our first encounter with friendly Filipinos after we had crossed the swamp. For accounts that vary slightly from my own recollections Cf. Jack Hawkins, *Never Say Die*, pp. 126-127, and Steve Mellnick, *Philippine Diary*, pp. 237-239.

Chapter Eight
Life With The Guerrillas

WE HAD SCARCELY SET FOOT ON THE BEACH AT MEDINA when we were swept into the world of the guerrillas. In his memoirs General MacArthur says he had begun to make plans for guerrilla activity in the Philippines before the fall of either Bataan or Corregidor. Soon after those capitulations irregular groups did, in fact, begin to take shape. On Mindanao the Japanese never made any serious effort to control more than the coastal towns and chief agricultural areas. In the primitive interior of the big island all regular authority collapsed. Local Filipino officials then sometimes became guerrillas or, more commonly, asked prominent local figures to try to maintain order.

These guerrilla leaders were an exotic lot. Some of them had been tribal chieftains; some were mere adventurers, even bandits. Before long they were joined by an array of comparably unconventional Americans. Some of these were civilians who had lived in the Philippines before the war. Many more were men who had escaped from Bataan or Corregidor or who had simply taken to the hills when ordered to surrender after the fall of Corregidor. Most of the latter were hardy, self-reliant young men from the farms and small towns of the south and west. They were determined not to surrender when they felt unbeaten, and especially not to surrender to an enemy for whom they felt an instinctive dislike and contempt.

The most influential of them was "General" Wendell Fertig. Originally a mining engineer from Golden, Colorado, Fertig had been an important mining consultant in the Philippines in the 1930s. He had fled, alone, after the fall of Corregidor and eventually gained considerable control over most of the guerrilla activity on Mindanao. Fertig said afterward that only eccentrics could wage this kind of warfare because conventional minds would never accept the seemingly hopeless odds against success.

The guerrillas had few arms and little ammunition but they did enjoy widespread support and sympathy. Many were on good terms with Americans who had stayed on after the Spanish-American War to engage in mining, lumbering, and agriculture. There were only a few of these now-aging veterans left but they could be of great help to the guerrillas for they lived as virtual feudal barons in remote valleys and jungle clearings. Many Filipinos had been willing to come to terms with their Japanese conquerors initially, but once it became evident that the victors were much given to torture, rape, and lesser brutalities, civilian Filipinos grew increasingly willing to sell or give food to the guerrillas, to furnish them with regular information about the Japanese, even to join guerrilla bands themselves. Thousands of men on Mindanao began to lead two lives: farmers or fishermen by day, guerrillas by night. As these bands merged with the various runaway Americans they became better organized. Guerrilla leaders established rudimentary local governments, issued their own money, gave themselves military commissions, and promoted each other. One scintillating outfit, supposedly organized for combat, contained about 200 commissioned officers plus ten enlisted men who did the paperwork. Most of its "strength" consisted of instant second lieutenants who had cut their insignia from tin cans. After Fertig came to dominate these groups most such "field" promotions were recognized by MacArthur's headquarters in Australia.

All these bands squabbled among themselves ceaselessly. Moslem Moros and Christian Filipinos got on badly. Many of the guerrilla leaders had postwar political ambitions. More than a few were easily distracted by women, or dominated by them. Among the Americans, middle aged civilians like Fertig, who had lived for years in the Philippines and who were familiar with Filipino psychology, had many differences with young, inexperienced American Army officers. Rank and the file Filipinos fought willingly when defending their own villages but were distinctly less enthusiastic for war away from home. Many lived to set ambushes but would desert if an ordinary straight-out fight started. Some of the American guerrilla leaders treated Filipinos patronizingly. Some of the Filipinos complained that they did not get their fair share of available supplies or of what MacArthur was able to send by submarine from Australia. About all that these variegated groups had in common was hatred of the Japanese and support from the civilian population.

The whole guerrilla operation on Mindanao was "coordinated" from Australia by General Courtney Whitney, a prominent Manila lawyer before the war who had become head of the Philippine Section of Intelligence on MacArthur's staff. Liaison between him and Fertig was maintained precariously by Commander "Chick" Parsons USN. Parsons was a wealthy man who had lived for years in the Philippines before the war and had acquired a knowledge of Philippine waters that made him an expert pilot for U.S. submarines coming into the area from Australia. Parsons was prone to act mysteriously and to turn up unexpectedly in unusual places, but he was highly respected by the guerrillas.

Authorities in Australia wanted the guerrillas to avoid contact with the Japanese and become gatherers of intelligence, but native Filipinos wanted them to fight the invaders. Caught in the middle, Fertig had to disobey the orders of his superiors periodically or forfeit the civilian support without which guerrillas cannot operate at all. So the irregulars ambushed Japanese patrols, picked off individual Japanese soldiers, made roads and trails unsafe for the invaders to travel, and attempted to restrict Japanese influence to the seacoast towns. Many of them also farmed or logged in order to produce what the guerrilla movement needed. A few directed Filipino laborers who built airstrips. One of the latter, whom I came to know after the war, was Carlyle Townswick who had soared dramatically from humble Private First Class to instantaneous Second Lieutenant on March 2, 1943. In Townswick's case, this meteoric ascent, typical among the guerrillas, was merited, for he and another American, with the aid of a Filipino crew, extended a 3,000 foot runway in Zamboanga Province to 6,000 feet. It then became the main airstrip for the Allied reconquest of the southern Philippines, handling over 500 planes during the six months Townswick and aides managed it in 1944-1945.

Whenever the Japanese tried to attack guerrillas they melted into the jungle and mountains, taking their supplies and radios with them. The invaders persistently underestimated the strength of the guerrillas, though the guerrillas were a running sore. They tied down thousands of troops who would have been useful elsewhere. They inflicted casualties steadily, a few at a time, until the total was in the thousands.

The guerrillas were also linked with coastwatchers. These intrepid men lived a lonely and precarious existence, isolated with their radios along remote headlands and seashores. They sent a steady stream of information to Australia about the movements of Japanese troops and ships. Oftentimes this was then relayed to American submarines closer by, whose crews grew increasingly skilled and bold in torpedoing Japanese vessels.

The Japanese replied with occasional sorties against the guerrillas but never committed enough troops to strike a mortal blow. Balked here, the invaders would then resort to wholesale torture of Filipino civilians to get information about guerrillas. What was obtained by such means usually did not prove valuable, and the Filipinos were merely hardened in their detestation of everything Japanese.

As soon as we arrived in Medina we were met by one of these local American military entrepreneurs, Lieutenant Colonel Ernest McLish. He had been attached to a Philippine Army regiment in Mindanao when Corregidor fell. Instead of surrendering he had fled into the jungle. He was young, brave, energetic, and an able commander of troops, though deficient as a strategist and a student of Filipino psychology. To us, McLish was munificently hospitable. After questioning us closely about our experiences in and out of Japanese prison camps, and explaining to us the whole Mindanao guerrilla operation, he put us up with local Filipino families and began to arrange various public functions that were mostly excuses for fiestas. For several days life was a whirl of wonderfully cooked American, Filipino, and Chinese food, embellished by liquor, real tablecloths and chinaware, glistening silver and glassware, beautifully dressed women, and even a dance orchestra. Coming on the heels of all we had endured in the preceding fourteen months, the reception was overwhelming. Though I tried as hard as my compatriots to enjoy it all I could not resist giving some of them the needle. At one of these seemingly endless dinners I happened to come onto several of my buddies, full of tuba and some fiery Chinese liquor of uncertain composition. Thus fortified, they had just begun an energetic attack on heaps of food. I made some half-joking, half-serious remark to the effect that it had not been long before that "You begged old Sam to pray for you. Now you are full and you forget old Sam, and God too." Though the jibe was as applicable to myself as to the others, the implied reproach made a sufficient impression on Dyess that he recorded it in his book.

One of the first things McLish tried to impress upon us was that any attempt to reach Australia in a small boat, whether a sailing vessel or one with a motor, was almost certain to fail, either from wind or weather or because we would be intercepted by one of the many Japanese patrol boats along the coasts. McLish also made it clear that nothing would please him more than to have all of us join his guerrilla forces. All but two of us were already commissioned American officers, while Paul and Bob could be instantly transformed thus. We would provide some welcome leadership, he said. We pondered these problems and options. It did seem unwise for the twelve of us to stay together, and particularly to travel together. The Japanese would have greater incentive to try to capture us, and if they succeeded they would get all of us. Moreover, most submarines were likely to be fully manned and so would not have room for ten or twelve extra men. Finally, some of us were more anxious to leave than others.

We soon decided that more information about many matters was essential. Mellnick had once been on MacArthur's staff and was known to the General personally. McCoy was still not entirely convinced that going to Australia in a boat of our own was impracticable. Ben and Victor had nothing obvious to do where we were. So the four of them, with a guide, headed westward along the coast. They hoped to contact "Chick" Parsons, MacArthur's personal representative on Mindanao. Through him Mellnick would send a message to Australia requesting our rescue. He and McCoy also wanted to find out why there had never been a reply to an earlier message sent by Shofner and McCoy before the rest of us had even gotten to Medina. Shortly afterward, Dyess and Boelens left. Ed had convinced McLish that landing strips could be built in some flat coastal areas he had seen. McLish agreed and sent Ed and Leo to try to sell the idea to Fertig.

As for the rest of us, Mike and I were given the job of trying to find supplies for the guerrilla forces, Hawkins and Shofner were assigned to Intelligence, and Marshall and Spielman were held in reserve for special tasks. The last two got impromptu commissions and decided to stay with the guerrillas until the end of the war. Soon they went even further. Spielman married the daughter of an old Spanish-American War veteran who had remained in the Philippines and acquired several sawmills. Marshall conducted a brief, personal paper war with the enemy. Japanese spies soon discovered our whereabouts, even our names. Not long afterward fliers were circulated under the signature of a Japanese captain in Surigao offering 1,000 pesos for the head of any of us. Paul responded by composing a declaration of his own, offering 1,000 pesos for the head of the captain. One dark night he had a guerrilla post it on the door of the captain's quarters. (Nobody ever tried to collect the reward.)

McCoy and Mellnick, meanwhile, after several close escapes from the Japanese, managed to negotiate the hundred miles that separated Medina from Fertig's headquarters to the west. Here they got a cold reception. No message about any of us had been sent to Australia! Fertig considered that all Americans on Mindanao were under his command, and he wanted all of us to become guerrillas. Fertig had an acid-tongued subordinate, "Colonel" Charles Hedges, whose good qualities I eventually came to understand and respect, but who was renowned principally for the colorful and emphatic profanity that embroidered his speech. Hedges summarized the situation with his habitual bluntness: if people wanted to fight, the war was right here. The Filipino guerrillas had helped all us American escapees extensively; indeed, without them we would not have survived. Now it was our turn to help them. In any case, no war would ever be won if people were allowed to run off to Australia whenever they chose. Though Fertig did not say so to their faces, he considered men who had recently escaped after long imprisonment to be not entirely rational: still in shock, really. Either they wanted to launch some suicidal attack on the Japanese at once, or they were obsessed to avenge themselves personally on some individual Japanese, or they were sick and hysterical.

I do not believe the suspicions of Fertig and Hedges, nor their ambivalent attitude toward us were justified. I think Fertig acquired these unfavorable impressions of us 'from his tempestuous and unrewarding contacts with Mellnick, McCoy, and Dyess. Both Steve and

Melvyn were graduates of Service Academies. They informed Fertig that they did not consider themselves outranked by ex-civilians who granted themselves commissions, adding that they had no intention of joining irregular forces commanded by such people. For good measure, they observed that Fertig had not properly prepared defensive positions in the mountains. They demanded flatly that they be sent to Australia on the first transportation available. Fertig considered their conduct to be so damaging to morale at his headquarters that he put them under what amounted to house arrest. Soon after, Dyess showed up. He and Leo Boelens had also narrowly escaped being captured by the Japanese several times. Ed went along with McCoy and Mellnick for another conference with Fertig. This time McCoy held a .45 in his lap. Soon a message was sent to Australia. A few days later a reply came authorizing McCoy, Mellnick, and Dyess to board a submarine that would arrive within a month. Nothing was said about the rest of us. The three decided that it would take ten days to get word to us of what had happened, and probably another twenty days for all of us to get to where they were. By then the submarine would have come and gone. Besides, it was not likely to have room for ten people. Hence they decided to go alone, and merely notified us of what had happened.

Our two guides, Ben and Victor, elected to stay behind at Fertig's headquarters. They reminded Ed, Steve, and McCoy not to forget their pardons. They did not. As soon as McCoy and Mellnick got back to the United States they went to Saranac Lake, N.Y. to see Philippine President Manuel Quezon who was under treatment there for tuberculosis. He granted the pardons at once.

Our three companions almost never got to the United States. After many heart-stopping adventures hugging the coastline in bancas, and more when they crossed the mountains to the southern coast of Zamboanga, they were finally picked up by a submarine forty miles offshore. The boat that took them to the submarine was the "flagship" of Fertig's lilliputian navy. How narrowly they escaped is indicated by the fact that the Japanese sank the "flagship" before it could get back to shore.

While Dyess, Mellnick, and McCoy were spending the better part of two months negotiating their departure I had become a guerrilla. McLish had given me quite general instructions. I was to look for any kind of supplies or commodities that might be useful to guerrillas and, in one way or another, procure them. He gave me some suggestions about what was needed and where I might find it, but otherwise left me on my own. He also assigned a bodyguard to me, a tough but delightful little fellow with the picturesque name of Wenceslao del Mundo, who was, for some reason, called Ben. Though he was

Filipino, Ben looked like a Caucasian. Like me, he had been in prison camp and had escaped. He hated Japanese passionately. He was quite intelligent, had attended college for two years in his native Cebu, had a great sense of humor, and was totally loyal. For the rest of my sojourn in the Philippines Ben went everywhere with me, more as a brother than as a subordinate.

If cats have nine lives, I must have twenty-nine. As at Clark Field, on Bataan, in the camps, and in the swamp, I had several close brushes with death as a guerrilla. One of them was due to mere absent-mindedness. One day I went in a motor boat down the coast to buy some carabao meat. I returned after dark and forgot to swing a lantern in a prearranged way to indicate my identity. Unknown to me, shortly before my return word had come to Medina that a Japanese attack was imminent. When Medina's defenders heard my motor boat in the dark they thought it was the spearhead of the anticipated attack and were all ready to shoot me to bits when Shifty recognized my voice. Afterward, he reprimanded me with memorable warmth, concluding that he *should* have shot me for forgetting the recognition signal.

Most of my career as a Philippine guerrilla was spent going back and forth from Talisayan to Mumbahao. Talisayan was a village on the north coast of Mindanao. Some five or six miles north of it, across a strait was the island of Camiguin. Mumbahao was a village on the north end of Camiguin, perhaps ten or twelve miles by sea from Talisayan. Camiguin is a beautiful little island topped by a symmetrical volcanic peak. Before the war it had been the site of a resort where Chinese merchants and rich Filipinos came to gamble in the casinos. It was thought that some Chinese still living on Camiguin had hoarded shoes, clothing, bolts of khaki cloth, hardware, and various small articles that would be useful to the guerrillas; hence my interest in the place.

Though I made perhaps a dozen trips to Camiguin I never enjoyed any of them. The sea was usually rough in the strait. To negotiate it I had only an old round-bottomed motor launch fueled by alcohol distilled from coconut oil. Every time I set out across the strait in that craft I was afraid either that a Japanese patrol boat would catch me or that my motor would die and leave me helplessly adrift in a tub that could easily capsize in a heavy sea. After a few harrowing trips I junked the motor boat in favor of a banca, a Philippine sailboat with outriggers.

On Camiguin, I was a combination governor, diplomat, policeman, investigator, merchant, and public relations specialist. On my first trip to the island I made a close friend, an Army enlisted man named Gus Mancuso. The main thing Gus did on Camiguin was to represent the United States. This might not seem like much but intangibles are often important in human affairs. For an American to be on Camiguin was evidence that the U.S.A. had not forgotten the Filipinos

156

thereabouts, that the Americans would try to come back some day. I would say that save for my dealings with Luis Morgan, which will be described later, the most important thing I did as an irregular was to play the same role as Gus, simply to *be there*, to remind the Filipinos by my presence that America was not through, that the war was not yet over. Gus, who liked to talk and drink tuba, knew Camiguin thoroughly and gave me a lot of information about what went on there and where I might procure various supplies. He also had a delightful Filipino wife with the unusual name of Ding. I looked forward to *being* on the island if not exactly *going* to it, since I could sit around for hours, drink tuba with Gus, and talk at length with both Mancusos.

When I had something serious to do in Mumbahao I would stay with Ding's aunt. Like all Filipinos with whom I had any contact, she would always give me the best of everything in the house: the best chicken (or the only one), the best bed, the best chair, or whatever. One night Ben and I had gone to sleep at her place when three drunk Filipino youths started a ruckus outside our window. I asked them to be quiet. They wanted to know who I was to tell them what to do. I went outside, accompanied by my bodyguard. Ben and I overpowered the most pugnacious of the troublemakers and trundled him off to the local jail. Next day, when he had sobered up, we let him out and all laughed about it. Thus was public decorum preserved on Camiguin.

In the course of my expeditions there I became acquainted with two local priests. One was Reverand Edward Haggerty S.J. . Before the war Father Haggerty had been Rector of a small college at Cagayan on the north coast of Mindanao. He had taken to the mountains when the Japanese landed. As nearly as I could estimate, he spent about half his time performing regular religious duties and the remainder aiding the guerrillas, who esteemed him highly. The Japanese knew about Father Haggerty and periodically forced him to flee into the jungle to avoid capture. He kept a diary when he could during these years, and published a book (*Guerrilla Padre In Mindanao*) based on it shortly after the war. He went to Camiguin with me two or three times. We talked a great deal and I still remember him vividly. Though he never said anything to me about it, he knew about the troubles Fertig had had with McCoy, Mellnick, and Dyess. It indicates how touchy and quirky some of us must have been that he agreed with Fertig and Hedges that recently escaped prisoners were seriously unbalanced emotionally. He says in his book that he soon realized that our peculiarities were due to the hard and sordid life we had endured in prison camps and would soon subside in the outside world. He also adds that he soon came to believe that "quiet, convincing" Mellnick and "voluble, explosive" McCoy could do more for the war effort somewhere outside the Philippines.

On one of our trips Father Haggerty told me about another

Jesuit, a Father John Pollock, who lived as a missionary in Mumbahao. Since I had gone to a Jesuit school back home, I went to see him. He was a tall, thin man who reminded me of pictures of Abraham Lincoln. I told him who I was, where I had gone to school, and what had happened to me in the war. He then told me that once in his travels he had stopped at Mount Saint Michael's, the Jesuit scholasticate near Spokane, and had become acquainted with Fathers Pete Owens, Edgar Taylor, and Curtis Sharp, all friends of mine. This would have been merely another "small world" story save that Father Pollock went into the sacristy and emerged with a bottle of Benedictine. At that time I did not even know what Benedictine was, much less that it had such a delightful taste. We went out to the edge of the jungle, sat on a log, opened the bottle, and gradually consumed it in the course of a five hour conversation. It was one of the most enjoyable days I spent during the entire war.

My principal official responsibility on Camiguin was to secure food and clothing for the Mindanao guerrillas. MacArthur's headquarters had authorized us to commandeer whatever we needed in such cases. The owner was to be given a receipt which the U.S. Government would redeem at the end of the war. I had learned that a particular Chinese family in Mumbahao had a hoard of useful things. Our agents even told me where it was hidden, in a barn in the forest. I went to see the Chinese family, whom I shall call the Chans. They were a middle aged couple with two fine looking sons about seventeen or eighteen. I began asking the father if he still had anything he had once sold in his store, beyond what was needed for his immediate use. He said "no" twice. I then reminded him that the guerrillas had declared hoarding to be a crime, that I knew he had hoarded much, and that I even knew where it was. I urged him to think of how badly the guerrillas needed what he had in order to better fight the Japanese, and promised him eventual payment for what was taken. He was adamant in his denial that he possessed any such goods, so I put him in jail. A few days later I came to get him. With great reluctance he followed me into the jungle to the barn where his wares were secreted. I took a hasty inventory, reminded him that if the Japanese found it they would pay him nothing, and assured him that I would prefer to have him give it to me in exchange for a receipt than to simply seize it. We went back to his house. He pondered. His sons took my side and tried to persuade their father that I was not stealing his goods but only keeping them away from the Japanese, and that he would be paid eventually. He began to waver, but his wife remained resolutely unconvinced. She argued vehemently against giving up the hoarded items, guarantees or not. At length, in desperation, she took the belt off her dress and attempted to strangle herself. The sight was so ludicrous that I burst out laughing. At the same time I had an inspiration. I took out my .45 and offered it to her, motioning that it was a far more efficient mode of suicide than her belt. At that the father and sons also began to laugh. This was too much for Mrs. Chan. She laughed too and relented. In two minutes the whole matter was settled. There is more to warfare than killing people. . .

This trip to Camiguin was nearly my last. Among the commodities I got from Mr. Chan's warehouse were several hundred burlap bags, badly needed on the mainland to hold rice that was about to be harvested. I filled the hold of a twenty foot sailboat with the bags and prepared to leave at once because one of our local operatives told me that the Japanese knew an escapee was on the island and that one of their patrols was coming to look for him. A brisk wind was blowing but we were on the lee side of the island so the water did not look rough. The skipper of the boat, who was much better acquainted with local sea and weather than I, reminded me that once we got into the strait we would be on the open ocean where the water would be much rougher. I knew this, but at the moment my imagination was petrified by the appalling possibility of being recaptured by the Japanese so I pressed the reluctant captain and his crew of thirteen to go, at once.

As the captain had foreseen, once we got into the strait the sea became violent. Soon we were hit by ten foot waves and tossed about like a cork. Water began to pour over the sides of the boat, but by now we were too far out to turn back. A huge wave broke the mainmast and flung the mainsail into the sea where it dragged and threatened to capsize the boat. The Filipino crewmen averted this disaster by cutting it loose with their bolos. This left us only the jib sail. I was scared witless. I remembered Bill Knortz, one of Fertig's ablest lieutenants, who had ventured into that same strait in a rough sea and had never been seen again. The captain, understandably, reproached me bitterly for having pressured him to leave.

In desperation, I pulled out all stops. I urged that we pray. Everyone said several "Hail Marys" enthusiastically. Then, thinking how much Filipinos love awards and decorations, I promised to recommend all hands for a Silver Star if we came through. Finally, we threw our hard-won sacks overboard. All this helped. Gradually, everyone got hold of himself. The skipper maneuvered the craft marvelously, sliding along the tops of the mountainous waves and keeping out of the troughs. Somehow, contrary to all logic, to all likelihood, we made it across. The crewmen leaped ashore, hugged one another with unrestrained joy, and assured each other that they were the world's greatest sailors. I felt utterly wrung out.

When Commander John Morrill neared Darwin, Australia in 1942, at the end of a thirty one day voyage with seventeen men in a thirty-six foot boat on the open sea, he thought of how many times, logically, all aboard should have died. He said he could not believe that they had all come through by sheer luck or circumstance: he was sure some Higher Power had looked after them. I felt the same: that once more God had seen me through a miracle. If each one of us is entitled to a certain number of miracles in his lifetime I vastly exceeded my quota in World War II. If miracles occur in response to prayers, perhaps I didn't.

I regret to add that the crewmen never got their Silver Stars. This was due about equally to my own negligence and to the press of circumstances. Under U.S. military regulations anyone may recommend anyone else for whatever award seems suitable recognition for some act of heroism beyond the call of duty. I ought to have submitted these recommendations at once but there seemed no obvious authority among the guerrillas close by so I put it off. Within a few days I became more than ordinarily fearful of being recaptured by the Japanese. Shortly after that I moved 100 miles away and became engrossed in General Fertig's troubles with an unruly subordinate, with a project of Leo Boelens', and with my own opportunity to get away to Australia. Before long I had forgotten the names of the crewmen. Then I *could not* recommend them for their Silver Stars.

Thus do many valorous deeds in war go officially unrecognized. The wearer of a chest full of medals has usually earned at least most of them, but many a soldier who deserved a medal quite as much never got it because he was killed in action, simply disappeared in a combat zone, was alone when he performed some heroic act, or gradually slipped from the consciousness of others just as the brave Filipino crewmen did from mine.

Not long after my heartstopping escape in the strait I had an experience which was nearly as unsettling, if in a less spectacular way. One day I was walking down a road near the coastal village of Salay when I met ten Filipinos. They said they had just been released by the Japanese at Cagayan. I immediately wondered why our enemies had been so uncharacteristically generous. Perhaps these people had agreed to become Japanese agents? I asked them if they had heard that ten Americans had escaped from Davao. They said they had. I inquired if they knew any of the names. They mentioned several of our party by name, then named other Americans whom the Japanese knew to be on Camiguin Island. They concluded with the remark that "Grashio" made periodic visits to Camiguin. Any sweat I exuded in the tropical sun at that moment was cold.

Within a day or two I got the message Dyess had dispatched just before he got aboard the submarine that was to take him to Australia. He said Leo Boelens, who had earlier gone to Baroy, a few miles from Fertig's headquarters, to build an airstrip, was suffering badly from dysentery and loneliness. I could do nothing about the dysentery but I could provide companionship so I immediately asked McLish for a transfer. He was agreeable, merely asking me to stop to see Fertig along the way. Ben and I went off under cover of darkness in a sailing boat, partly because this was an easier way to travel than through the jungle, partly because the overland route was deemed unsafe. The voyage was hairy for both the Filipino crew and myself. For them, to be caught with an American aboard meant certain death, most likely a lingering, painful one. For me, all sailboats were imported from Hell. They seemed flimsy, the sea splashed over them, Japanese power boats could run them down or shoot them up at any time, and they were utterly dependent on the wind. I marveled at the nonchalance with which Filipinos sailed these rickety bancas, and especially at their composure when becalmed. They had an odd superstition that whistling would stir up the wind. Though it seemed to me uncanny how often a breeze would in fact spring up, I never became a True Believer in this mode of navigation. Any prayers I had neglected to say earlier in my life were always made up when I was at sea.

In some way that surpassed my understanding, the Filipino crew evaded the Japanese and got us ashore. Soon we were at General Fertig's headquarters. He greeted me warmly and treated me generously. Whether he had been chastened by his acrimonious encounter with Dyess, Mellnick, and McCoy, or he feared what they might have said about him in Australia, or he had merely changed his mind about escapees, I do not know. Whatever the case, he gave me three good meals from delicacies brought in by occasional submarines from Australia, briefed me about his whole organization, told me what Leo Boelens had been doing, and assured me that I was quite right to want to be with Leo. Further he promised that I could go out on the next submarine, and said he would send a runner to tell me when and where to meet it whenever he got precise information. As a going away present he gave me some cigarettes.

Now I had to get back onto that wretched boat, try to slip unobserved into narrow, shallow Panguil Bay, and get ashore at Baroy. The crew buried me, with our rifles, under a heap of gunny sacks and guided our banca through the entrance to the bay. As they proceeded unconcernedly, fishing boats moved in and out all around us and a Japanese sentry walked his tour on a pier that seemed only spitting distance away. At this crucial time when my most devout wish was to attract no attention from anyone some of the Filipinos proposed that we shoot the sentry! I was aghast. To do such a thing would stir up a hornet's nest and ruin us utterly. It was all I could do to dissuade my hot-headed associates without making so much noise in the process to be discovered myself.

At length we glided into Baroy safely in the dark. I soon found out where Leo was. Next day some friendly natives gave me a small Filipino horse to ride. With my sidekick Ben I now started along a jungle trail through Moro country. The Moros were alleged to be friendly to the guerrilla movement and obedient to Fertig but many things about them were disquieting. For instance, they had never abandoned their ancient religious conviction that to kill Christians would ensure them a place in heaven. And long after the Spanish-American War they had persisted in the strange practice of periodically clamping an elastic vine around their genitals. The resulting pain caused them to run amok. In this state they would kill anyone they met. It had been because of this that the .38 calibre revolver had been replaced by the .45 as standard U.S. Army issue. It had been discovered by hard experience that no slug smaller than a .45 would stop a Moro in his tracks when he was amok. Mindful of these sobering considerations, I did not feel altogether at ease as I made my way into the domain of these allies in our common struggle for a democratic world.

Suddenly the little horse I was riding froze in his tracks. His eyes bulged, his ears shot up, and the hair on his mane rose. Ben nodded to me and went a short way on the trail alone. Soon I heard a shot. There in the path lay a python, thicker than a man's arm and about ten feet long. It had been lying on a tree limb overhanging the trail, for no purpose that seemed good to me. The horse had either seen or sensed it. Ben was proud of himself for having killed the sinister creature, one of only three snakes I can recall having seen in the Philippines. Carlyle Townswick, the builder of the Zamboanga airstrip, said he once caught a huge python, cut seventeen feet of steaks off it, and found them tasty. Maybe this mere ten footer would have looked like potential steaks to me during the black days in Camp O'Donnell but now that I was better fed I was pleased to see the loathsome monster dead.

It was good to see Leo again after an absence of two months. He was managing a Filipino crew who were building an airfield. When completed it would be about 300 feet wide and a mile long, sufficient to accommodate B-29 bombers. Aside from clearing and leveling, his main task was to throw rocks into a huge carabao wallow located in the middle of the projected runway. I stayed with Leo several weeks before my submarine arrived. While there, something took place that I often read but never expected to see; a plague of locusts. Vast, incredible clouds of them darkened the sky for many minutes at a time. When they passed through trees or cornfields they left behind only leafless trunks and limbs or stalks. Billions of them chewing all at once made a considerable grinding noise. Though the locusts were a disaster in most ways, the Moros attacked them with their customary pertinacity. They and some other Filipino tribes regarded locusts as a delicacy. To capture them the Moros dug pits, then pounded the earth nearby. This caused the locusts to pack together in the pits, where the Moros scooped them up by the sackful.

Once Leo and I attended a Moro feast, the object of which

162

was to improve relations between these unpredictable little freebooters and the guerrillas. Some unusual items were on the menu. Locust, deep fried in coconut oil, was better than it sounds, much like popcorn. Monkey meat was also good, very dark but resembling mutton in flavor. Most of the rest was fruit: mangos, bananas, papayas, and a pink, crisp, sweet, light fruit called tambis.

Not long afterward I learned about some less appealing culinary tastes of the Moros. One day an American submarine sank a Japanese ship close in. Thirteen Japanese soldiers managed to swim ashore, only to be captured by the guerrillas. They were put into a barbed wire enclosure south of Baroy. Ben and I went to seem them. Since I was not a heavy smoker I still had some of the cigarettes Fertig had given me. When I came up to the enclosure all the Japanese save the captain of the ship arose and saluted. The captain squatted with his head down and his arms locked around his knees, a picture of oriental resignation. Ben reminded him sharply that an American officer was present. He did not move. Ben then slapped him a couple of times. I told Ben to stop, then went into the enclosure and offered the men cigarettes. Each took one and saluted me when I left. Only the captain remained obdurate, sulky, unmoving; convinced, presumably, in that strange Japanese manner that we Occidentals could never fathom, that he had disgraced himself by the mere act of saving his life. If so, his disgrace did not last long. A few days later a Filipino turncoat helped all the Japanese escape. Alas, for them! The Moros caught them and killed every one. To verify their deed they brought back the head of one of the Japanese. They added, matter-of-factly, that they had eaten the hearts and livers of the others to show their hatred for everything Japanese.

As the reader might surmise from incidents like this, I never knew exactly what to think of the Moros. They and the Christian Filipinos hated each other. Each had committed many single and multiple atrocities against the other for many decades past and even during the war. Father Haggerty, who knew the Moros well, disdained them as treacherous semi-savages who lacked idealism and were tepidly pro-American only because they judged that in the long run this would be more profitable than to be pro-Japanese. Possibly some of Father Haggerty's hostility to the Moros was due to them being Moslems who hated Christianity; but I really do not *know* if this was the case. All I can say, finally, is that nobody else in the Philippines regarded the Moros with either admiration or affection.

Independence movements have flourished all over Asia and Africa in our century. By now most of them have ended in the establishment of independent nations in what were formerly parts of European or American empires. Most of the time the leaders of these "struggles for liberation" have been educated natives. Their standard cries have been that "we" must have "freedom," "we" must have independence and the rest. If independence is gained, they, of course, are the ones who shortly become presidents and premiers, cabinet ministers and ambassadors, army officers and commissioners of police, chief of bureaus and managers of national airlines. It is they who get expense accounts, chauffeured limousines, and country homes. It is they who dine on lobster, steak, caviar and champagne. But what of the vast majority of their countrymen who fish and chop wood and follow the ox in the field as their ancestors have always done? Do *they* really want independence? When I was with Leo Boelens in August of 1943, and work was not pressing, I often talked with ordinary uneducated or half-educated peasants on Mindanao about the Philippine independence they were to receive in 1946. Not a single one said he welcomed the prospect. Many of them had been at odds with their own government for decades or generations. Most thought they had been treated better by the Americans than anyone else, and they did not want to break the link. Of course most, or even all, of them may have told me this just to make me feel good or to curry favor with Americans, but I doubt it. They always seemed sincere. Thus even though the Filipinos certainly earned their independence and deserved to have it, I have always been skeptical about how many of them truly desired it.

When I had visited General Fertig he had told me a great deal about a particularly troublesome subordinate of his, a mestizo (half-Filipino, half-American) named Luis Morgan. Morgan was an ex-police chief: a hard drinker and inveterate womanizer; ambitious, treacherous, and cruel; but also brave, tough, and reasonably able. Morgan already headed his own guerrilla force when Fertig had begun to pose as MacArthur's man from Australia. Morgan had then planned to use Fertig as a front man; Fertig had hoped that he could, ultimately, reduce Morgan to obedience and make use of his unquestioned bravery and prowess in the field. Neither had succeeded. Morgan had once slaughtered a band of Moros, thereby complicating Fertig's task of winning Moro support against the Japanese. Morgan had also plotted ceaselessly to supplant Fertig as chief of the whole Mindanao guerrilla operation and had once mutinied openly. By the summer of 1943 Fertig was convinced that Morgan was mentally unstable and that his only alternatives were to execute Morgan, an act which would alienate many Filipinos, or somehow get rid of him. He had met Morgan and told him he was to be promoted: sent to Australia where he could be added to MacArthur's staff. There he would be given a regular American commission and would train a Filipino division in jungle warfare. One day he would lead it back in a successful Allied invasion of the Philippines. Morgan was highly suspicious of the motive behind this "promotion" but he did nothing. Fertig intended to send Morgan out on the same submarine that was to take me, and asked me to urge Morgan to go with me. Though I did not know it, Fertig subsequently received orders from Australia to deal with Morgan himself. He chose to ignore the orders, planning to plead afterward that they had arrived too late.

Leo arranged a meeting with Morgan for me. I told him everyone with any knowledge of the situation in Mindanao knew what an outstanding job he had done but that only Fertig would ever get credit for it because he was the only one in regular contact with MacArthur. If he, Morgan, was ever to be appreciated he would have to get to Australia and tell authorities there what he had been doing. Morgan gave me no firm reply but did say he would meet me at the rendezvous point when the submarine arrived. I never expected to see him again.

One day a Filipino courier brought me word that I was to report to Fertig's headquarters at a certain date to prepare to meet a submarine soon after. I was simultaneously gladdened and saddened. Leo Boelens and I had grown close in our weeks together. Somebody had left a stack of old *Reader's Digest* magazines in the area. Many afternoons Leo and I had gone to a beautiful waterfall near the field and had passed the time reading *Reader's Digest* articles to each other. The night before I left I offered, as I had done several times before, to stay with him until his airstrip was completed and then take my chances of getting out with him on another submarine sometime in the future. He had always refused, just as he had always refused to discuss with Fertig the numerous ills that still afflicted him from many months in prison camp. Fertig surely would have arranged to have had him evacuated had he known how sick Leo really was.

On this last night I awoke about 2:00 A.M., Leo was still up, writing a letter by the light of a feeble coconut oil lamp. When he finished, he sealed it, gave it to me, asked me to open it only when I was aboard the submarine. When I did open it, at length, it said the same things he had said to me in person several times: that if I refused an opportunity to go to Australia those in high places there would conclude that the life of a guerrilla could hardly be unpleasant if the escapees did not *want* to be repatriated. This would make matter difficult for all our buddies. Therefore I must go, now, alone. He appreciated my concern for him, but he believed a pilot was a more valuable man in the overall war effort than an engineer. Finally, he said, we must not think about our individual desires but the needs of the nation in the war. His duty was to stay and complete the airstrip. Mine was to go.

There never was a more level-headed, reliable, unselfish man than Leo Boelens. No American ever treated his Filipino workmen with greater concern and fairness. He was a true patriot in the fullest sense of the word: one of the finest men I have ever known.

Notoriously, good often goes unrewarded, at least in this world. Less than a month later a Japanese patrol came into the area where we had been. Leo got advance warning and went into the jungle. Then he was told that all was clear and came back, too soon. A Japanese sniper shot him; other Japanese captured him. He was taken to Baroy, put to death cruelly, and buried secretly. Afterwards, Filipinos found his body and gave it a Christian burial. Leo was the only one of the ten of us who never made it back to the United States.

When I came to the place where I was to meet the submarine I was flooded with contradictory emotions. I was elated at the prospect of going home to see my wife and family, and to tell the American people all about the horrors of life in Japanese prison camps. At the same time, I could never put out of my mind memories of my fellow prisoners back in Davao. What were they enduring now because ten of us had escaped? The thought bedevilled me constantly. I thought too, about Leo, sick but determined to do his duty, come what might. I thought about Jack Hawkins and Shifty and Mike and Spielman and Marshall. All were being left behind. Of course things eventually turned out well for all of them save Leo. The three Marines were rescued by another submarine a couple of months later, while Marshall and Spielman cast their lot with the guerrillas and made it through till the end of the war. Spielman even stayed on afterward. But I could not foresee this *at the time* and my heart was heavy as I awaited the submarine.

My melancholy reverie was broken abruptly when there arrived, of all people, *both* Fertig and Luis Morgan! Fertig wished me well and gave me a $100 bill as a going-away present. Morgan, to my amazement, got on board with me without a word. Perhaps Luis half-expected his fate. When he reached Australia he was simply removed from the war by higher authorities. Several years later he was killed in an airplane crash. Many months after my dealings with Morgan I was awarded a Bronze Star for what his superiors judged I had done to neutralize him.

NOTE: Fertig is the subject of a laudatory biography by John Keats (*They Fought Alone*), rendered in that strange literary form, the "nonfiction novel." The tangled and murky dealing of Mellnick, McCoy, and Dyess with Fertig are described from Fertig's side by Keats, pp. 219-244; from the side of our representatives by Mellnick, *Philippine*

Diary, pp. 261-265. Fertig's side of his many troubles with Morgan is given by Keats, pp. 82-95, 271, 286, 292-299.

McLish's name is also spelled McClish and McLeish by various writers. The estimate of him given here is mostly my own though it was Fertig, his nominal superior, who deemed McLish an indifferent strategist who lacked skill in dealing with Filipinos. Cf. Keats, p. 254. For an estimate, contrasting in some ways, Cf. Jack Hawkins, *Never Say Die*, p. 148.

Chapter Nine
To Australia And Home

At LENGTH THE USS BOWFIN ROSE SLOWLY out of the ocean like some giant primordial beast. When the American Flag went up atop it, I trembled with excitement. Dozens of people near me on shore, Filipinos and Americans, burst into tears or cleared their throats unconvincingly. Some Filipinos took me out in a small banca. Despite having been out of prison camp five months by now I had not yet shaken either malaria or dysentery. I had regained some of the strength I had lost but I doubt that I weighed over a hundred pounds. I started slowly up the rope ladder that the submarine crew had hung over the side of the vessel. When I neared the top a husky Navy man grabbed me and hauled me aboard bodily. For the first time since December 8, 1941 I felt truly safe.

The sailor was Lieutenant Cone, a classmate of Jack Hawkins at Annapolis. He wanted to know all about Jack, and would have taken the submarine to get him at once had this been possible. Overall, I have never seen a more outstanding group of servicemen than the crew of the BOWFIN. All were volunteers, each one had been hand picked for this ship, and every man did his job with skill and care. Had all the people in our armed services performed at this level the war would have been shorter.

It would also be hard to beat the sailors for hospitality. I was taken downstairs to meet the skipper, a much-decorated Commander Willingham, and the crew. The first thing they did was give me some clothes. I had been living either in camps or hand-to-mouth with the guerrillas for so long that clothing had come to mean whatever I could get my hands on. I had also suspected that I might be issued new garb aboard the BOWFIN so just before I left shore I gave most of what I was wearing to an ill-clad Filipino. When I actually went aboard I was attired resplendently in a G-string and little else. The crew soon outfitted me acceptably, save for headgear. Several hats were tried but all were too big. Years afterward I thought of a story about Yogi Berra, the New York Yankees' catcher. On the first day of spring training one year the equipment manager asked Yogi what size cap he wanted. Berra supposedly replied, "How do I know? I'm not in shape yet." Yogi had a point, for those who were unable to outfit me with a hat finally expressed their exasperation by measuring my head. I discovered that it, like the rest of my body, had shrunk during the many months of captivity.

Once I was suitably attired I was taken to the officers' dinning room, a cubicle about the size of a restaurant booth. The table was covered with clean linen, glasses, and polished silverware. Some cookies and coffee were placed before me and I was asked what I would like for a serious meal. I was so excited that I was unable to lift a cup of coffee to my lips. In an effort to calm me, the Captain urged me to try again. This time I spilled some but then relaxed sufficiently to drink the rest. By then I was able to say I would like a hamburger and some ice cream. There was no hamburger on board so I was given a steak, which I ate with relish. That settled me down sufficiently for ordinary conversation. The Captain and many others stayed with me till 2:00 A.M. talking about all my experiences, the inhuman treatment accorded the prisoners, and progress of the war. In particular, they asked me innumerable questions about friends of theirs I might have encountered.

It seems to me that I had been asleep about ten minutes (though it must have been something over three hours) when the klaxon sounded deafeningly. Half asleep, I supposed it was some practice exercise. Suddenly somebody grabbed me bodily and told me the Captain wanted me on the bridge to identify a ship. When I got there he thrust a pair of binoculars into my hands. I could tell at once that the boat did not belong to any of the Mindanao guerrillas. The Captain then moved the submarine just out of range of machine gun tracers coming from the ship and began to fire his four inch gun. Since the enemy vessel was small and could not match the BOWFINS's artillery there was no point in wasting torpedoes on it. Soon the ship was hit once then several times. Fire broke out on it; then it broke in two and sank. We departed.

Readers may think it was heartless and uncivilized to make no effort to rescue the Japanese sailors left struggling in the water many miles from land, but there were sound reasons for leaving them. To start with, a submarine is extremely crowded. There is little room for extra people. Equally pertinent was the attitude of the Japanese. In the European Theater if German or Italian sailors were plucked from the water they were glad to save their lives and made no trouble for their rescuers. All experience with the Japanese, by contrast, had indicated that they could not be trusted. They fought to the death everywhere, and they had shot or stabbed medical corpsmen and doctors who had tried to treat them. In any group of Japanese sailors there were likely to be a few who understood the workings of submarines. If a number of them were packed on board and one man among them grabbed some crucial valve or switch he might send the submarine and all its crew to the bottom. The willingness of Japanese pilots to fly suicidal kamikaze missions against American ships in the last months of the war is further proof, if any is needed, that reluctance to take Japanese aboard submarines was a sound instinct. On a big surface ship the situation was different. These prisoners could be thrown into the brig where they could do no harm.

The BOWFIN already had an illustrious history. On the voyage that preceded my rescue it had sunk five or six Japanese ships off the China coast. These successes had particularly delighted the chief gunner. He had served on Corregidor aboard the TROUT when it brought a load of gold off that beleaguered island. Now nothing pleased him so much as an opportunity to shoot back at anything Japanese. He got one more chance on this particular trip. We sank a small Japanese communications vessel in the Indian Ocean, again with gunfire alone.

The rest of the trip to Australia was routine. Our skipper, a top notch seaman much admired by his crew, ran submerged for only six hours out of the whole ten days. Unhappily, I was unable to appreciate his expertise because I lay on my cot most of the time suffering from my assorted ills compounded by seasickness. One day an enlisted man named Reid Lee came in to see me. He was from Colville, only seventy miles from Spokane. Moreover, his uncle, Ray Cantrell, a Pan American pilot, was a close friend of mine. We talked for hours. I seemed halfway home already.

It is Navy tradition to have some sort of reception when a ship comes in. When we landed at Perth on the distant west coast of Australia we were met by a Navy band and a great crowd of people offering fresh milk to all aboard. Three of our passengers, Napalillo, Offert, and Owens, were overcome. They were members of Lieutenant John D. Bulkeley's torpedo boat crew who had brought MacArthur off Corregidor. Later they had refused to surrender, preferring, like many, to take their chances in the jungle with the guerrillas. Like my self, they had been picked up by the BOWFIN along the Mindanao coast. Now tears rolled down their cheeks unashamedly, partly from surprise, partly from sheer gladness, partly because they knew they would soon be back in the regular service again.

Life in war always seemed to me to be a succession of extremes. Either I was being starved, or was sunk in misery, or was sure I would die of some disease, or expected to be killed in the next three minutes; or else I was exulting about something, celebrating, shedding tears of joy, or being feted as a hero. Maybe life was placid in the Quartermaster Corps, or in the Pentagon, but it never seemed to be anywhere I was.

After being taken off the submarine I was sent to an Australian hospital in Freemantle to be treated for my malaria and dysentery. The three days I spent there were somewhat like attending one's coronation. Australian volunteer hospital workers, the counterparts of Gray Ladies in American hospitals, came in every day to give me candy, special foods, a razor, and other such welcome commodities. On the second night most of the BOWFIN's crew came to see me, armed with a gunny sack full of beer. We traded stories for hours. Also in the hospital were several Italian war prisoners who had been taken in the North African Desert when Tobruk fell. Now they were janitors, waiting in undisguised contentment for the war to end. One of them was from Calabria, the south province from which my parents had emigrated to America. They had spoken the Calabrese dialect around the house, so I now had a long talk with my fellow countryman, once removed.

After my brief sojourn in this delightful hospital I was flown across the wasteland of central Australia to the eastern coast. I even had distinguished company all the way, Commander "Chick" Parsons!

There used to be a joke during World War II to the effect that Germans fought for Hitler, Russians fought for Communism, Japanese fought for the Emperor, and Americans fought for souvenirs. At least one Australian valued them too, for at the refueling stop in Melbourne somebody stole an array of exotic daggers and a Moro hat I had collected in Mindanao.

My destination proved to be a guerrilla training camp near Brisbane. Here I was told that my arrival was a military secret, that if the Japanese learned that I had been taken off Mindanao by submarine this might jeopardize the evacuation of others. For the same reason, I was not to communicate with my family. The message was crushing. I yearned to let my wife, parents, and sisters know that I was safe at last. In addition, I was thoroughly tired of guerrilla troops. The daily sight of primitive irregulars, probably from New Guinea and locally called fuzzie-wuzzies, did not intrigue me. I wanted badly to get into the city of Brisbane and especially to report to 5th Air Force Headquarters. One day I got hold of a lieutenant and told him my grievances. A couple of days later I was picked up in a staff car and taken to see General George C. Kenney, Commanding General of the 5th Air Force.

Kenney was a fine man who enjoyed unusual rapport with his subordinates. He greeted me warmly and began immediately to talk about prison camps, even though he had discussed the same subject at length with Dyess several weeks earlier. At the end of our conversation he asked me my rank. I told him "second lieutenant." (I had been proclaimed a captain while with the guerrillas but I was uncertain of the status of these backwoods promotions.) The General told me that I was now a first lieutenant and would soon be made a captain. To top off a magnificent day, he sent me to my new home, Braeland House, a three story mansion which housed three Air Force colonels, Bill Hudnell, Roscoe Nichols, and Ben Caine. They took me in hand, treated me as an honored guest, and tried to put some weight back on my bare bones. My short stay with them was marvelously pleasant.

One day I went back to see General Kenney. He began our conversation in the most promising way possible by saying I could have anything I wanted. I said I would like to fly again. He replied that I should wait until I had regained more weight and strength; adding that, meanwhile, I should go to his tailor and have some uniforms made that fit me. I did so, and when I was paid I went to reimburse him. The General refused to take a penny, saying the uniforms were his gift to me.

A couple of weeks later Colonel Hudnell asked if I would like to fly over to Amberley with him that afternoon. I was jubilant. In prison camps I had thought often of flying, and of the new planes that must be coming off the assembly lines, planes that I might never see, much less fly. We went up in a C-43, a small, single-engine biplane. We flew a short distance to a fighter base where many new P-40N5s were parked. After having witnessed the devastation wrought by the Japanese among aircraft lined up in neat rows at Clark Field perhaps I should have been horror-stricken to see so many planes parked wingtip-to-wingtip again. Not so. Things were different now. The Japanese were no longer on the march. Now I was impressed immediately by what those rows of planes indicated about the latent might of the United States. Second thoughts followed quickly. If only the guerrillas in the Philippines had some of these scores of planes! I could not but wonder, too, why it had been "impossible" to spare at least one of them now and then. . .

Colonel Hudnell asked me if I would like to check out one of the new P-40s. I was enthused. He showed me the instruments and instructions, and explained to me the changes that had been made in the P-40 since I had last flown one eighteen months before. I was heartened by his confidence and took off in high spirits. I flew around for an hour, had an airborne look at the camp where the fuzzie wuzzies were drilling and sweating, and took special care to make a good landing. This broke the ice. Soon I was flying twice a day, routinely. A short time later Colonel Hudnell asked me if I would like to fly a P-47, a new plane that had been developed while I was in prison. He thought I should catch up with the other American pilots who were flying the latest planes. Within a few days I was on my own with the P-47. Within a couple of weeks I had logged some twenty hours in the air, gotten my weight back up to a portly 115 pounds, and felt back in the groove again. Only six months earlier I had been trying to drive Mike Dobervich's brahma bull through the comote fields of Davao. That seemed light years away now.

Despite the immense satisfaction of flying again, I was still profoundly dissatisfied to remain under orders not to tell anyone about my past experiences and not contact anyone in the United States. One day General Wilson, Chief of Staff for the 5th Air Force, called me in. He asked if I had written to my wife. I said I had been ordered not to do so. He replied that I should write, but should caution her not to say anything to anyone. He added that when she wrote back to me she should address the letter to him, with her return address on it. Incredible though it may seem, after receiving no mail from the U.S.A. in nineteen months, and after all that had happened to me in the interim, I could not think of anything to write to my wife. All I can remember now is that I finally managed to ask the name of the daughter I had never seen.

There happened to be in Brisbane at the time one of the most colorful figures in the Pacific war, a pilot with the singularly appropriate name of Paul I. (Pappy) Gunn. Pappy was a legend in the 5th Air Force. Before the war he had been the manager of Philippine Airlines. Before that he had been one of the pioneers of aviation in the Orient. Now he was about fifty years old and commander of a transport unit in Australia. Pappy was a first rate technician, an expert maintenance man, and an excellent bomber pilot even though twice the age of most combat pilots. Because his whole family had been interned in Santo Tomas, Pappy regarded the war as a personal vendetta between himself and Japan. His side of it was pursued passionately and with exceptional ingenuity. Eventually he devised a way to mount eight .50 calibre machineguns in the nose of a B-25, a particularly lethal combination for strafing ships and ground targets that was employed with great effectiveness in the Battle of the Bismark Sea, March 3-4, 1942.

Pappy took a liking to me at once and treated me like a son. One day he offered to fly with me just to give me some experience. I was both honored and overjoyed. We flew for several hours over northern Australia and the ocean. Pappy took special care to show me how to fly just above the waves so as to evade enemy radar. Quite possibly this gave me unwarranted confidence that nearly ended my career a week or so later.

Shortly after my sojourn with Pappy I asked to go to Doba Dura in New Guinea to see some old classmates who were stationed there. Thus began an adventure that changed my status abruptly. I landed in Port Moresby, without instructions, and paid my respects to Brigadier General Paul B. Wurtsmith, the Commander of the Fifth Fighter Command under General Kenney. I also met Pat Sullivan, a fighter pilot who had recently been shot down over central New Guinea, perhaps the only place in the world more primitive than central Mindanao. Some cannibals had wanted to make soup out of Pat but he had managed to escape them and, after many adventures, had made his way out of the Stone Age and back into the twentieth century.

At Doba Dura, where a fighter group was located, there was a great party with some of my old classmates. Local supplies of gin and lemon powder were reduced appreciably. One of those at the party was the Group Operations Officer, "Killer" Kirsch, with whom I had trained at Kelly Field. During the course of what proved to be a long evening I asked if I could fly a regular mission up to Buna and Salamaua the next morning, just to see if there was anything worth shooting at or bombing along the way. As Operations Officer, Kirsch should have known of the regulation prohibiting escapees from returning to the war area from which they had fled, and refused to let me go, but he probably thought there was little danger so he not only let me go but went along with me.

Though we found nothing worth bombing, I almost killed myself on the way back. Instead of cruising along routinely, "Killer" and I repeatedly dove our planes down to water level, raced just above the waves, and then climbed again. One such dive and pass came close to being my last. I scraped the ocean with my belly tank, a chilling reminder that I had gotten rusty and had no business yet in a combat area where split second reactions are often the difference between life and death.

It must be emphasized that there was no *reason* whatsoever to indulge in such carefree bravado. Why did I do it? If someone had asked me immediately afterward I probably would have said something about the animal exuberance of youth or my sheer exultant joy at being in the air once more, unfettered. If a psychologist had been asked he probably would have remarked merely that I had the right profile for a fighter pilot. Had friends of my youth been queried, a fair number of them surely would have said, "Same old Sam." Though I never got into any trouble of the sort that interests the police, from early youth I had always liked action, physical contact, excitement, and adventure. More than once these proclivities had nearly ended my life before I ever got into an airplane. On one occasion back home, when I was in the eighth grade, I had climbed some thirty feet to the top of a huge storage bin full of wood blocks in a local fuel yard, until I reached the very top. Suddenly my movements precipitated an avalanche which threatened to bury me. I struggled frantically to get to the side of the bin, and was able to grab a pole there for a second or two before the cascading blocks pounded into me, broke my grip, and engulfed me. When I regained consciousness, perhaps half an hour later, I was near home, atop the shoulders of a schoolmate, Benjamin Nicodemus. Half a century ago kids were not passed routinely from one grade to another in school merely because they were still alive at the end of the term. Promotion had to be earned. As a result many grade schools contained "students" who were sixteen, seventeen, even eighteen years old. Ben, who was an Indian, was one such. He was eighteen years old, six feet tall, husky, and strong; a grown man, though still in the eighth grade. Not surprisingly, he was the pitcher on our school base-ball team, of which I was the catcher. Fortunately for me, Ben was not given to loitering in the library after classes. On this day he was strolling around our baseball field, which lay next to the fuel yard. He heard my cries and dug me out from under the woodpile. I had suffered only a broken wrist and a great many bruises, though I might well have died had I lain unconscious under the pile all night.

Another time that same year I had decided to go for a walk on the logs in the McGoldrick Lumber Company's mill pond, without the "corked" shoes loggers wear, without previous experience walking on logs, and without being able to swim. Soon the inevitable happened. I got on a log too small to control and too far away from others to get off. In I went. I grabbed the log but could not get back on it. This time I should have cashed my chips for sure for it was late in the fall and the water in the Spokane River was icy; but I had a second great stroke of luck. Another school friend, Leo McKenna, happened to come by. Providentially, he was a strong swimmer. He jumped in, clothes and all, and rescued me.

On still another occasion, perhaps the next year, I took an absurd risk in the company of Paul Giesa, who had done so much to quicken my interest in flying. One day the two of us climbed up inside one of the towers of Saint Aloysius Church near our homes, then made our way outside to the ladder that went up the cross atop the tower. Paul, who was absolutely fearless, climbed to the very top and stood on the cross, utterly unattached, in the open air, some 150 feet above the street. That was too much for me, but I did climb the outside ladder up to the top of the cross where I could overlook the city. On several other occasions Paul and I crawled up underneath the Division Street Bridge that spans the Spokane River, to catch pigeons. In these latter cases mere bravado was diluted somewhat by the consideration that the country was sunk in the Great Depression, our fathers did not make much money, and pigeons were edible.

Football and boxing had also attracted me, and I did a fair amount of the latter both inside and outside the ring. That outside derived considerably from the pugnacity of another of my friends,

Joseph (Boo) Shields. Boo had a marked proclivity not only for getting into fights himself but for involving his companions. I still recall with chagrin allowing Boo to talk me into fighting Bob Jones, a mutual friend some forty pounds bigger than myself.

Another time, when I was twenty-one, I had ridden the rods with a couple of kindred spirits, Buck Baker and Bill Skeffington, more than 2000 miles from Spokane to Pontiac, Michigan, just to see what it was like. The experience was harsh and sobering, though it might have possessed marginal utility in that it conditioned me a bit for becoming a guest of the Japanese railways three years later.

Of course my present superiors knew nothing about these youthful escapades but they did learn almost at once of my ill-advised expedition with Killer Kirsch. Back at the base there was a message from General Wurtsmith asking me to report to him at once at Port Moresby. He was not pleased that I had flown into a combat zone without orders, and informed me that I should return to Brisbane. Authorities there were equally disenchanted. No doubt all of them were thinking of all the trouble they would be in and all the bad publicity that would follow if I managed to get myself killed while in their keeping. Apparently they decided that for my own good and their peace of mind they had better get me out of that part of the world. Next day I was on my way back to the United States.

The haste with which I was sent home reminded me of another lefthanded vote of confidence I had received some three years earlier, that time from my own mother. I had just gotten my private pilot's license. It had seemed like a great occasion to me so I asked my mother to accompany me on my first flight. She was extremely fearful but finally consented to go, explaining that if I was killed she would want to be along in any case. . .

Chapter Ten

The Last Half
Of The War

Whenn I left Australia I was on a thirty day leave. When it expired I was to return for assignment to the Intelligence branch of the 5th Air Force. Presumably, this was where I would spend the rest of the war, at a desk job in a rear area, for as I had just discovered, there were strict regulations that forbade one who had escaped from the Japanese or evaded them as a guerrilla from returning to combat zones in the Pacific.

No doubt most people would have been filled with joy to have been in my situation on the flight back to the United States: only a lunatic would have been sad. Even so, I was more thoughtful than jubilant. Every time we made one of several stops it reminded me anew how vast was the Pacific Ocean and how much of it American forces must control by now. Then I recalled the scores of new planes lined up on airfields near Brisbane. If only the nation had been properly prepared in the 1930s, if only a fraction of that might had existed in 1941-42, all those thousands of men who had perished wretchedly in Japanese prison camps would be alive, and the thousands still incarcerated might now be free and enjoying good health instead of hanging on in half-starved misery, wondering how many more such months, or years, lay before them. The thought oppressed me until the end of the war.

San Francisco was shrouded in one of its periodic fogs when we arrived so we landed at Travis Field in the Napa Valley. Later in the day I was taken to Hamilton Field and debriefed at 4th Air Force Headquarters. Here, as in Australia, I was reminded repeatedly that my past was a military secret, that I was not to discuss life in prison camps with anyone. At the moment I thought this merely silly. Within a few days the gag was to become exceedingly irksome.

When my debriefing was completed I called home. In the long months when no one knew what had happened to me my father had lost considerable weight from worry and had come close to a nervous breakdown. Now he was incoherent with excitement and elation. He was finally able to tell me that my wife was working as a draftsman at Boeing Aircraft in Seattle. I called her there, flew in the next day, and spent two days of joyful reunion. Neither Devonia nor my father, for all his worrying, had ever doubted that I would get back some day. Then I went on to Spokane for another tumultuous reunion with family, friends, neighbors, and not least, Judy, the little daughter I had never seen. At first she was wary of me but a few kisses and hugs dissolved the barriers.

Only a few days had passed when I received a message from Washington directing me to report to the Pentagon for further debriefing. This proved to be an unsettling experience. Right off I was told still another time that I must say absolutely nothing about anything that had happened to me. Everyone in Washington seemed frightened lest a public statement by an escapee jeopardize the chances of other prisoners to escape or bring Japanese reprisals down on them. The State Department debriefings were the worst. People there did not seem to think I had any problems worthy of their attention. When I told them that within a few days I had gotten scores of letters and phone calls from all over the United States beseeching me for information about husbands, sons, and brothers who had been missing for months, and that I had been besieged personally by many people in Spokane who knew that I must have *some* knowledge which I was refusing to divulge to them, State Department functionaries merely told me in a patronizing way what I was and was not allowed to do. To them, no doubt, it appeared that I had such a fixation about prisoners that I had lost sight of the war as a whole. To me, they seemed unreasonable, even inhuman; preoccupied with Europe when American soldiers were starving, rotting, and dying in squalid prison camps; far too concerned about the reactions of Japanese and too little about the fate of Americans abroad and the anxieties of their loved ones at home.

Though I never got any real satisfaction from anyone in Washington, the military people at least understood my plight and tried to help. General Miller White, the War Department Personnel Chief, listened to me sympathetically, then told me to go home and await instructions. I did, and soon got a letter authorizing me to reply to queries about prisoners and men missing in action. The letter also contained a number of stock replies to such requests, boiled down to single paragraphs. I was instructed to reply to each letter by citing one of these paragraphs verbatim. It was better than nothing, but not much.

After the shocks and disappointments of Washington I went to Chicago for quite a different reason: to buy an automobile. Cars were hard to secure during World War II: an ordinary person had to "know somebody" to get one. The man I knew in Chicago was Don Maxwell, Managing Editor of the *Chicago Tribune*, whose acquaintance I had made on my way to Washington, in circumstances that will be described in due course. With his aid, I secured a 1941 Buick and started off westward. Several flat tires later I made it back to Spokane, only to be sent immediately to Fort Wright Hospital. Here I stayed for six weeks of rest, recuperation, and repairs. The hospital commandant was Colonel Bill Kennard, who had been one of the Senior Flight Surgeons in the Philippines early in 1942, and who had barely managed to get out just before the surrender of Bataan. Perhaps for this reason he took a personal interest in me and treated me with great kindness. Looking back, it is apparent that I did not realize how many things wcre the matter with me nor how badly I needed a complete rest. My old nemesis, malaria, had come back. hospital dentists discovered that malnutrition and lack of care had turned my mouth into a disaster area. Several hours a day for many days Lieutenant Colonel Sud Rule worked on my teeth until he had pulled and replaced or filled, every single one.

Many years after the war was over I could reflect that my experiences in the Philippines had made me a stronger and better person. They certainly made me more appreciative of my own country, especially of American freedom. I also emerged with a vastly increased capacity to take in stride the hardships, vexations, and disappointments that are an inescapable part of life but which many people find extremely frustrating and burdensome. I have always savored the many friendships I made with my fellow prisoners. Shared dangers and sufferings draw people closer. Most of all, surviving the Death March and the camps increased my sheer determination to live, without which doctors tell me I would never have survived heart surgery in 1977-78.

But all this, as usual, constitutes realization after the event. In the last months of 1943 my state of mind was entirely different. At that time, merely being taken out of circulation for six weeks probably did me more good than either the dental care or the treatment for malaria. Almost from the first day I had gotten back to the U.S.A. I had been nervous and restless. After having lived so long packed in so closely with so many people what I craved above everything else was privacy, yet everywhere I was feted, lionized, and made the center of attention day and night. Of course, this was inevitable, and I would have been less than human had I not enjoyed it to some degree, but it soon palled. Worse was the avalanche of questions, calls, and letters from people who sought news of missing menfolk. I did not resent being deluged with such requests, indeed quite the reverse; but it was maddeningly frustrating to be unable to divulge what I knew, especially when some of the beseechers were aware that I was holding back on them and when I was convinced that no sufficient reason existed to hold back. Under this pressure I fell into fits of depression. Often I could not sleep. Other nights I had frightening dreams about the camps and the Japanese. It seemed that everyone around me was preoccupied with trivialities. I had no patience with anyone who complained about anything small, and said many sharp things to those close to me. Though I did not realize it at the time, my feelings were not unusual among returned war prisoners whose experiences were similar to mine. Three who endured the same difficulty in readjustment were Ernest Gordon; and in the Vietnamese War, Commanders Richard Stratton and Jeremiah Denton. For them the shock of return was even greater than for me since Gordon was a prisoner for three and a half years, Denton and Stratton for six. In the latter cases, six years came at the end of the 1960s and early 1970s, the years when pornography gained public acceptance, long hair for men became fashionable, and prominent people who gave aid and comfort to the enemy became celebrities, even in some quarters heroes, rather than traitors. Stratton said all of it together nearly made him vomit.

In my own case, it indicates the good sense of my wife, parents, and friends that they did not take my dark and petulant moods seriously. The worst of them did not last long, though I still suffered from occasional depressions until the end of the war.

Strangely, I had not been plagued by insomnia, chilling dreams, or depressions either with the guerrillas on Mindanao or in Australia. On Mindanao I was occupied most of the time and happy to be with all the Filipinos who were so friendly and grateful. In Australia the joy of flying regularly again seemed to blot out nearly everything else. Maybe I would have been plunged into gloom and sleeplessness there eventually; what befell me at home was only a delayed reaction to the shock of returning to the outside world, one that was bound to occur *sometime*.

The main reason for my irritability, I am sure now, was concern for the prisoners still in Japanese hands. I did not have a bad conscience exactly, for war prisoners are expected to seek opportunities to escape. It was rather that I never knew what happened to those left behind in Davao. I feared that the freedom of ten of us might have been purchased at the price of the lives of as many as a hundred of them, or that our flight had caused 2,000 of them to be treated in some more shameful and degrading way. Of course we had all thought of this before we had left Davao, and had talked about it many times. We had made the considered judgment that the opportunity to let the whole world know what went on in Japanese camps would create sufficient pressure that conditions in all such camps would be improved. This would justify whatever punishment might be inflicted on those left behind in Davao. I was not surprised to be forbidden to speak about the circumstances of our escape, but none of us had ever dreamed that our government would forbid the dissemination of news about enemy cruelties. Now I found myself muzzled, seemingly unable to do anything to help those left behind, and at the same time ignorant of what had happened to them. The whole purpose of our escape seemed thwarted, mocked every day. Thus the prisoners were always on my mind. I felt chronically uneasy about everything connected with them. It seemed to me that nobody inside or outside Washington save the next-of-kin attached sufficient importance to trying to help them in some way. Everybody seemed preoccupied with the European war. I never entirely shook this complex of disappointments and misgivings until V-J Day.

I was not the only one who was frustrated. Dyess, Mellnick, and McCoy had also been muzzled. Not long after we got back to the States word spread that some American prisoners had escaped from the Japanese. Yet official Washington was obsessed with the conviction that to publicize this would induce the Japanese to take reprisals against all those who were still in their camps. All of us considered this utterly wrong, a total misreading of Japanese psychology. We were convinced that publicity would cause the Japanese to improve treatment of prisoners to avoid losing face all over the world. Yet many weeks passed and Washington remained obdurate.

Just why, is still difficult to understand. The sensitivity of the Japanese to loss of national honor had been demonstrated in the past. When wholesale atrocities in Nanking in 1937 had been widely publicized in the United States, Tokyo had punished the officers responsible. When British Foreign Secretary Anthony Eden had spoken bitterly in the House of Commons in 1942 about Japanese administration in Hong Kong, conditions there improved noticeably and rapidly. One of MacArthur's biographers says the General asked permission from the War Department to publicize our stories but was turned down "Because of delicate negotiations then under way indirectly with Tokyo to get an internee exchange and Red Cross parcels to allied prisoners in Asia. . ." It is likely that this was a consideration of at least some importance since I had been told the same thing when I was first summoned to Washington. I do think, however, that our rulers were worried primarily about something else: that the revelation of wholesale Japanese atrocities might produce such a storm of public outrage that the whole Allied grand strategy of giving priority to the European war would be imperiled.

Whatever the case, Dyess came much closer than I to being destroyed by the consequent frustration. Instead of being welcomed back as a hero and allowed to tell the world about the valor of those who had fought and died on Bataan and the agony of those who had survived the Death March, Ed was informed by the Pentagon that he knew too much and must remain silent. For several weeks he was kept at a resort hotel in White Sulphor Springs, West Virginia to rest and "recover."

While there Ed began to negotiate with representatives of various newspapers and magazines to publish what he could tell them about the Death March, life in prison camps, and our escape. All of these people chattered incessantly about rights, slices, cut-ins, percentages, residual, and agents' fees at a time when he was interested only in getting our story the greatest possible publicity so it would have the maximum impact on the country. Eventually he made a deal with the *Chicago Tribune* which, with associated newspapers, could guarantee that a serial presentation of his experiences would reach twelve-to-fourteen million readers each day, if official clearance could ever be secured.

When I had been summoned to Washington for debriefing, Don Maxwell of the *Chicago Tribune* had asked me to stop in Chicago to see him en route. He was anxious to prevent me from telling the story to some other newspaper or magazine. He met Devonia and me and took us to his home for breakfast. There he told us the *Tribune* already had Dyess' story. They wanted to have a monopoly of it, he said, so it could be broken dramatically and thereby make the greatest possible impact on the country. He wanted me to sign a contract which amounted to a promise to honor the *Tribune's* monopoly. I did not know what to do. Maxwell suggested that we call Dyess. We did. Ed told me to do whatever I liked since it did not appear that the story would be cleared by the War Department in the near future anyway. So I agreed to cooperate, signed the contract, and was rewarded with the princely sum of $100. Our nation might be embroiled in the most momentous war in human history, but the newspaper business was still a business.

Throughout the last months of 1943 pressure mounted to force publication. Dyess' father remarked loudly and often that those who favored suppression did not understand Japanese psychology, and that Ed knew everyone in the prison camps would want the story told. He made scathing comments about "pencil pushing officers who would probably faint if they smelled gunpowder," by whom he meant those responsible for the suppression. Colonel Leroy Cowart, the father of my friend whose shoes had been taken by the Japanese on the Death March, denounced the policy of suppression on the ground that Americans needed to be awakened to the real nature of our brutal and ruthless enemy. Albert C. MacArthur, President of the American Bataan Club, declared that suppression of the story was a major mistake of the same sort that had made Bataan possible in the first place. Now, he charged, the same bankrupt politicians in Washington who had been responsible for America's unpreparedness were trying to persuade the people to forget their dereliction by suppressing what Dyess had to say.

Eventually high authorities either gave way before the mounting pressure, or simply changed their minds. In late January, 1944, the ban was lifted and the whole story began to appear in the *Chicago Tribune* and other newspapers. It was a nationwide sensation. Predictably, shoals of politicians and Administration officials turned 180 degrees within a day or two. Such figures as Secretary of State Cordell Hull, Alben Barkley, later to be Vice President, and Representative Andrew May demanded revenge on the Japanese at once. Presidential Secretary Stephen Early discovered that there was no longer a reason to keep information about Japanese atrocities secret. Elmer Davis, Director of the Office of War Information, said his office had been willing to release the story at any time: that they had been restrained by higher authority. A few months late *The Dyess Story*, edited by *Tribune* writer Charles Leavelle, was published in book form.

The financial side of the whole matter was nearly as dismaying to me as the political side. During our escape the ten of us talked a good deal about the possibility of making some money by recounting our experiences if we ever got home. We agreed that for five years we would share equally in whatever was reaped. When LIFE printed its account of our adventures on February 7, 1944, each of us received what was for that day a sizable sum of money. The legal officer at Fort Wright assure me that it was a gift and so not taxable. He even helped me fill out the pertinent tax form. Some years afterward the IRS decided that the payment had been taxable after all and so required me to pay a tax, with interest and penalty. I had learned another of life's hard lessons: fame is evanescent and gratitude is fleeting: the pursuit of money is serious and permanent.

My original orders to return to Australia in thirty days for reassignment had to be shelved while I lay for weeks in Fort Wright Hospital. During the same weeks Dyess got out of his hospital and began to implore General H H. Arnold to let him return to the Pacific to fight the Japanese. The General refused to bend the rule against this, but he did tell Ed he could form a new pursuit group that would be based in England. I had written to Ed as soon as I got home. Once he found out that he would be able to fly again, though in Europe, he asked me to join him as commander of one of his squadrons. I was jubilant and agreed at once. Ed soon got my orders changed to fit this new situation.

Then fate intervened. The last time I had actually seen Ed had been in the Philippines. Now he wrote to say that he was going to fly from California up to Spokane sometime around Christmas. Then a Christmas card come from him and his wife. It was postmarked December 21. On December 22, I got a long distance call from Don Maxwell. He told me he had just learned that Ed had been killed in a plane crash in Burbank, California. I was stunned. I called the Dyess home in Albany, Texas. Ed's father answered. I began by saying that I had heard that Ed had been in an accident. The elder Dyess could not say a single word. It was shattering. To me Ed Dyess had been not merely a superlative commanding officer but a friend and big brother as well. He and I had saved each other's lives. Together we had endured numberless dangers and hardships, followed by brief triumph. Now, after having survived starvation and brutality, disease and humiliation, swamps and jungles, Japanese bombs and bullets, this man of extraordinary character, talent, and promise had been killed merely because the engine of a P-38 had malfunctioned on an ordinary training flight. Every circumstance of his death seemed to mock reason and justice, even mere proportion. Ed was one of the outstanding individual heroes of the Second World War yet ever since his return to the United States all his deeds in the Orient had been shrouded in mystery. He had been silenced so thoroughly that only a few intimates even knew where he was stationed. Perhaps the final irony, according to witnesses, he need not have died at all: he could have landed his plane in a street and saved himself at the risk of demolishing some automobiles and their occupants. It was typical of Ed that he chose to risk his own life rather than hit the cars. He pulled up his crippled plane, struck a church steeple, and crashed. One man, who had been in an automobile below, sent a telegram to Ed's parents that read thus: "Please accept sympathy of a man spared from disaster by the final brave deed of your son. Sincerely, J.M. Fladwed."

Now Ed would never know if the story he wanted so badly to tell would ever be released. For me it was hard to understand and accept. The optimistic belief of Occidental peoples that history is the record of man's progress, is only about 250 years old. Ancient and Medieval men thought life, whether of individuals or whole societies, was cyclical and tragic. Perhaps they were wiser than we.

At the time of Ed's death I was recovering from one of my malarial attacks so I could not go to the funeral. About a month later I attended a memorial service for him in Hollywood. Edward Arnold was master of ceremonies. Several hundred airmen from March Field who were about to embark for the Pacific Theater were there. I was to be one of the speakers, but when my turn came I could get out only half a dozen words before I broke down. Soon after, I flew to Texas to visit Ed's parents. Here I had better control of myself and made a short speech. Ed's mother drove me to the cemetery the next day. I felt empty, utterly drained.

Some ten or twelve years after the war Dyess Air Force Base, one of the largest SAC bases in the country, was dedicated to Ed in Abilene, Texas. If Ed was watching in the Great Beyond he probably laughed, for it was a bomber base while he had been a fighter pilot.

With Dyess' death my orders had to be changed again. This time I was assigned to Geiger Field near Spokane. It was mostly a place to hang my hat since my main activities in the last year and a half of the war were traveling and making speeches. Invitations poured in from everywhere. I spoke to Rotary Clubs, Kiwanis Clubs, Chambers of Commerce, Elks Clubs, and Italian Clubs; to industrial groups, labor groups, and Veterans of Foreign Wars; to the YMCA, the Bataan Relief Organization, and the Red Cross; in theaters, churches, and schools; on Flag Day, Bataan Day, Armistice Day, and Corregidor Day; but most of all I spoke endlessly at rallies to sell war bonds. When I first came home Jimmy Keefe, then manager of the Orpheum Theater and later Senior Senator in the Washington State Senate, asked me to appear at a "Buy Bonds" show at the Orpheum. I spoke three times. The event was a great success from the standpoint of bond sales, and the Athletic Round Table in Spokane gave me a one thousand dollar bond in appreciation. Naturally, I was pleased to be so well received in my home town. A few weeks after *The Dyess Story* broke, the Treasury Department had me speaking at similar rallies all over the country. The usual format was to have three or four of us from different branches of the service describe some of our combat experiences and then urge the listeners to buy War Bonds.

Pappy Boyington did much public speaking after the war and said he did not like it. I found it wearing, but rewarding. I accepted all reasonable invitations. This meant that I traveled all over the country, sometimes on an organized circuit, much of the time merely in response to single invitations. I never tried to keep track, but I would guess I spoke in at least half of the states of the union plus Alaska. I held forth in public auditoriums mostly, but often in plants and factories. On one memorable (and exhausting) occasion I gave fifteen speeches in a single day in Jersey City.

At first I was strongly motivated. I was convinced that the best thing I could do to help all the prisoners still languishing under the yoke of Japan was to give vigorous, stirring orations about my bloodier experiences in combat, in the camps, and especially on the Death March. I hoped thereby to stimulate more vigorous prosecution of the war. This approach was quite successful. Large crowds attended the War Bond rallies everywhere, accounts of the Death March invariably left many listeners crying, and bond sales skyrocketed. In the 1940s the country was till susceptible to patriotic appeals, and I felt a real sense of accomplishment when great numbers of people from all economic and social levels bought bonds. Many factory workers supported the bond drives strongly, both by their purchases and by their efforts on the job. The Treasury Department was pleased too, as they indicated by giving me their Silver Award.

I never became disillusioned with selling war bonds but I did gradually tire of the grind. Also, the main focus of my interest began to change. After every speech wives and relatives of prisoners would flock around me to show me pictures and ask questions about their menfolk whom I might have known or seen. I grew anxious to spend more time with them and less making speeches, though military and Treasury authorities alike were understandably anxious to keep me on the War Bond circuit. Overall, I don't know whether all the speaking was beneficial to me personally or not. It got me out of the doldrums I had been in after returning to the States, it gave me something worthwhile to do, and I had the satisfaction of seeing tangible results flow from my efforts; but at the same time I could never forget my own prison camp experiences or get prisoners off my mind when I talked about the subject virtually every day.

One of the spinoffs from speaking at bond rallies was that I met many celebrities and gradually became something of a celebrity myself. The latter really began in Australia. From there till the end of the war everywhere I went I was treated as a hero, given awards, asked to speak, taken to expensive night clubs, fed steaks, plied with drinks, introduced to famous people, and photographed endlessly. I had my picture painted, sat for sculptors, even became the subject of a cartoon done in comic strip style but with a highly patriotic message. No publicity gimmick was left unused. Once I signed my name to a 400 pound bomb that was addressed to Tojo, "In appreciation of your hospitality." Another time I spoke to 50,000 people at Forest Lawn Memorial Park in Los Angeles at 6:30 A.M. to jointly commemorate Easter and Bataan Day. I felt like visiting royalty permanently on tour. I cannot say I hated all this adulation, for much of it was enjoyable and all of it was flattering, but it did wear me down. I longed to live normally again, and wondered how public figures could stand to spend their whole lives in such an atmosphere.

Some places where I spoke politicians and entertainers on the make would try to sit up on the stage with me, insinuate themselves into proceedings and, above all, have themselves photographed with me; but they were exceptional. Most of the sponsors and hosts treated me splendidly and most of the real celebrities I met were sensible, often impressive people. At one time or another I met Jane Powell, Edward Arnold, Brenda Marshall (whose parents were civilian internees in Santo Tomas), Bernard Baruch, Helena Rubinstein, Pat O'Brien, Frank Capra, Fiorella LaGuardia, Jack Dempsey, General H H. Arnold, Joseph Cotton, Joan Fontaine, Cedric Hardwicke, Ralph Bellamy, Bing Crosby, several presidents of corporations, and others I have since forgotten. All those I can recall by name were level-headed individuals who were never presumptuous or patronizing. I have pleasant memories of several of them. Pat O'Brien was an interesting and convivial man. As a kid I had gone to his movies. Now I spent two hours with him one day in the Masquer's Club in Hollywood drinking, trading questions, and discussing our varied experiences. (Someone whom I have since forgotten had secured me an honorary membership in that club, typical of the frenetic existence I led at that time.) I liked Frank Capra, a colonel in the Signal Corps, who had a flair for words. Near the end of the war he was composing speeches to be addressed to soldiers returning from Europe who needed to be motivated to continue the war in the Pacific against Japan. He wrote a speech for me which contained a much-quoted passage,"I can't tell you very much about the education or training of the Japs but I can tell you what the result is. The finished product is a lying, rotten, bullying son-of-a-bitch." At the time, I loved that line and delivered it with vehemence in many a speech. Crowds like it too, invariably reacting with cheers or murmurs. Once in Chicago I got an especially appreciative response to it from Marine General Alexander Vandegrift who had won the Congressional Medal of Honor on Guadalcanal.

In New York I had an interesting visit with Mayor LaGuardia when both of us spoke on the same occasion for Russian War Relief. In the same city I had my picture taken with William Green, then President of the American Federation of Labor; and was promised some cosmetics by Helena Rubinstein, which I negligently forgot to pick up. In Philadelphia Jack Dempsey and I were to appear on the same program. There was a delay, during which Dempsey and his old manager Jack Kearns reminisced about various of Dempsey's fights, particularly the one against Tommy Gibbons in 1923 which nearly bankrupted the town of Shelby, Montana. The appearance in Philadelphia was memorable for another reason too. One of those who came to hear me was Bartholomew Passinante, a pilot who had lost a leg when the Japanese bombed and strafed Iba Field on the first day of the war. After the speech he took me to his father's restaurant where we had some delicious mostaccioli and reminisced for hours. In Hollywood, Bing Crosby brought me to a rehearsal for the Kraft Hour and called me up on the stage during proceedings. Though he did not remember it, I had met him once some years before when I had driven the Gonzaga University Quartet to Hollywood to appear with him on that same program.

Despite it all, the sense of frustration never left me. Every time I ate another steak in another plush night club with another Big Name I thought of the starving prisoners left behind to a fate still unknown to me.

The most permanently satisfying thing I did during the remainder of the war was to try to answer the innumerable requests for information about servicemen know to be prisoners or who were missing in action somewhere in the Far East. Once the ban was lifted on news about Japanese atrocities and our escape military authorities close to me were extremely cooperative. One such was General William Lynn, Commander of the 4th Air Force. Soon after my return to the States General Lynn had presented me with the Distinguished Service Cross, which had been awarded to me in Australia by General MacArthur. Now he not only authorized me to address prisoner-of-war organizations and visit next-of-kin at my discretion, but assigned a plane to me. Colonel Bill Kennard, who had taken such good care of me at Fort Wright Hospital, loaned me his personal secretary to handle the voluminous correspondence that had accumulated. She was an efficient and understanding lady who took my dictation and eventually typed 2,100 letters for me. Phone calls also came by the hundreds, and in Spokane itself many people came in person to inquire about missing menfolk. None of them had heard anything beyond what was on "form" postcards the Japanese occasionally allowed prisoners to mail. On these cards the writer merely checked "good," "average," or "poor" after a few stock questions about his health and disposition.

One letter has stuck in my memory to this day because it called back to my consciousness a particularly embarrassing experience when I had been in flight training at Kelly Field. One day several of us cadets had been sent on a crosscountry training flight to Austin, Texas. On our return I saw some of the other planes, which were far behind me, veer off to the south. I wondered why they were all going the wrong way, and proceeded westward. Eventually it dawned on me that it was not *they* who were off course! By then I was short of fuel. Near Uvalde I had to make a forced landing in an oat field with a fence in the middle. Luck was with me. The ground was muddy and the plane stopped quickly. Filled with some trepidation and more chagrin, I had to phone my section commander, Major Dike Meyer, back at Kelly. He flew out promptly and landed. He siphoned gasoline from his own plane into mine, prepared to take off, and told me to follow him. Unfortunately the mud was too sticky for him to get his own plane off the ground. Darkness fell. Eventually, the man in whose field we had landed put us up for the night, bunking the Major and me in the same bed. Needless to say, I gave him plenty of room.

The usual punishment for a foulup of this sort was to wear a "dumb bell" around one's neck for a week. I fully expected to be awarded one once we got back to the base but nothing happened until graduation. On that occasion, April 25, 1941, when the Commandant, Colonel Davies, presented me with my commission he added the wry observation that everyone knew I was one of the best navigators in the outfit. I did not miss the point. Afterward I was always careful when computing my course before taking to the air. I also learned another lesson: that sometimes it is best not to punish or humiliate a subordinate who has made a mistake.

Now three years later, a letter arrived one day from a man in

Uvalde, Texas inquiring if the Sam Grashio about whom he was reading in the newspapers, was the same person who had once landed in his oat field!

I received permission to work with next-of-kin at just about the time I began the War Bond tour. Between the two, they kept me busy until the war was over. As with war bonds, I accepted almost all invitations to speak to organizations concerned about prisoners. Most individual contacts were made after these speeches. It was extremely gratifying when I was able to identify a picture, or provide some information to an anxious wife or mother. Of course it was disappointing to have to say, as I did innumerable times, that I did not know the person in question or had never heard anything about him. Even in such cases though, it was possible to offer a little comfort if a Japanese "form" card had been received for that indicated that the writer had already survived for some time in camp. Since conditions in camps improved somewhat as time passed anyone who had suffered a few months had a fair chance to live considerably longer.

My own spirits were buoyed by regular contacts with these people. Invariably, they were highly appreciative of any information I could give them. Though knowledge of atrocities was widespread by the early months of 1944 they did not blame their own government for this. Some would complain that more attention should be paid to the Pacific than to the European Theater of war but I never heard one charge that the country had let down a husband or son. They were patriotic, they had a sense of duty, and they demonstrated both by their generous purchases of bonds. Most of them were warm and hospitable as well. Many times I was invited to their homes to share meals. Usually I would be treated like the missing brother or son. Many wrote me letters and cards of appreciation. Some continued to write for years afterward. They represented the best side of America then. They still do.

I seldom flew to see individuals, but I did make an exception for the parents of my old Alabama buddy, Bert Bank, later to be an Alabama state representative and senator. In the spring of 1944 I flew to Tuscaloosa. Bert's parents were overjoyed to see anyone who had seen their son, and overwhelmed to think that anyone would come to see them personally to tell them about him. Bert's father gave me a roll of silver dollars to give to my own children. Happily for his parents, and for Bert, he was eventually rescued by the Rangers from Cabanatuan where the Japanese had returned him after moving all the prisoners out of Davao.

Once, too, shortly after the end of the war I had a chance, along with three or four other ex-prisoners, to talk privately with General Wainwright who had just been feted at the Davenport Hotel in Spokane. Wainwright had had to endure the humiliation of surrendering Corregidor and spending years as a prisoner of the enemy. Though he had subsequently received the Congressional Medal of Honor he was a humble man and assured us that the Medal belonged to all of us who had shared a similar fate. I was touched profoundly.

By now the reader is probably convinced that I had become obsessed with prisoners and their plight. I suppose I had. To this day prisoners from all our twentieth century wars are a remarkably close knit group. When the fighting ended in Europe my principal feeling was, "Now we can concentrate on the war in the Pacific. We should be able to get the prisoners home sooner." When the Atomic Bombs were dropped I gave no thought (at that time) to their ethical or geopolitical implications. My first reaction was, "Ah! Now the prisoners will be home soon." When Japan surrendered at last, my spirits soared. Now the prisoners would be coming home for sure! My only remaining anxiety was about how many of them would be left.

On V-J Day I was assigned to Hamilton Field to greet the returning prisoners and help them in any way I could. I met them when they arrived, got hotel reservations for their next-of-kin, coordinated transportation for all concerned, and tried to smooth out any problems that developed. It was a great thrill to see several men I had known well in the camps, particularly those of the 21st Pursuit Squadron. Best of all was meeting Bert Bank. We spent several days telling each other all that had happened since I had disappeared into the jungle outside Davao more than two years before. It was from Bert that I learned at last that Major Maeda had not slaughtered the helpless prisoners still in camp when we escaped. That news lifted a cloud that had hung over me for twenty-eight months.

———————————

NOTE: Among many who have recorded a sense of letdown and depression after release from prison camps were Ernest Gordon, *The Valley of the Kwai*, pp. 244-251; Jeremiah Denton, subsequently a U.S. Senator from Alabama, in *When Hell Was In Session*, pp. 238-240; and Richard Stratton in Scott Blakey's, *Prisoner At War*, pp. 311-370. Stratton's feelings appear to have been closest to my own, though his anger and disgust at what had happened to the U.S.A. while he was in captivity much exceeded my own. Gordon and Denton were disappointed and dispirited but took it more philosophically.

The American government appeared to have learned nothing from its efforts to prevent escapees from Japanese prison camps talking about their experiences. Twenty-five years later, in the Vietnam War, political and military authorities once more wanted to suppress any mention of the ill-treatment of prisoners by the enemy, apparently from fear that public clamor about it would raise the price for their release. Once more, they were dead wrong in their reading of enemy psychology; and once more they changed their approach only under public pressure. Commander Jeremiah Denton, who was imprisoned by the North Vietnamese for more than six years and tortured atrociously on many occasions, notes that when the brutality of the North Vietnamese began to receive some international attention in the late 1960s the torturers relented somewhat. In 1969 the National League of Families of American Prisoners and Missing in South East Asia was organized and began to exert pressure on politicians and newspapers. Before long Washington politicians began to give way, much publicity was directed towards the inhumanity of the North Vietnamese, and the latter largely abandoned the torture of prisoners. Cf. Denton, *When Hell Was In Session*, pp.98, 125-126, 210-214.

History may not repeat itself but it contains a great many close parallels.

Chapter Eleven
Epilogue

IT WAS NEAR THE END OF THE WAR that I made a fateful decision, to make my career in the Air Force. I did so with mixed feelings. Several people I had met, in Spokane and elsewhere, had offered to back me in businesses of different sorts. On more than one occasion I had been sorely tempted to accept, but love of flying was still in my blood. When I was able to pass a series of mental and physical examinations that were prerequisites for a regular commission I decided to stay. I have never regretted it. Life in the Air Force has been good to me and for me, and has afforded me an opportunity to serve our country. It is hard to ask for more.

Some might conclude that the real reason I could not leave the Air Corps was that I had a lifelong compulsion to risk my neck. That is not so, at least on the conscious level, though I can understand how a reader of this book might reach that conclusion. The numerous adventures of my youth, combined with my ambition to become a fighter pilot, my many close escapes from death, the alacrity with which I went off on a regular mission against the Japanese in New Guinea when I was rusty as a pilot and only half-recovered from life in prison camp, my decision to make the Air Force my career, and some dangerous missions for which I volunteered later in life, could easily lead one to conclude that I was one of those rare, psychologically abnormal people who genuinely like war, to whom the danger and excitement of violence and combat are the very cream of existence, a reckless glory hound constantly in search of more medals. I can only say that it is not so. I had a reckless streak in my makeup, to be sure, and excitement had always attracted me, but I never consciously pursued fame and glory as some adventurers do. I never sought death at any time. Quite the contrary: without a grim, dogged determination to live, bolstered by religious faith that I *would* live, I would never have survived prison camp. I never went on a combat mission without being nervous and apprehensive at the outset, though like a boxer who hears the bell, this feeling usually left me once I was in the air. The night before our escape from Davao anticipation and impatience gripped me strongly but they were mingled with uneasiness and inability to sleep. Many time in combat, in the camps, on our escape, and with the guerrillas I was badly frightened. Of my many narrow escapes from death, in a few cases I knowingly accepted danger in the line of duty, but many times it was otherwise. Some risks, such as those involved in the escape from Davao, simply could not be avoided. Sometimes I undertook risky ventures without fully realizing the dangers inherent in them. Often I barely got away alive due merely to accidents. Most of my close scrapes with death when flying were caused by nothing more romantic than malfunctioning equipment. The only time in my life when I have felt completely at peace and indifferent to death has been since December, 1977, when I survived open heart surgery and many weeks in the hospital.

Having said all this, there is no denying that I have had an extraordinary number of close calls. For instance, in Detroit in 1944 I was to appear in an air show. Because I had been so busy I had not flown four hours in the preceding month, a prerequisite for flight pay. Consequently, I asked the colonel in charge of the air show if I might go out one afternoon and fly my time. He gave me permission and a new P-39. I taxied to the main runway of the Detroit Municipal Airport. Halfway down, at takeoff speed, the engine sputtered. A tall iron fence and, with macabre appropriateness, a cemetery, lay directly ahead. I did the best I could: I pulled back the throttle and hit the left brake and left rudder as hard as possible: the left tire overheated and blew, a providential development which enabled me to turn sharply to the left. The plane would have stopped soon, undamaged, if only someone had not parked a flatbed trailer with a bulldozer on top right in that part of the airport. I slammed into it and damaged the plane extensively, but walked away unscratched.

At home after the war I once took off from Walla Walla for Spokane in a Beechcraft, only to have the left engine catch fire and force me to make an emergency landing at the village of Othello.

Not long after that I had another close call in an A-24 when I was merely getting in flight time, as in Detroit. This time, just for company, I took along Colonel Sud Rule, the dental surgeon who had spent so much time fixing my teeth at Fort Wright Hospital. We cruised around until the fuel began to run low, only to discover that the landing gear would not extend. I tried everything I could think of to jar it loose. Nothing availed. Soon the choice was to take to our parachutes at once and let the plane crash, or try to slide in on the plane's belly. I asked Doctor Rule which he preferred. He wanted to try to land. On the field the Crash and Fire crew had emergency gear and foam all ready to attempt to rescue us when we came in. Then at the last possible moment the landing gear inexplicably came down and we made a normal landing

In 1958 I had a similar experience at Paine Field in Everett, Washington. Captain Ed Cleary wanted me to fly a T-34, a new plane recently purchased for the local aero club. We took off in the T-34 to pick up another plane not far away. The plan was for Captain Cleary to check me out in the T-34 on the way. Then I would fly the T-34 back alone and he would fly the plane we were going to get. Once more, the landing gear would not come down. We tried everything, including diving and then pulling out sharply, in an effort to shake the gear loose. Nothing worked. We flew until we were nearly out of gas so as to minimize the risk from fire if we had to make a belly landing. The ground crew then put foam on the runway, fire trucks and ambulances assembled, and a crowd lined up to watch us try to come in. Because I had never flown a T-34 before I asked Ed to land it. He did a beautiful job, cutting off the engine and setting the propeller at horizontal just before we slid in on our belly. The plane wasn't even damaged much.

In the same year I had still another close call at Paine Field. This time Lieutenant Bob Huntley, a young fighter pilot who was also an excellent Instrument Flight Examiner, went up with me one day to give me my annual instrument check. The weather was awful but we climbed above it into the sunshine at 32,000 feet. Abruptly, we had a flameout which cut out all our navigational aids and silenced our radio. There we were, somewhere over the Cascade Range whose highest peak, Mt. Ranier, towers over 14,000 feet, above a solid overcast and out of contact with the ground.

What to do? Bob and I talked it over on the intercom. We decided to descend to 25,000 feet and attempt an air start. No luck. We decided to try several more times until we were down to 16,500 feet. This was as low as we dared to descend anywhere near Mt. Ranier since we needed a couple of thousand feet to fall safely if we had to take to our parachutes over some of the most forbidding terrain in North America. Two more attempted air starts failed. Then at 17,000 feet, on the last try we would have room for, my prayers were answered. We got flame, regained our radio communications, and with the most exquisite care worked our way back down to Paine and safety.

My narrowest escape came in 1964. I have never understood how I survived that time. I was at Tyndall Field in Panama City, Florida to check an F-106, a supersonic jet two-seater. I was in the back seat, with Captain Sam Rudasill in the front. Our plan was to build up to Mach-2 speed, and then with reduced power climb to 60,000 feet, drain off our Mach-2 air speed and descend. I accelerated to Mach-2 and initiated the climb but something went wrong. Instead of "coasting" we shot right through 60,000 feet and suddenly lost our pressurization system. This was a desperate emergency for at 62,000 feet nitrogen bubbles form in the blood, much as when a diver has the bends, and cause death almost at once. We must have reached nearly 63,000 feet before we started our descent. My throat at once felt warm and dry. I shouted at Sam to descend immediately and then advised Jacksonville Center of our emergency. Though Sam was woozy neither of us lost consciousness and we came down safely. Once more all the emergency gear was waiting. We were taken by ambulance to the base hospital and run through a battery of test to see if we had suffered any irreparable damage. We had not, though according to all flying and medical lore both of us should have been dead.

If Ed Dyess had been alive he probably would have said that anybody who could survive fire from his own antiaircraft batteries, and land a plane safely in a strong wind with his bombs hanging, had not been predestined to perish in some mere peacetime mishap.

There is an old saying in the military services, "Never volunteer for anything." I don't think this is good advice for anyone with ambition but it does enable people who are content merely to drift through life to avoid a fair amount of trouble. The most unrewarding experience I ever had in twenty-five years of military service resulted from volunteering for a mission in the Near East. Early in 1948 hostility between Jews and Arabs in Palestine had escalated to continuous terrorist activity just below the level of open warfare. Later in the same year a brief war did break out, which ended with the establishment of the state of Israel.

Several months earlier, though, it was not certain that matters would turn out thus. At the time the United Nations decided to send an international peacekeeping mission to Palestine. The United States was to contribute some of the troops so quotas were established for various American military installations. When I saw the quotas for March Field, near Riverside, California, where I was currently stationed, I asked to have my name put on the list. By now I had fully recovered from all that had happened in World War II. After the war I had returned to college to finish my education, graduating from the University of Washington in 1947 with a B.S. in Psychology. Now I was restless for action again, anxious to see a different part of the world, and curious to see if some of the psychology I had studied so recently might be applicable to the troubled Near East. My commanding officer, Colonel Clifford Reese, tried to talk me out of volunteering, saying there was no role for a fighter pilot in such a mission. He predicted that I would be assigned to some dull desk job. When I remained insistent Colonel Reese eventually authorized me to go. I went to the Pentagon for briefing by the Intelligence Section. there I ran into Steve Mellnick for the first time since our escape from Davao. Steve agreed with Colonel Reese that my proposed new adventure was likely to prove a bummer. Undaunted, I pressed on. Soon I met some of my fellow UN observers. One was Captain John D'Angelis of Nesquehoning, Pennsylvania. John had been one of those adrift for many days in the south Pacific with Captain Eddie Rickenbacker. He and I soon became friends. We even lived together for a time with a Czech Jewish

Family in Tel Aviv when it proved impossible to find hotel accommodations in Palestine.

My initial assignment in the Near East was to lead a convoy that carried food daily from Tel Aviv to the Jews in Jerusalem. The supplies were hauled by trucks driven by Jews. I went ahead in a jeep and secured a safe conduct from a British major before leading the trucks into a No Man's Land along the route. The major was the recipient of the Victoria Cross, but by 1948 he was an alcoholic who had to be contacted before 10:00 A.M. if any meaningful business was to be transacted. On August 18 he was already drunk even at that early hour and said my convoy could not go through because we had been using the UN Flag to smuggle contraband to the Jews. I assured him that I had inspected all our trucks and that they held nothing but food. He replied that the Arabs were angry and suspicious, and that he could not allow me to proceed. I consulted the other members of the Truce Commission. We decided that we could not give way, lest we provide the Arabs an excuse to stop us any time they chose. So we put UN observers on the running boards of the trucks and set out.

It was an important decision. Right in the middle of No Man's Land an old British fortress stood on a hill, commanding the road below. It was occupied by Jordanian troops. Just as we came abreast of it a burst of .50 calibre machinegun fire kicked up the dust immediately ahead of the jeep in which I was riding. I ordered the driver to slow down. The firing stopped. The driver then resumed his normal 25 m.p.h. There was another burst of machinegun fire. This time I was convinced that the jeep was no place for me. I jumped out of it, rolled over a bank, and landed in a patch of thistles. Blood ran down my face from a cut on my head and I injured a shoulder badly enough that I was unable to raise one arm. As soon as I collected my scattered wits I took out a white handkerchief and waved it with my good arm. The Jordanians ignored the sign, if they saw it at all, and shot up the whole convoy. Meantime, D'Angelis had also bailed out of the jeep, though he had waited for it to stop first. He had also taken to the ditch below the road embankment. Now he dashed over to me and asked why I had jumped while the jeep was still moving. I replied that I thought the bottom of the ditch was safer. John was silent for a few seconds. Then he replied gravely somewhat as follows: "Sam, the greatest man who ever walked this part of the world was Jesus Christ. He spent his whole life trying to pacify these people and persuade them to do what was right. They nailed Him to a cross for it. What in hell are two dagoes like us doing here?"

John was right. Jews and Arabs were implacable in their mutual hatred. Neither cared a nickel for the UN mission nor the principles it represented. I once saw a heavily decorated French colonel, and a French captain who was flying his plane, with UN markings, secure a flight clearance from the Egyptian Air Ministry in Cairo only to be fired on by Egyptian troops as they came in to land, and finished off by those same troops when the plane was on the ground. Another time a planeload of Jewish refugees from behind the Iron Curtain landed near Tel Aviv. It was the responsibility of the UN Truce Commission to check the passengers in such cases since Jewish men of military age were to be taken off the plane and interned to prevent them from joining Jewish armed forces. In this case ground authorities flatly refused to allow those on the plane to debark despite all my orders and entreaties. I called our mission headquarters in desperation. Finally they told me to leave. The passengers, meanwhile, had stayed on the plane. I never learned how many there were or where they went. Soon after, September 17, 1948, Jewish terrorists murdered Count Folke Bernadotte, the Swedish head of the Truce Commission. Protests were ignored in all these cases, and many more.

Three months of this was enough for me. I had met some Arabs whom I liked and respected, and I must admit to a certain admiration for the fixed and fierce determination of the Jews to defend what they plainly intended to make their national homeland. But to try to persuade either side to compromise their dispute, or to accept third party arbitration in good faith, was hopeless. Neither side wanted anything save to route the other. It was impossible to predict what any of the factions, official or unofficial, would do in any given circumstance. Everyday my own life was in danger. I was never so happy to leave an assignment as that one. Back home when I composed a critique of my mission I wrote that no settlement would ever be reached in Palestine until the refugee problem was settled. Headlines relating to that part of the world in 1948 could still be used in 1994.

A postwar sojourn that proved more pleasant came in 1952. Its roots lay back in the Philippines. One of the pilots I got to know fairly well there was Hank Thorne, Commander of the 3rd Pursuit Squadron. Hank was a cool man, respected by all who knew him. Virtually all his planes and many of his men had been wiped out at Iba Field on the first day of the war. Hank himself was evacuated before Bataan fell. After the war he was a colonel in the Pentagon when I went there to seek an assignment in Italy. Hank put in some good words for me, and I was eventually picked to head an American Military Assistance Advisory Team there. The overall objective was to promote standardization of equipment, training, and procedures among the members of NATO. Specifically, we were to help the Italians transform their military aviation program, which had been built around the conventional P-47s, to new F-84E jets. Italian pilots had to be trained to fly the F-84, their maintenance men to service it, and their administrative people to properly translate technical orders and learn American requirements.

This was an agreeable assignment both professionally and personally. The Italian Commander to whom I was attached as tactical air adviser was Colonel Gino Callieri. He was an able pilot himself, and a friendly, intelligent man. He understood the necessity of learning to use the latest equipment and the advantages of standardized procedures. He cooperated with me fully and cordially. When my tour was over I considered that I had accomplished a good deal and had made many friends among Italian Air Force people as well.

Personally, the interlude was enjoyable. Italy is a varied and delightful country from a tourist's standpoint. Italians customs were familiar to me. I knew the Calabrese dialect well enough to talk to the natives readily, and I was there long enough to improve my command of formal Italian appreciably.

As usual with my assignments, though, trouble developed. This time it was of different sort than in the past. One day I stopped in the town of Udine in northeastern Italy, some sixty miles from Treviso where I was stationed. There was a restaurant in Udine that I fancied. By the merest chance I ran into a man whom I shall call Charlie and struck up a conversation with him. He spoke English. He said he was an American citizen who had been born in Italy but had lived most of his life in the United States. He had gone back to Italy just before the war, and then was not allowed to leave when the war began. We had a long and pleasant conversation in the restaurant. At the end of it Charlie asked me what I thought of Lucky Luciano, the gangster who had been deported from America to Italy. I replied that I knew nothing about him other than what had appeared in the newspapers. Charlie said one could not believe what was in the papers and asked me if I would like to meet Luciano. Without thinking seriously, I said offhandly that it would be all right. He said he would introduce me someday if the opportunity arose. That was all, and I promptly forgot about Charlie.

About a month later my godparents, Mr. and Mrs. Pete Mele, were visiting Italy with their daughter Eleanor. They came to see me. I took them to Trieste where there was an American community. On the way back to Treviso we stopped for dinner at my favorite restaurant in Udine. In the middle of dinner in came Charlie. Everyone was introduced, we all drank some wine together, Charlie chatted amiably with the Meles, and we returned to Treviso.

Perhaps a month after that I was transferred to the American Embassy in Rome. One day a colonel there asked me to come to his office to discuss some work I had done in the north. When I kept the appointment the colonel was not there. Instead there were two men I had never seen. They told me they were waiting for Charles Siracusa, an important figure in the U.S. Treasury Department with a special interest in drug smuggling. Soon Mr. Siracusa came in. He was a small, dynamic man who immediately asked me if I had ever known any criminals. I replied truthfully that I knew a couple of people who had had legal troubles but that I did not regard them as criminals. He continued to ask me oblique questions until I grew irritated. I said I had never been in any trouble, and asked him to come to the point. He told me brusquely to cool off, that he would ask the questions. Then I recalled Charlie in Udine and his talk about Luciano. I asked Siracusa if this was whom he had in mind? He said it was indeed; that one of his agents had noticed that my car bore diplomatic license plates, and had also observed me talking to Charlie. Charlie, it developed, had an extensive criminal record in the United States and had been deported. Siracusa was concerned that he might be trying to use me in some way. Thus did I learn what most parents tell their small children: don't talk to strangers.

Save for occasional close calls flying, the rest of my career in the Air Force was uneventful. In 1962 when I was at the Canadian National Defense College in Kingston, Ontario the opportunity arose to take an official trip to the Middle East and southern Asia. In the course of this trip I had a chance to stop off in Rome and renew acquaintances with the Italian Air Force people with whom I had worked a decade before. They had a delightful party for me, and we reminisced till 3:00 A.M.

My last assignment was Deputy for Operations for the 25th Air Defense Division at McCord Air Force Base in Tacoma. In 1965 the Division had considerable responsibility. All the American air defense weapons, and some Canadian as well, were under its operational control at McCord. We were charged with the air defense of the Northwest from British Columbia to San Francisco. The commanding officer was Major General William Elder, who had been Ed Dyess' roommate at flying school in 1937. The two were similar in important ways: patriots, first rate pilots, utterly honest, and possessed of a realistic concept of loyalty to subordinates. I could not have asked for a finer superior officer than General Elder.

By now I had spent twenty-five years in the Air Force and was well past forty. I had learned a lot, particularly about principles of management, which was to prove valuable to me when I eventually undertook a new career in the field of education at Gonzaga University. Still, I was getting restless again: the desire for action had not left me. Moreover, the Vietnam War was heating up and our nation seemed as unready as in 1941, though this time the unpreparedness lay more in the realms of psychology and morale than in material shortages. I asked for an assignment in Vietnam. The request was rejected. The reason was not illogical: what was needed in Vietnam was personnel trained in fighter ground support while my current background was in air defense operations; but it was keenly disappointing nevertheless. Consequently, I decided to retire.

When I was commissioned in 1941 my first commanding officer had been William E. Dyess. When I retired in 1965 my last commanding officer was William E. Elder, Ed's friend, classmate, and roommate. One gave me a good start, the other a good ending.

My employment at Gonzaga University started October 1, 1965, the same day I retired from the Air Force. The new job brought with it a very special blessing in the person of Father John Francis Gubbins, known by his friends, and he had many, as Father Frank. This saintly Jesuit Priest became my boss and before too long, he was my role model and mentor. He possessed excellent judgment which I am sure proved to be invaluable to the many individuals who sought his prudent advice.

My first endeavor under his competent supervision, was student recruitment and subsequently in the fund raising function where I remained until November 1977; at that time I terminated my employment at Gonzaga due to ill health.

Father Gubbins died on November 9, 1979. The example set by this virtuous man continues to be a dynamic inspiration in my life; a day does not pass without fond memories of a true friend, a good boss, and an excellent teacher. Having been closely associated with Father Frank for twelve years is one of the best things that could have happened to me; I am deeply grateful for that privilege.

When I left the Island of Mindanao, 29 September 1943, aboard the USS BOWFIN 287, I did so with a desire to someday return to the Islands. I was leaving a place I had learned to hate but still loved. The beautiful Filipino people and the pristine beauty of the Philippine Islands had touched me very deeply, notwithstanding the Infamous Bataan Death March, the horrors of the prison camps, and the cruelties of our Japanese guards.

I have often questioned why our principle adversaries in World War II, Japan and Germany, became economic giants in the world, due in part to the help received from the United States, but the loyal Filipinos who fought alongside us, did not receive similar assistance. This they desperately needed and in my judgment richly deserved.

Over the years, I wanted to learn first hand what impact this apparent neglect had on the grass roots level of Philippine society. Were the Filipinos the same warm, lovable and kind people I left in 1943? Did they still love America and Americans? An opportunity to get answers to my curiosity and concern was given to me in Albuquerque at a national reunion of the American Defenders of Bataan and Corregidor in the spring of 1985. There Dave Oestreich, a former member of the

34th Pursuit Squadron and a survivor of the Bataan Death March, asked if I would be interested in being a tour leader on a trip back to Manila and other places on the island of Luzon to revive memories of World War II. My immediate reply was an enthusiastic yes.

Dave was with the General Travel Service in Bellevue, Washington and in recent years had planned and led several tours to the Philippines. He was exceptionally knowledgeable in the political affairs of that area and had many friends there, in prominent positions in and out of government. He knew where to go and had the influence to get Tour Groups to those places where they wanted to go and to do what they wanted to do. I was confident that if Dave obtained a sufficient number of Bataan and Corregidor Veterans, and others of similar interests to make the trip, he would organize an itinerary and agenda second to none. This he did.

Saturday evening, January 18, 1986, twenty-three people, veterans and some of their spouses, gathered at the San Francisco International Airport. Following a Happy Hour hosted by the Philippine Airlines, a very happy and excited Tour Group boarded a PAL 747, destination Manila. Most of us who had served on Bataan had not been back. We were uncertain what our reactions would be.

High over the Pacific, I was reminded that on November 1, 1941, with other members of the 21st and 34th Pursuit Squadrons and other military units, including the 27th Bomb Group, I had sailed from San Francisco to Manila on the President Coolidge. Twenty days later, we had arrived at Pier Seven. What a difference in the time enroute to Manila since 1941! The next morning, close to fourteen hours flying time, we would be there. I had flown jet fighters at Mach 2 speeds; still I was highly impressed with the remarkable progress made in commercial aviation in the past 45 years.

On arrival in Manila we were met by a group of Filipino Scouts who had served on Bataan. They saluted smartly and their greetings were warm and emotional. Eight of our veterans were survivors of Bataan and fought alongside the Scouts at Aglaloma, the Battle of the Points and elsewhere on Bataan. Our respect for these exceptionally brave men has remained high over the years.

Following a quick processing through customs, we departed for the luxurious Manila Hotel where we received a cordial reception from another group of Scouts. Here we observed welcome banners prominently draped on the balcony rails above the Hotel's main lobby.

After an orientation and greetings session with the Hotel management, Dee and I went to our room. There, attractively arranged on the table, were mangoes, bananas, and other goodies. Shortly, the call I was anxiously awaiting came from a desk clerk. He advised that Magdaleno Duenas was waiting for Dee and me in the lobby. (Duenas is discussed in a prior chapter covering our escape. I had written to let him know of our forthcoming trip to Manila.) Forty-three years had gone by since I had last seen this old friend. Seeing him, again brought to mind, how important he was to the success of our escape and the great respect our group had for him. My reunion with Magdaleno remains one of the highlights of my journey back to the Philippines.

Following a fast change of clothing, we went to City Hall. Upon arrival, we were met by a band playing stirring marching music. After an excellent musical reception, we were escorted to Mayor Bagatsing's office by one of his aides. We completed our courtesy call then joined the Mayor and members of his staff in a delightful luncheon ceremony. Speeches were made, each praising our noble efforts in the defense of their homeland during WWII. We then departed to start our tour of Metro Manila.

Santo Tomas, the oldest University in Asia and Malacanang, the Presidential Palace, were canceled from our itinerary. Political unrest arising from the election, just a few weeks away, made visits to those places inadvisable. Teedie Woodcock and Jane Fredrickson were particularly disappointed in that decision; they had been incarcerated at Santo Tomas as Civilian Internees for forty-two months by the Japanese. Understandably, they were quite anxious to see Santo Tomas. The rest of our planned itinerary remained as scheduled.

On this first day of our arrival in Manila, with a police escort, and the competent performance of Bobby Fulcher, our tour guide, an air conditioned motor coach transported us to Intramuros or the "walled city" also known as "Spanish Manila," with its narrow streets and stone walls. It was behind these stone walls that the Spanish Governing Body ruled the Philippines from the 16th to the 19th centuries. Here, also was Bilibid, used by the Japanese as a POW Camp. Many Americans were incarcerated here in a transient status enroute to other POW Camps on Luzon and Mindanao and also Japan. Some were held in Bilibid during the entire duration of the War. Corporal Maurice Freeland, a member of the 21st Pursuit Squadron was one of those. Freeland, who was Dyess' driver lost both legs at Aglaloma and survived forty-two months as a POW. When he was returned to the United States he was hospitalized in the General Walter Reed Hospital in Washington, D.C. . I visited him there in 1945. During our ensuing conversation, in addition to a great deal of reminiscing, we discussed Aglaloma Bay on the west coast of Bataan and the part he played on board the off-shore boats commanded by Ed Dyess (covered in an earlier chapter). I commented that I had the highest respect and admiration for the courage and perseverance he demonstrated fighting at Aglaloma and also as a Japanese Prisoner of War. I stated that I knew all too well what I had experienced as a POW with my two legs intact, and asked him, "how in God's Name" did he endure the horrors of the Prison Camp for those long forty-two months with both his legs amputated?

202

He replied by asking me to help him into his wheel chair and wheel him down the hall about six rooms from where he was located, to meet another patient. We entered a private room and there in the bed was a WWI "Basket Case," no arms, no legs but with a big smile on his face when Freeland introduced us. After a short visit with this inspiring Veteran whom I shall never forget, I wheeled Freeland back to his room. On the way he turned his head toward me and remarked, "you see Major, I didn't have it so rough." I was speechless, and unable to control a very heavy lump in my throat. Maurice Freeland has been dead several years. Prior to his passing he was the principal of a high school in San Jose California. I am very sure that many people's lives were enriched by his heroic example. I know mine was.

From the "Walled City" we went to San Agustin Church and marveled at its baroque altars, richly carved doors and ancient icons

The first day of our tour ended with a sentimental visitation to the American Military Cemetery at Fort Bonifacio. This superbly maintained Memorial, subsidized by the United States Government, is located six miles South-East of Manila. It covers 152 acres of land which is part of the former United States Military Reservation at Fort William McKinley. 17,206 of our Military are buried there. Forty percent of these Americans were originally buried in temporary cemeteries in New Guinea, the Philippines, other islands in the Southwest Pacific, and also in the Palau Islands of the Central Pacific. Most gave their lives in the defense of the Philippines and East Indies, in 1941 and 1942.

Eddie Page, a long time friend of mine, joined our Tour Group primarily because he wanted to locate the burial site of his younger brother, Lieutenant Charles Page. Chuck with his friend Lieutenant Truett Majors, both members of the 17th Pursuit Squadron, were killed in action while serving as assistant fire direction officers on detached status with Battery C of the 91st Coast Artillery, Philippine Scouts, located near Bataan Field. They were to provide an aircraft identification capability for the Battery in its defense of Bataan Field. On January 5, 1942, during a Japanese raid on the field, Battery C opened fire on the attacking bombers with its 3-inch anti-aircraft guns. A faulty fuse of WWI vintage resulted in a virtual muzzle burst, instantly killing Page and Majors, along with several Filipino Scouts.

Chuck and Truett were at Pier 7 when the 21st and 34th Pursuit Squadrons arrived in Manila on November 20, 1941. With other members of the 17th Pursuit, they gave us a cordial welcome, followed by a generous reception at their quarters. Their hospitality could not have been better. While viewing Chuck's grave-site, I remembered that November 20, 1941 with a great deal of nostalgia.

After Warsaw, Poland, Manila was the most ravaged city in the world during WWII. Touring Manila and its environs, I was impressed with the excellent restoration of Manila's infrastructure.

There are two Hemicycles, (curved structures) each with 24-pairs of thin walls, located within the Cemetery. The Names and Particulars of 36,280 of our Missing are inscribed on these walls. The number of Missing include 16,913 United States Army and Air Corps, 17,528 United States Navy, 1,727 United States Marine Corps and 58 United States Coast Guard. These Military Personnel died in the service of their Country, in the region from Australia, Northward to Japan, Eastward to the Palau Islands, and Westward to China, Burma, and India. Either their remains have not been identified or they were lost or buried at sea. They include names from every State in the Union, also from the District of Columbia, Panama, Guam, the Philippines, Puerto Rico, Australia, New Zealand, and Canada. On the partitioned walls, facing the list of the Missing, are these inscriptions:

"Here are recorded the names of Americans who gave their lives in the service of their Country and who sleep in unknown graves 1941, 1942. Included on these rolls are the names of Filipino Scouts who shared with their American Comrades in the defense and liberation of the Philippines."

In the morning of our second day in Manila, we started on a scenic trip to Tagaytay Ridge with its breath-taking over-view of Lake Taal. It is interesting to note that here is the only Volcano within a Lake, within an Island and also within an Ocean.

Enroute to the Ridge we visited a Jeepney factory. The Jeepney is one of the principle means of transportation in and around Manila. This highly decorated vehicle originated in 1945 when the departing American Forces abandoned their popular Willys Jeeps following the liberation of the Philippines. In the process of reconstruction, repair and some external modification of this windfall by diligent Filipinos, the Jeepney was born and today provides a very popular mode of travel in cities, towns and villages throughout most of the populated areas of the Philippines. Passengers usually pack into these attractive vehicles like sardines. Obviously, safety does not occupy their attention or concern; they ride precariously, in crowds, on fenders, hoods, and roofs of the Jeepneys.

Our next stop, enroute to Lake Taal and Tagaytay Ridge, was at an early day Spanish Cathedral which is home for the world famous Bamboo Organ. Built in 1824 by Father Diego Cerra, a Spanish Priest, today its a popular tourist attraction. We were disappointed that this unique musical instrument was not scheduled to be played on the day of our visit. We were informed that it can be heard every Sunday and during the week-long Bamboo Festival in February.

Proceeding to Tagaytay Ridge, the highway climbed through numerous papaya and coconut groves to a Swiss style chalet. Here we had lunch and enjoyed an exhibition of native dancing.

The drive through the Philippine countryside was a welcome

change from the hectic pace observed on the streets and sidewalks of Metro Manila. Out here in a rural area, it was a pleasure to see the friendly, happy, easy-going way of life. It reminded me of the time I spent on Mindanao with the guerrillas. There in the boondocks, despite the presence of the Japanese, and the uncertainty of survival, the natives' way of life was also friendly, and relaxed. Back then, the population of the Philippines was 17 million. When I returned in January 1986 with the Tour Group, the population had grown to over 57-million. With the teeming pedestrian and vehicle traffic I saw in the Manila area, it seemed to me that all the additional people had come to Manila and its environs to eke out a living.

When we arrived at Tagaytay Ridge in the early afternoon, a layer of haze obscured the panoramic view of Lake Taal that we had expected to see. Nevertheless, the overview of Lake Taal and the Taal Volcano was very interesting and the cool air at our elevation, 2,296 feet, was invigorating; it helped condition us for our arrival back in hot and humid Manila.

Northward from Manila, we drove through the scenic countryside to Nueva Ecija Province and the recently completed Monument and Memorial at Cabanatuan (Japanese Prison Camp No. 2 was located here). They were erected to honor the greatest number of American Prisoners of War to die in a prison camp in any of our Nation's Foreign Wars. Three thousand Americans perished there during WWII.

The last time I had traveled this route had been in October 1942. Then I was going in the opposite direction in a box-car heading for Bilibid Prison in Manila. On board the train were 1000 American POWs enroute from Cabanatuan to the Davao Penal Colony in southern Mindanao.

The names of my comrades who died at Cabanatuan are engraved on a stone wall. I stood motionless there, scanning the long list of those who died miserably without even the reverence of a dignified burial. Many of those whose names appeared on the wall were my friends who suffered the deprivations and humiliation experienced on the Bataan Death March and the "Hell Hole," Camp O'Donnell. Among those listed was Melvin E. McKnight. He died in his sleep on the floor next to me on August 21, 1942. He was a P-40 pilot in the 20th Pursuit Squadron, commanded by then Captain Joe Moore. Teedie Woodcock, Jane Fredrickson and I, with the other members of the Tour Group in attendance, placed a floral wreath at the base of the Monument and offered a silent prayer. I can fully understand and appreciate the emotions experienced by many of our Vietnam Veterans who visit the Vietnam Memorial in Washington D.C.

Tony Hillman, NBC's Producer in its Hong Kong Office, and two of his TV Cameramen accompanied us in our cruise across Manila Bay, on board the Mari Jean to Fort Drum and then to the "Island

Fortress," Corregidor. This NBC team remained with our group for several days. Part of their resultant production was shown on the Tom Brokaw National News in February, 1986.

The trip to Fort Drum and Corregidor brought to mind Christmas Eve 1941. On that memorable evening, my good friend Leo Golden and I joined a shipload of other military personnel for an unknown destination. Like most on board, our main concern was to avoid being captured by the Japanese who had broken through our lines and, according to our intelligence, were about to arrive in Manila.

We circled Fort Drum, the "Concrete Battleship" situated about three miles south of Corregidor and saw the devastation wreaked by Japanese bombing, strafing and shelling of that concrete fortification.

Malinta Tunnel, MacArthur's Headquarters prior to his departure for Australia, came into clear focus as we approached Corregidor. This supposedly, impenetrable "Rock," also left no doubt of the success of Japanese bombings, shelling and strafing. "Topside," "Middleside" and also "Bottomside" were terribly devastated. All that remains of Corregidor's above ground facilities that once were formidable buildings, are just ugly reminders of the barracks and support structures they used to be; the shells of the buildings that are still left seem to stand defiantly against the elements.

We toured the Pacific War Memorial and Battery Hearn before leaving Corregidor for the Bataan Peninsula. The Memorial was a disappointment because of the unkept condition of the grounds and facilities. Unlike the meticulously maintained American Military Cemetery at Fort Bonifacio, the Memorial does not receive financial support from the United States to properly maintain the grounds and the Memorial structures. I recently learned (Feb., 1994) that private funds have been provided to correct the situation.

Battery Hearn with its twelve inch gun and maximum range of eight miles, pointed seaward, verified what I had heard many times on Bataan; the Japanese invasion points and their subsequent offensive positions made that artillery piece useless against the enemy. Obviously in 1941 our intelligence had not been abreast of current reality. That gun and others on Corregidor were installed there in the early part of the 20th Century before aviation became a serious factor in warfare. A fixed seaward direction of fire at that time could be justified in, say, 1910 but certainly not in 1941. It was interesting to learn that Battery Hearn's twelve-inch gun was restored to an operational condition by the Japanese, using American POWs to do the work.

About three miles north of Corregidor is Mariveles, at the Southern Tip of the Bataan Peninsula. Today, Mariveles is a Historical Landmark; the infamous Bataan Death March started there. Coming back to Bataan after almost forty-four years was the highlight of the journey back to the Philippines for those of us who fought and surrendered on Bataan. Lieutenant General Joe Moore commanded Mariveles Field. Although the Field was no longer there but occupied by industrial buildings, like the rest of us he was still very enthusiastic about seeing the area again.

As the Mari Jean approached the pier at Mariveles I noticed a tense silence amongst the Bataan Defenders. We were all focused on a scene that was not familiar to us. The landscape was completely changed. Open areas forty-three years ago are now a part of an industrial complex.

Robert Brown, a former member of the 34th Pursuit Squadron and a Death March survivor, recalled that for six hours before the March started, his group was held in the Mariveles area as hostages so the American Forces on Corregidor would not open fire on that area where the Japanese were preparing for the invasion of Corregidor. This was one of many violations of the Geneva Convention which requires POWs to be removed from the combat zone as soon as possible. He also recalled that before he started on the Death March, he traded his WWI helmet for a sailor's cap. That navy head gear protected him from the scorching sun that many succumbed to during the long march.

After a short tour of now industrialized Mariveles, we traveled north in another air conditioned motor coach. We followed the route of the "Death March" through Little Baguio. My memories of that area are vivid and pleasant. The 803rd Engineers served Leo Golden and I a delicious Christmas dinner there on December 25, 1941.

Further north we located the site of Cabcaben Airfield where Dave Oestreich and his group were held as hostages to discourage the guns of Corregidor from opening fire. Unfortunately, the artillery personnel on the "Rock" were not aware that our POWs were being held by the Japanese within the range of their weapons. The cannons from Corregidor fired and, according to Dave, killed about fifteen Americans.

I also had vivid memories of Cabcaben. It was at this airfield that I had two close encounters with death; once attempting to land with six 30 lb. fragmentation bombs hanging precariously on the bomb racks of my P-40E. They had failed to release when I pulled the salvo handle over shipping in Subic Bay. The other incident took place on the morning of April 8, 1942, the day before we surrendered. On that occasion, very low on fuel, I landed just seconds prior to an attack on the airfield. Thanks to the courage of a brave airman who hurriedly towed my P-40 to a revetment and with the help of our good Lord, I barely missed being a target of Japanese dive bombers and a statistic on someone's list of victories.

As we drove past the site of the Bataan Airfield, about three miles north of Cabcaben, I had strong memories of the P-40 pilots, several of whom were classmates of mine in flying school, who were no longer alive. Many were killed in action because of the overwhelming advantages enjoyed by the Japanese. Others did because of faulty equipment or lack of proper training. Most however succumbed to starvation. Then there were those who died miserably in filthy Japanese Prison Camps and on board unmarked Hell-Ships. Who can ever explain and justify the deplorable state of our readiness when the Japanese hit Pearl Harbor? Americans should never allow such a disgraceful disaster to happen again. Our credibility as the only Super Power in the world today demands that we remain the world's strongest power.

Riding in an air conditioned motor coach on a paved, well maintained road that followed the route of the Bataan Death March, was indeed a dramatic contrast to the hot and dusty trail over which we stumbled, crawled, and walked during the "March." The dense mosquito ridden jungle that "best" characterized Bataan has been logged off and now one sees a pleasant countryside. Further north we arrived at the Mt. Samat War Memorial and Museum. The Mt. Samat Cross can be seen from much of Central Luzon. The Memorial is located on the Orion/Bagac Front Line where some very fierce fighting took place. We proceeded along that imaginary line to Montemar, our luxury resort on the South China Sea. Montemar is a private club two kilometers south of Bagac on the west coast of Bataan. Here one can enjoy golf or tennis, swim in a fresh water pool, and truly relax on a sweeping white sand beach. What I appreciated the most about Montemar was the privacy: one didn't have to share these beautiful facilities with thousands of other tourists. Moreover, the food was excellent and the employees could not have been more gracious. On arrival at Montemar we were greeted by "Rancho Grande," played by a band, strumming guitars and other stringed instruments.

After a good breakfast, we departed for Aglaloma, an area where most of the Bataan Defenders on the tour had experienced bitter combat against the Japanese.

Transportation on this leg of our tour was about an hour trip on board a flotilla of motorized bancas that brought us to Barrio Quinawan. We shed our footwear, rolled up our trousers and slacks, and waded ashore to be greeted by a group of very friendly Barrio people. They served us chicken, pork, rice, a variety of vegetables and tropical fruits, coconuts and coconut milk. The hospitality and generosity of these kind and gentle people touched me very deeply.

We explored old positions and points around the bay and five of the tour group, Dave Oestreich, Bob Brown, Omar McGuire, Stanley Korczyk and myself were interviewed by Tony Hillman, NBC Producer in the Hong Kong Office. All of us were asked why we wanted to come back to Bataan. The common reply was in essence, "I wanted to come back because we love these people and I wanted to see if they are the same kind of people who loved Americans and America. This response did not surprise me at all. We returned to Montemar, some enjoyed dancing that evening, we all enjoyed the excellent San Miguel Beer and we were all very favorably impressed with the congenial Filipinos who did their best to make us feel at home. I don't believe anyone of our group felt otherwise. I am sure the time spent at Montemar will be long remembered by all of us.

The next morning following an early breakfast we departed for Olongapo and Subic Bay. Enroute we visited Orani and the school house where the 34th Pursuit Squadron established its headquarters. This part of our tour was of particular interest to Bob Brown and Dave Oestreich who were members of the 34th and arrived there on December 26, 1941 from Del Carmen.

At Olongapo we visited the Memorial to the Oryoku Maru, the most horrible of the "Hell Ships." It was a somber reminder of December 15, 1944 when it was sunk by our own navy bombers. It was without markings to properly identify it as transporting American POWs. The survivors of that infamous "Hell Ship" were then loaded on another unmarked Japanese ship and it too was sunk by our navy. The third ship, with about 400 American POWs arrived in Japan, where those still alive were used as slave laborers. Only around 400 of more than 1,600 who started that terrible trip at sea survived.

We toured the naval facilities at Subic Bay, saw the USS Midway receiving periodic maintenance and then had a pleasant overnight stay at the White Rock Resort on the shores of Subic Bay. Like Clark Field, the lease agreement with the Philippine Government, authorizing use of Subic Bay has been terminated.

From Subic Bay we again headed north to Basa Air Base, home of the Fifth Fighter Wing, commanded by Brigadier General Mapua. The General and his staff gave us an excellent briefing and also hosted an excellent lunch. A static display of aircraft included an F-51, an F-86, and a T-34 that received my immediate attention. As covered in an earlier chapter, on my initial check out in the T-34 at Paine Field, Everett, Washington, I had to land wheels up due to a landing gear extension failure.

Our next stop was Clark Field, no longer used by the United States Air Force. The Commander of Clark and his staff spoke to the Tour Group about operations, problem areas, future plans and Base/Community relations. I am sure General Joe Moore's thoughts went back to December 8, 1941. On the take-off roll, with Randy Keator as his wingman and Japanese bombs trailing him down the turf airfield, he and Randy got airborne to engage the enemy in raging combat when the odds were heavily stacked against them. Both General Joe and Randy were recipients of the DSC for their courageous actions on that day over forty-five years earlier. Second Lieutenant Jesse Luker, a classmate of mine all through flying school, was killed on take-off that same day by a bomb going off in the cockpit of his P-40B. Looking at the now surfaced runway at Clark, I could visualize the powdery dust that obscured one's vision on take-off that next day and was responsible for Bob Clark's crash into a parked B-17 and instant death.

The visit to Camp O'Donnell was not a pleasant experience. Our Air Force was using that former "hell hole" as a radar facility in support of Clark field and other USAF activities in the area. I asked one of the airmen assigned there, why the Memorial to those who died there was erected where it was? He told me that in the process of excavating to install radar antennae, the workers uncovered one hundred and fifty bodies; An example of the mass burials common in Japanese Prison Camps. It was decided to erect the Memorial there and install the new radars in another location. There were no good memories of that filthy, stinking hole, that had followed the Bataan Death March.

A very pleasant experience was next on our itinerary; Baguio, the City of Eternal Spring and the luxurious five star Hyatt Terraces Hotel. Also as an additional bonus, we could see the Super Bowl Game.

While in Baguio, we had the pleasure of meeting Mayor Bueno, a former fighter pilot with the Philippine Air Force. The Mayor is a personable, dynamic individual who made a very favorable impression on all of us. A tour of Baguio included Mines View Park, the Presidential Summer Palace, and Igorot Village in Imelda Park. Here I learned that the Igorots will allow one to take their picture only if you put their stated price on the "barrel" before you operate the shutter. A short stay at the Philippine Military Academy and Camp John Hay, often called the most beautiful American base in the Far East, finished our tour of Baguio.

Our last day in Manila was a time set aside for shopping or whatever else one wanted to do before our Farewell Banquet that evening in the Manila Hotel. On that joyful occasion the Bataan Veterans of our group were presented the Philippine Defense Medal by the Adjutant General of the Philippine Armed Forces, followed by a very warm goodbye from Colonel Espinoza representing the Ministry of Tourism.

We departed Manila for San Francisco on January 30, 1986 in a comfortable PAL 747. At our cruising altitude we were blessed with a favorable jet stream that brought us back to San Francisco, nonstop, in just over nine hours. The food and service were superb. Dave Oestreich, our travel agent and fellow Bataan survivor, organized a tour that could not have been better. No one was disappointed.

Meeting Saburo Sakai, Japan's leading living Ace and my foe in the sky over Clark Field on December 8, 1941, was distinctly an unexpected privilege in my life. I had read about his incredible accomplishments as a Zero Fighter Pilot in the Japanese Imperial Navy. His 64 victories was indeed impressive. A Fighter Pilot of any nation will respect that record, even though it belongs to a former adversary.

I never had the slightest clue that it was Sakai who shot that hole in the left wing of my P-40E on the first day of WWII. To have an "eye ball to eye ball" contact with this extraordinary Fighter Pilot was an exciting experience. Nearly fifty years ago he was my enemy, I am proud to have him as my friend today.

My reunion with Saburo Sakai was occasioned by an invitation from Helen McDonald, Curator of Exhibits & Programs for the Museum. She informed me that in May of 1991, the Museum would sponsor the fourth in a series of Symposia on the War in the Pacific. This Symposium would be held in Austin, on 9-10 May. It would deal with the attack on Pearl Harbor plus what they called "the Other Pearl Harbor, the Philippines."

William Bartsch, Author of Doomed At The Start, a very well researched and written account of the 24th Pursuit Group in the Philippines during 1941-1942, gave Helen my name, and recommended that she invite me to participate in the Symposium. She obtained my telephone number and mailing address from Lieutenant General Joseph Moore who would be a featured participant in the Symposium. I have known General Moore since Bataan days and had served with him in Wiesbaden, Germany at USAFE Headquarters in 1955. I remembered that in early March, 1942, he brought me an RCA cablegram from the Island of Cebu sent by my wife Devonia, advising that I had become a father of a new baby girl on March 8, 1942. The message was dispatched immediately following the birth of my daughter before my wife had named her, consequently, I did not know Judith Ann's name until October, 1943, after I arrived in Brisbane, Australia. In Fredricksburg, Texas, General Moore and I discussed the evening in early March 1942, at Cabcaben Field on Bataan, when he brought me the good news. That message was the only correspondence I received from home during the entire time I spent in the Philippines.

Moore's and Bartsch's involvement in the invitation made it easy for me to say "yes" to Helen. I have never regretted being a part of the Symposium. It was very well organized and gave me the opportunity to meet some outstanding Veterans of the Pacific War and dignitaries in diverse "walks of life." They all contributed to a wealth of knowledge that provided new insights into many old controversial issues of the Pacific War that still evoke many question marks in the minds of many. Who should bear the stigma of Pearl Harbor and Clark Field? Who are the real culprits? Were General Short and Admiral

Kimmel scapegoats? Is General MacArthur completely blameless for what happened in the Philippines?

Helen named several of the people who would appear on the program, including Saburo Sakai. She explained that my presence was important because Saburo was identified as the Zero Pilot who shot the hole in the wing of my P-40 over Clark. I was curious to know how it was determined that it was him? She explained that Sakai's report of his encounter with me correlated with mine. Bill Bartsch, who studied the reports carefully, concluded that indeed it was Saburo who shot the hole in the left wing of my P-40. After discussing the matter with Sakai, with his lovely daughter Michiko translating, there is no doubt in my mind that it was he.

I first met Saburo Sakai on 6 May 1991 at the Admiral Nimitz Museum in Fredricksburg. Rear Admiral Charles Grojean, USN (Ret) and Helen McDonald were there to introduce us. It was a very pleasant occasion. Saburo was congenial, warm and seemed to be as genuinely happy to meet me as I was to meet him. We spontaneously embraced and gave each other a hearty handshake. Almost fifty years had gone by since our encounter over Clark. At that time he did his very best to blast me out of the sky. He was a Samurai; his first priority was to destroy the enemy and if necessary, to die for his country. For him, there was nothing more honorable. His multiple victories and the many heroic actions associated with those victories, attest to his unswerving dedication and adherence to the Bushido Code.

Keith Ferris, the founder of Society of Aviation Artists and former president, produced a splendid oil painting of his conception of the Japanese attack on Clark Field. Appropriately titled, "Too Little Too Late," I can vouch for the realism depicted in his painting. Before the Symposium, General Moore, Keith Ferris, Saburo Sakai and myself, countersigned 1000 limited edition fine prints of Ferris' painting. The Greenwich Workshop, Inc., in Trumbull, Connecticut did a superior job in producing the print and also a video tape that accompanies it. Concurrent with our signing project, Brigadier General Kenneth Taylor, a classmate of mine in flying school, Zenji Abe, leader of a flight of Val Dive Bombers that sank the Arizona and Craig Kodera, an aviation artist and professional pilot, were busily engaged in another room of the LBJ Library and Museum, signing 1000 limited edition fine prints of Kodera's oil painting, titled "This Is No Drill." The painting is a tribute to Ken Taylor who got airborne during the surprise attack on Pearl Harbor. He was the first American Pilot to experience combat in WWII when he shot down two Japanese aircraft at Pearl. He was credited with shooting down six enemy aircraft in the Pacific War.

Sakai told the audience that he knew his target was Clark Field and the mission briefing defined their time of arrival over Clark to be concurrent with the time of the Japanese attack on Pearl Harbor. He was one of forty-four Zero pilots who escorted fifty-four Betty bombers from Formosa to Clark Field. Fog covered the base on Formosa and delayed their take-off. Their arrival over Clark was around nine hours after the attack on Pearl Harbor. Sakai expressed his reaction to this turn of events as follows: "On one hand I was happy for my country, but my honest reaction was disappointment, we wanted to be the first fighters to engage in battle with the United States. His comments concerning his encounter with me over Clark Field were reassuring and complimentary: "Mr. Grashio's reaction to my approach was quick, which I admired," said Sakai. "The way he got away from me was perfect." His kind words continued: "Fifty years ago Mr. Grashio was my enemy, I shot at him, damaged his airplane. Today I want to let him know that he too was a gentleman and his life has always been as meaningful as my own."

The time I spent with Saburo was not all serious, there also was time for play. I challenged him to some rounds of Indian Arm Wrestling while we were in the foyer of the Lyndon Baines Johnson Library. After giving him a short period of instructions, he accepted my challenge and the contest started. The instructions I gave him must have been very poor, because four times consecutively I won. Now, he was still the champ in the air but I was the champ on the ground. We both enjoyed a round of good laughs followed by a discussion with Zenji Abe and Kazuo Sakamaki[1] concerning our wrestling contest. With my meager understanding of Japanese and Saburo's gestures I was able to understand the essence of what he was telling his two Japanese friends; I had on a better pair of shoes than his and they provided me a more stable platform and a decisive advantage.

In Austin, while signing posters with other veterans of Pearl Harbor and Clark Field, it was my privilege to meet two Medal of Honor recipients, both retired officers of the United States Navy. Lieutenant John Finn, the oldest living Medal of Honor recipient was at Kaneohe Naval Air Station in support of Pearl Harbor during the Japanese Attack on December 7, 1941. John remained at his post manning anti-aircraft guns after he was wounded. Recovered from his wounds he continued to fight in the Pacific War. I sat next to John while we were signing the posters and asked him if he was related to Father Francis Finn, a Jesuit Priest who wrote books for children. I remembered reading his books while in grade school and was impressed with the religious lessons his writings conveyed. Father Finn S.J. was John's Uncle. He was surprised that I remembered him after the passage of more than sixty years since I had read many of his books. Like his Uncle, the Jesuit Priest, I will not soon forget one of the great heroes of Pearl Harbor, Lieutenant John Finn.

The other Congressional Medal of Honor recipient is

Captain Donald K. Ross U.S.N. (Ret), a very congenial, jovial individual who kept us all in good humor during the signing session. It was obvious that his comrades and friends had a great respect for him. I liked him the minute I met him. The following citation speaks for itself:
"For distinguished conduct in the line of his profession, extraordinary courage, and disregard of his own life during the attack on the Fleet in Pearl Harbor, Territory of Hawaii, by Japanese forces on December 7, 1941. When his station in the forward dynamo room of the USS NEVADA became almost untenable due to smoke, steam, and heat, he forced his men to leave that station and performed all the duties himself until blinded and unconscious. Upon being rescued and resuscitated, he returned and secured the forward dynamo room and proceeded to the after dynamo room where he was later again rendered unconscious by exhaustion. Upon again recovering consciousness he returned to his station where he remained until directed to abandon it."

At the completion of the two day symposium in Austin, many of the participants traveled to Fredricksburg to see a reenactment by the Gulf Coast Wing of The Confederate Air Force of the air battles over Pearl Harbor and Clark Field. I sat next to Sakai during this thrilling Air Show at the Gillespie County Airport. When the P-40, in a diving descent came screaming across the spectators' viewing area with the Zero in a close stern chase, simulating in a very professional manner, Sakai's near kill on my P-40, we looked at each other, smiled and shook our heads. I know what went through my mind, "Thank God we are both here as friends."

Before Sakai left the Fairgrounds he came over to where I was standing, took off a white cap I was wearing, removed his own, a navy blue color and the same brand as mine, put his cap on my head and mine on his, symbolizing our friendship.

During interviews by the news media I was asked how I feel today towards the Japanese who eventually took me prisoner on Bataan? My answer, "I hold no animosity toward them. This symposium has helped heal some old wounds. I'm proud to have Sakai as a friend. His cap is on a shelf above my desk at our summer home in Idaho. It keeps fresh in my mind a great warrior that I met at the Admiral Nimitz Museum on May 6, 1941."

---

[1] Note: Ensign Sakamaki was a crewman aboard a midget submarine that was a part of the attack force. Following a futile effort to enter Pearl Harbor, the midget sub was stranded on a coral reef. Sakamaki set the fuse for a self-destruct mechanism which failed to detonate and he swam for shore. He was captured at Bellows Field in Hawaii at 5:40 A.M., December 8, 1941. The submarine was recovered by U.S. forces and today it is a popular display at the Admiral Nimitz Museum. Sakamaki was our first Prisoner of War.

Bibliography

Primary Sources—Books by Participants in the War

Aida, Yugi. *Prisoner of the British: A Japanese Soldier's Experiences in Burma*. Translated by Hide Ishiguro and Louis Allen. London: Cresset Press, 1966.

Arnold, H.H. *Global Mission*. New York: Harpers, 1949.

Bank, Bert. *Back From The Living Dead*. Tuscaloosa; privately printed in 1945.

Bertram, James. *Beneath the Shadow: A New Zealander In The Far East*, 1939-1946. New York: John Day Co., 1947.

Boyington, Gregory. *Baa! Baa! Black Sheep*. New York: Putnam's, 1958.

Boyle, Martin. *Yanks Don't Cry*. New York: Random House, 1963.

Brereton, Lewis. *The Brereton Diaries*. New York: William Morrow & Co., 1946.

Chennault, Claire. *Way Of A Fighter*. New York: Putnam's, 1949.

Conroy, Robert. *The Battle Of Bataan: America's Greatest Defeat*. London: Macmillan, 1969.

Considine, Robert, ed. *General Wainwright's Story*. Garden City, New York: Doubleday, 1946.

Dew, Gwen. *Prisoner Of The Japs*. New York: Knopf, 1943.

Dyess, William E. *The Dyess Story*. Ed. Charles Leavelle. New York: Putnam's, 1944.

Eisenhower, Dwight D. *Crusade In Europe*. Garden City, New York: Doubleday, 1948.

Gaskill, Robert C. *Guests Of The Son Of Heaven*. New York: Vantage Press, 1976.

Gilkey, Langdon. *Shantung Compound*. New York: Harper & Row, 1966.

Gordon, Ernest. *Through The Valley Of The Kwai*. New York: Harper & Bros., 1962.

Gunnison, Royal Arch. *So Sorry, No Peace*.

Haggerty, Edward, S. J. *Guerrilla Padre In Mindanao*. New York: Longmans, Green & Co., 1946.

Harmon, Tom. *Pilots Also Pray*. New York: Crowell, 1944.

Hawkins, Jack. *Never Say Die*. Philadelphia: Dorrance & Co., 1961.

Howell, John B. *42 Months Of Hell*. Muskogee, Oklahoma: Hoffman Printing Co., 1970.

Ind, Allison. *Bataan: The Judgment Seat*. New York: Macmillan, 1944.

James, D. Clayton, ed. *South To Bataan, North To Mukden, The Prison Diary Of Brigadier General W E. Brougher*, Athens: University of Georgia Press, 1971.

Keith, Agnes Newton. *Three Came Home*. Boston: Little, Brown & Co., 1947.

Lee Clark. *They Call It Pacific*. New York: Viking Press, 1943.

MacArthur, Douglas. *Reminiscences*. New York: McGraw Hill, 1964.

McCall, James. *Santo Tomas Internment Camp*. Lincoln, Nebraska: Woodruff Printing Co., 1945.

McCoy, Melvyn. and Mellnick, Steve, as told to Welbourn Kelley. *Ten Escape From Tojo*. New York: Farrar & Rhinehart, 1944.

Mellnick, Steve. *Philippine Diary, 1939-1945*. New York: Van Nostrand Reinhold, 1969.

Miller, Ernest B. *Bataan Uncensored*. Long Prairie, Minnesota: Hart Publications, 1949.

Morrill, John, and Martin, Peter. *South From Corregidor*. New York: Simon & Schuster, 1943.

Quezon, Manuel. *The Good Fight*. New York: D. Appleton Century, 1946.

Redmond, Juanita. *I Served On Bataan*. New York: Lippincott, 1943.

Reynolds, Quentin, ed. *Officially Dead: The Story Of Commander C.D. Smith*. New York: Random House, 1945.

Romulo, Carlos. *I Saw The Fall Of The Philippines*. Garden City, New York: Doubleday, Doran & Co., 1943.

Sayre, Francis B. *Glad Adventure*. New York: Macmillan, 1947.

Steven, Frederic H. *Santo Tomas Internment Camp*. Privately published, 1946.

Stewart, Sidney. *Give Us This Day*. New York: Norton, Popular Library ed., 1947.

Stimson, Henry L., and Bundy, McGeorge. *On Active Service In Peace And War*. New York: Harper, 1948.

Strong, Tracy, ed. *We Prisoners Of War*. New York: Association Press, 1942.

Townswick, Carlyle G. *Too Young To Die*. Privately printed, 1979.

Whitcomb, Edgar D. *Escape From Corregidor*. Chicago: Henry Regnery Co., 1958.

Primary Sources—Magazine Articles By Participants

Deane, Philip, "I Was a Captive in Korea," Reader's Digest, August, 1953, pp. 65-70.

Harrison, Thomas D., "Why Did Some G.I.s Turn Communist:," Collier's, November 27, 1953, pp. 25-28.

Beller, Edwin L. "I Thought I'd Never Get Home, I and II," Saturday Evening Post, August 20, 1955, August 27, 1955.

van Landingham, Charles, "I Saw Manila Die," Saturday Evening Post, September 27, 1942, pp. 12-13, 70-74; October 3, 1942, pp. 24-215, 61-65.

Secondary Works—Books

Baldwin, Hanson W. *Battles Won And Lost*, New York: Harper & Row, 1966.

Barrett, Jeffrey. Unpublished manuscript.

Beck, John J. *MacArthur And Wainwright: Sacrifice Of The Philippines*. Albuquerque: University of New Mexico Press, 1974.

Belote, James H., and William M. *Corregidor: The Saga Of A Fortress*. New York: Harper & Row, 1967.

Blakey, Scott. *Prisoner At War: The Survival Of Commander Richard A. Stratton*. New York: Doubleday (Penguin Books), 1978.

Calvocoressi, Peter, and Wint, Guy. *Total War: Causes And Courses Of The Second World War*. New York: Penguin, 1979.

Congden, Don, ed. *The War With Japan*. New York: Dell, 1962.

Craven, W.F., and Cate, J.L., eds. *The Army Air Forces In World War II: I, Plans And Early Operations, January, 1939 To August, 1942*. Chicago: University of Chicago Press, 1948.

Denton, Jeremiah A. *When Hell Was In Session*. Clover, South Carolina: Commission Press. 1976.

Edmonds, Walter D. *They Fought With What They Had*. Boston: Little, Brown & Co., 1951.

Emerson, Dorothy. *Among The Mescalero Apaches: The Story Of Father Albert Braun O.F.M.* Tucson: University of Arizona Press, 1973.

Falk, Stanley L. *Bataan: The March Of Death*. New York: Norton, 1962.

Greenfield, Kent Roberts. *The Historians And The Army*. Port Washington, New York: Kennikat Press, 1954.

Hubbell, John G. *P.O.W.: A Definitive History Of The American Prisoner-Of-War Experience In Vietnam, 1964-1973*. New York:L Reader's Digest Press, 1976.

Hunt, Frazier. *The Untold Story Of Douglas MacArthur*. New York: Devin-Adair, 1954.

Hyde, H. Montgomery. *Room 3603*. New York: Dell, 1964.

James, D. Clayton. *The Years Of MacArthur*. Boston: Houghton Mifflen Co., 1975. 2 vols.

Keats, John. *They Fought Alone*. New York: Lippincott, 1963.

Kleinfeld, Gerald R. and Tambs, Lewis A. *Hitler's Spanish Legion: The Blue Division In Russia*. Carbondale, Illinois: Southern Illinois University Press, 1979.

Knightley, Philip. *The First Casualty*. New York: Harcourt, Brace, Jovanovich, 1975.

Lea, Homer. *The Valor Of Ignorance*. New York: Harper & Bros., 1909.

Lochner, Louis P., ed. *The Goebbels Diaries 1942-1943*. Garden City, New York: Doubleday, 1948.

Major, Ralph N. *Fatal Partners: War And Disease*. Garden City, New York: Doubleday, Doran, 1941.

Morison, Samuel E. *History Of U.S. Naval Operations In World War II, Vol VI, Breaking The Bismarck Barrier 22 July, 1942-1 May, 1944*. Boston: Little, Brown & Co., 1950.

Morison, Samuel E. *The Two Ocean War*. Boston: Little, Brown & Co.,1963.

Morton, Louis. *The Fall Of The Philippines. Washington, D.C.: Chief of Military History, Department of the Army, 1953*.

Morton, Louis. *The War In The Pacific. Strategy And Command: The First Two Years*. Washington, D.C.: Chief of Military History, Department of the Army, 1962.

Pogue, Forrest C. *George C. Marshall: Ordeal And Hope, 1939-1942*. New York: Viking, 1966.

Reischauer, Edwin C. *Japan: the Story Of A Nation*. New York: Knopf, 1974.

Sherwood, Robert. *Roosevelt And Hopkins*. New York: Harper's, 1948.

Tasaki, Hanama. *Long The Imperial Way*. Boston: Houghton Mifflen Co., 1950.

Toland, John. *But Not In Shame: The Six Months After Pearl Harbor*. New York: Random House, 1961.

Toland, John. *The Rising Sun: The Decline And Fall Of The Japanese Empire, 1936-1945*. New York: Random House, 1970.

Zich, Arthur, ed. *The Rising Sun: World War II*. Alexandria, Virginia: Time-Life Books, 1977.

Secondary Works—Magazine Articles and Commentary

Bouscaren, Anthony T., "Korea, Test of American Education," Catholic World, April, 1956, pp. 24-27.

Collier's, editorial, September 30, 1955, p. 106.

Commonwealth, July 1, 1955, p. 318.

Cooke, Alastair, "The Evil Truth Behind The Germ Warfare 'Conference'," Reader's Digest, March, 1954, pp. 443-46.

Craig, William, "The Battle of Stalingrad," Reader's Digest, July, 1973, pp. 209-255.

Edmonds, Walter D., "What Happened at Clark Field," Atlantic Monthly, July, 1951, pp. 19-33.

Hill, Gladwin, "Brain-Washing: Time for a Policy," Atlantic Monthly, April, 1955, pp. 58-62.

New Republic, editorial, November 9, 1953, p. 8.

Newsweek, February 7, 1944.

Sondern, Frederic, "US Negroes Make Reds See Red," Reader's Digest, January, 1954, pp. 37-42.

Time, November 2, 1942, pp. 36-38; July 12, pp. 49-50; 1951-1956.

Index

Organizations

25th Air Defense Division, 199
4th Air Force, 177
5th Air Force, 171, 173, 177
27th Bomb Group, 201
91st Coast Artillery, 203
803rd Engineers, 207
31st Infantry, 33
116th Observation Squadron, 1
3rd Pursuit Squadron, 197
17th Pursuit Squadron,203
20th Pursuit Squadron, 30, 205
21st Pursuit Squadron, 2, 9, 10, 15, 22, 76, 85, 190, 202
34th Pursuit Squadron, 1, 23, 201, 203, 207, 209
194th Tank Battalion, 50

A

A-24, 193
Abe, Zenji, 212, 213
Abes-san, 103, 104, 105, 109, 110, 111
Abilene, Texas, 184
Abrina, Candido, 121
Acenas, Juan, 126, 135
Admiral Nimitz Museum, 212, 214
Africa, 43, 114, 163
Aglaloma Bay, 22, 23, 29, 41, 201, 202, 208
Aida, Yugi, 64, 79, 80, 84, 88
Air Force, 172, 192, 199, 200, 210
Akobe, 29
Alaska,185
Albany, Texas,7, 184
Allied, 19, 61, 66, 79, 90, 123, 152, 164, 181
Allies, 11, 117
Amberley, 172
American Embassy, 198
American Federation of Labor, 187
American Flag, 33, 80, 147, 168
American Headquarters, 66, 70, 73, 77
American Military Assistance Advisory Team, 197
American Military Cemetery, Fort Bonifacio, 203, 206
Anderson, Lieutenant Marshall, 23

Annapolis, 119, 120, 168
Antonio, Lieutenant, 147
Arabs, 195, 196, 197
Army Air Corps, 1, 7, 8, 19
Arnold, General H.H. Edward, 183, 186
Asia, 163, 181, 199, 202
Ata, 145, 146
Atomic Bomb, 115, 132, 190
Augusan River,147, 148
Ausmus, Colonel Delbert, 148
Austin, Texas, 188, 211, 213, 214
Australia, 29, 35, 38, 41, 62, 96, 119, 120, 122, 143, 144, 151, 152, 153, 154, 155, 159, 160, 161, 164, 165, 166, 168, 170, 171, 173, 177, 180, 183, 186, 188, 204, 206

B

B-17, 4, 8, 9, 38, 39, 210
Bagac, 208
Baguio, 15, 38, 207, 210
Baker, Buck, 176
Baker, Lieutenant Bill, 29
Balanga, 57
Bamboo Organ, 204
Bank, Bert, 62, 72, 81, 85, 93, 97, 115, 118, 131, 189, 190, 215
Barkley, Alben, 183
Barnum, P.T., 34
Baroy, 160, 161, 163, 166
Barrio Quinawan, 208
Bartsch, Bill, 212
Baruch, Bernard, 186
Basa Air Base, 209
Basin, Wyoming, 120
Bataan Death March, 43, 45, 61, 200, 201, 205, 206, 208, 210
Bataan Defenders, 207, 208
Bataan Field,16, 203
Battery Hearn, 206
Battle of Bismark Sea, 173
Battle of the Points, 201
Bellamy, Ralph, 186
Bellevue, WA., 201
Benedictine (liquor), 158
Benson, Lieutenant Gordon, 108, 131
Beri beri, 31, 72, 74, 106, 107
Bernadotte, Count Folke, 197
Berra, Yogi, 168

Bertram, James, 63, 64, 74, 83, 116, 131
Bible, 91
Bilibid, 68, 69, 97, 121, 147, 202, 205
black market, 74, 75, 84, 92
Bluemel, Clifford, 38
Boeing, 177
Boelens, Leo, 118, 119, 120, 126, 131, 154, 255, 160, 161, 162, 164, 165, 166
Borneo, 11, 61, 63, 66, 70, 75, 77, 78, 89, 93
BOWFIN, 168, 169, 170, 171, 200
Boyington, Gregory (Pappy), 9, 78, 91, 93, 94, 104, 115, 131, 215
Boyle, Martin, 45, 94
Braeland House, 172
Braun, Father (Colonel) Albert, 111, 133, 217
Brereton, General Lewis R., 4, 13, 215
Brisbane, Australia, 171, 173, 176, 177, 211
British, 11, 13, 19, 51, 56, 59, 64, 79, 80, 84, 95, 107, 114, 115, 132, 181, 196, 215
British Columbia, 199
British Expeditionary Force, 56
Brokaw, Tom, 206
Brougher, General W. E., 41, 52, 59, 79, 88, 89, 94
Brown, Robert, 207, 208, 209
Browning, 142, 144
Buddha, 91
Buena Vista,148
Bulkeley, Lieutenant John D., 170
Buna, 174
Bunker, Colonel Paul, 148
Burbank, California, 183
Burma, 59, 95, 114, 204, 215
Burns, Lieutenant, 27
Bushido Code, 61, 96, 116, 212

C

C-43, 172
Cabanatuan, 17,61, 65, 68, 69, 71, 72, 73, 74, 77, 83, 85, 89, 93, 96, 97, 102, 103, 106, 108, 110, 111, 117, 118, 120, 121, 124, 141, 189, 205
Cabcaben, 15, 16, 27, 28, 29, 37, 207, 211
Cagayan, 157, 160
Cairo, Egypt, 197
Calabrese, 171, 198
Calabria, Italy, 171
Callieri, Colonel Gino, 198
Cambodians, 45

Camiguin, 156, 157, 158, 159, 160
Camp John Hay, 210
Canada, 204
Canadian National Defense College, 199
Cantrell, Ray, 170
Capas, 54, 55, 57, 97
Capra, Frank, 186, 187
Carberry, Father Richard, 133, 134
Cascade Range, 194
Cateel, 144
Catholic, 82, 92, 133, 218
Cebu, 17, 30, 36, 156, 211
Cerra, Father Diego, 204
Chan, Mr., 159
Chennault, General Claire, 7, 8, 13, 63, 215
Chicago, 66, 178, 182, 216, 217
Chicago Tribune, 178, 182, 183
China, 13, 16, 61, 63, 64, 77, 78, 83, 92, 115, 204
China coast, 67, 74, 77, 78, 170
Chinese, 29, 62, 63, 78, 79, 86, 114, 116, 153, 156, 158
Christianity, 163
Christians, 44, 92, 162
Clark, Bob, 9, 210
Clark Field, 4, 5, 6, 8, 9, 11, 13, 14, 16, 21, 22, 32, 33, 40, 113, 156, 172, 209, 210, 211, 212, 213,214, 218,
Clark, Lee, 216
Cleary, Captain Ed, 193, 194
Coast Artillery, 121
coastwatchers, 152
Cole, Joe, 4, 5
Coleman, Lieutenant L. A., 3
Colville, WA., 170
Communism, 171
Communists, 86
Congressional Medal of Honor, 40, 187, 190, 213
Corregidor, 12, 17, 18, 22, 25, 29, 30, 33, 36, 37, 39, 40, 41, 42, 47, 48, 49, 56, 57, 61, 62, 68, 90, 102, 119, 120, 121, 123, 126, 131, 148, 150, 152, 170, 185, 190, 200, 201, 206, 207, 216, 217
Cotton, Joseph, 186
Cowart, Colonel Leroy, 182
Cowart, Lieutenant Leroy, 50
Crellin, Lieutenant, 27
Crosby, Bing, 186, 187
Crossland, 27
Culion, 36
Cummings, Father, 92

D

Dale, Lieutenant Gene, 129
D'Angelis, Captain John, 195, 196
Daniels, "Ship", 97
Davao, 31, 61, 66, 67, 71, 80, 81, 82,
    84, 85, 98, 100, 101, 102, 103, 106,
    107, 108, 111, 112, 115, 117, 118,
    119, 120, 121, 124, 126, 133, 141,
    160, 166, 173, 180, 189, 190, 192,
    193, 195
Davao City, 100, 103, 121, 123, 142,
    143, 146
Davao Penal Colony, 138, 142, 205
Davenport Hotel, Spokane, WA. 189
David, Senor Eligio, 143
Davies, Colonel, 188
Davis, Elmer, 183
de Juan, Casiano, 80
de la Cruz, Benigno (Ben), 127, 128,
    131, 135,136, 137, 138, 139, 142,
    144
Death March, 24, 30, 33, 40, 45, 46,
    50, 51, 52, 53, 54, 55, 56, 57, 58,
    59, 60, 61,63, 64, 68, 69, 76, 78,
    81, 87, 93, 100, 104, 117, 119, 135,
    179, 181, 182, 185, 207
del Mundo, Wenceslao (Ben), 155,
    156, 157, 161, 162, 163, 175
Dempsey, Jack, 186, 187
Denton, Commander Jeremiah, 180,
    190, 191, 217
Detroit, Michigan, 193
Detroit Municipal Airport, 193
Devonia (Grashio), 30, 36, 178, 182,
    211
Dew, Gwen, 42, 72, 78, 94
Ding, 157
diphtheria, 74
Distinguished Service Cross, 188
District of Columbia, 204
Division Street Bridge, Spokane, WA.,
    175
Doba Dura, 173, 174
Dobervich Lieutenant Mike, 96, 99,
    106, 119, 130, 138, 139, 143, 149
Donaldson, Lieutenant I. B. (Jack), 37
Donohoe, Jack, 48, 65, 74, 81, 88, 91,
    113
Duenas, Magdaleno, 146, 201
Dyess, Captain William Edwin, 2, 3,
    4, 6, 7, 8, 9, 10, 15, 18, 22, 23, 26,
    27, 28, 30, 35, 36, 37 38, 39, 40,
    47, 50, 55, 67, 76, 84, 85, 87, 91,
    96, 98, 99, 103, 105, 106, 110, 115,
    118, 119, 120, 123, 126, 127, 130,
    136, 138, 140, 142, 143, 148, 153,
    154, 155, 157, 160, 161, 166, 171,
    181, 182, 183, 184, 195, 200, 202
dysentery, 19, 31, 37, 49, 50, 54, 69,
    72, 73, 74, 75, 87, 98, 107, 160,
    168, 171

E

Early, Presidential Secretary Stephen,
    183
East Asia, 53, 65, 113, 191
East Indies, 19, 60, 113, 203
East Pakistanis, 45
Easter, 31, 186
Eden, Anthony, 181
Egyptian, 43, 197
Egyptian Air Ministry, 197
Elder, Major General William E., 199,
    200
Eleanor, Mclc, 111
Elephantiasis, 72, 73
Eleventh Division, Philippine Army,
    52
England, 43, 56, 183
European Theater, 169, 189
Everett, WA., 193, 209

F

F-106, 194
F-51, 209
F-84E, 197
F-86, 209
Falk, Stanley, 41, 54, 63, 116, 131
Far East, 1, 13, 15, 63, 83, 85, 93, 187,
    210, 215
Ferris, Keith, 212
Fertig, "General" Wendell, 150, 151,
    152, 154, 155, 157, 159, 160, 161,
    162, 163, 164, 165, 166, 167,
fiestas, 143, 144, 153
Fifth Fighter Command, 174
Filipino Scouts, 41, 201, 203, 204
Filipinos, 8, 11, 15, 18, 21, 24, 29, 31,
    34, 38, 41, 47, 52, 53, 55, 56, 58,
    61, 62, 63, 66, 68, 69 79, 81, 82,
    83, 84, 89, 99, 102, 106, 109, 115,
    117, 119, 126, 128, 133, 134, 141,
    142, 143, 149, 151, 152, 156, 157,
    159, 160, 161, 163, 164, 166, 167,
    168, 180, 200, 204, 209
Finn, Father Francis, S.J., 213
Finn, Lieutenant John, 213
Fladwed, J. M., 184
Flying Tigers,7, 8, 13
Fontaine, Joan, 186
Forest Lawn Memorial, 186
Formosa, 2, 94, 148, 213

sun treatment,49, 60, 135
Surigao, 154
Sutherland, General Richard, 25
Swedish, 111

T

T-34, 193, 194, 209
Taal Volcano, 205
Tacoma, WA., 199
Tagaytay Ridge, 204, 205
Talisayan, 156
Tarlac, 17, 52, 82
Tasaki, Hanama, 64, 77
Taylor, Edgar, 158
Taylor, General Kenneth, 212
Tel Aviv, 196, 197
Terauchi, Field Marshal, 20, 56
Thai, 63
Thailand, 76, 115
The Greenwich Workshop, Inc., 212
Thorne, Hank, 197
Toka, 105
Tokyo, Japan, 19, 27, 31, 56, 63, 103, 181
Toland, John, 41, 64
Tonelli, Mario (Motts), 39, 40, 103, 111
Tour Group, 201, 203, 205, 208, 209
Townswick, Carlyle, 13, 94, 152, 162, 216
Travis Field, 177
Treviso, Italy, 198
Tropical ulcers, 49, 72, 73, 75
Turks, 44, 45, 92
Tuscaloosa, Alabama, 189, 215
Tyndall Field, 194

U

Udine, Italy, 198, 199
UN, 195, 196, 197
United Nations, 92, 195
United States, 29, 34, 76, 86, 88, 90, 113, 123, 134, 144, 155, 156, 166, 172, 173, 176, 177, 178, 181, 184, 195, 198, 199, 200, 202, 203, 206, 213
United States Air Force, 209
United States Army, 204
United States Coast Guard, 204
United States Marine Corps, 204
United States Navy, 204, 213
University of Washington, 195
USS Midway, 209
USS Nevada, 214
Uvalde, Texas, 188, 189

V

Vandegrift, Marine General Alexander, 187
Victoria Cross, 196
Vietnam, 30, 45, 86, 88, 94, 190, 199
Vietnam Memorial, 205
Vietnam Veterans, 205
Vietnam War, 83, 85, 91, 95, 199
von Richtofen, Baron, 1

W

Wainwright, General Johnathan P., 38, 59, 78, 115, 189, 217
Walla Walla, WA., 193
Walled City, 203
War Bonds, 185, 186, 189
War Crimes Trial, 56
War Department, 7, 178, 181, 182
Warsaw, Poland, 203
Washington Air National Guard, 1
Washington, D.C., 202
West Pakistanis, 45
West Pointer, 121
Whitcomb, Edgar, 32, 33, 62, 91, 115, 131, 132, 216
Wiesbaden, Germany, 211
Wilde, Oscar, 82
Williams Lieutenant Gus, 4, 5
Willingham, Commander, 168
Wilson, General, 173
Woodcock, Teedie, 202, 205
Word War I, 1, 2, 56, 117
World War II, 6, 8, 13, 32, 45, 64, 74, 76, 83, 86, 92, 116, 117, 160, 171, 178, 195, 200, 201, 217, 218
Wurtsmith, Brigadier General Paul B., 174

Y

Yuki, Lieutenant, 97

Z

Zambales mountain range, 20
Zamboanga, 152, 155, 162
Zapanta, Vincente, 149
Zero, 3, 6, 7, 8, 13, 211, 212, 213, 214

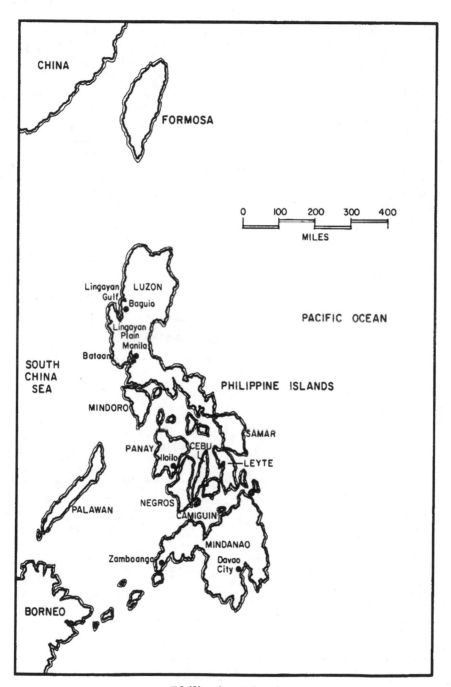

Philippine Islands

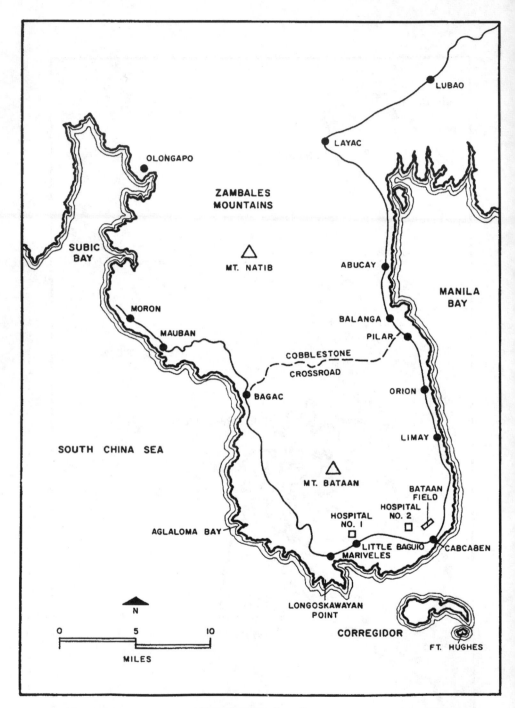

Bataan Peninsula

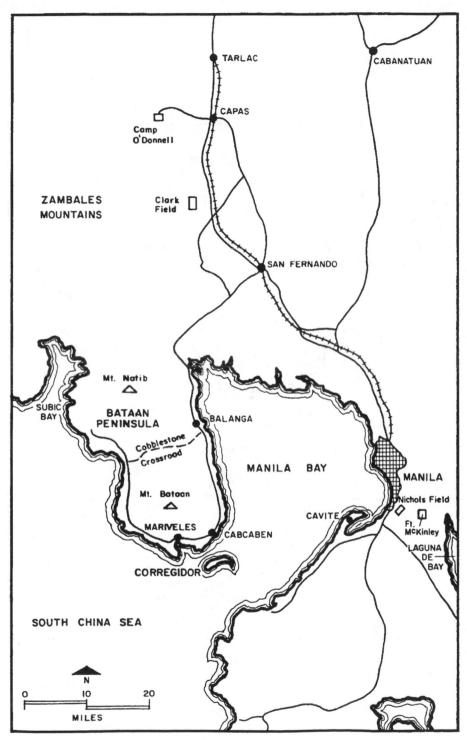

Manila Bay and Vicinity

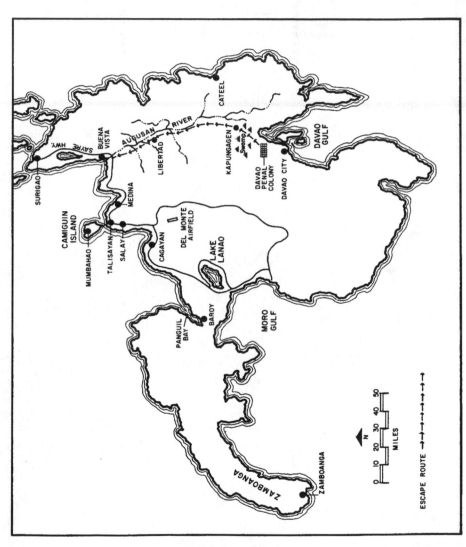

Mindanao Island

Putting lower classman in a brace. Randolph Field, Texas, 1940.

With my beloved mother at Hamilton Field, California just prior to leaving for Manila in October of 1941.

Artist's conception of one incident I saw on the Death March.

Artist's conception of beating I received in warehouse at Tarlac.

232

My wife Devonia (Dee) upon my return to the U.S. in November 1943.

Ed shortly before his fatal crash in December of 1943.

I received this letter from Ed Dyess 12/22/43 the day prior to his death in a P-38.

Dear Sam —
    I was to leave here for
Spokane this morning, but O-O
Kept me on the ground So
now I'll have to put it off until
after Xmas as the weather is supposed
to be bad all day tomorrow. Listen
"Knuckle head" if it isn't too much
of a secret Just where in the hell do
I find you after I get there, or have
you moved into the Jail to feel at home.
Still love you both.
                                    Marasen & Ed

234

With General Henry H. Arnold and Melvin H. McCoy at the I Am An American program at Soldiers Field, Chicago, 1944.

With two Congressional Medal of Honor recipients. Left: Charles E. "Commando" Kelly. Right: Ernest Childers, Chicago, 1944

Five members of our escape group reunited at the Marine Barracks at Quantico, VA. in 1944. Left to right, Major Mike Dobervich, USMC; Lt. Colonel Austin Shofner, USMC; Commander Melvin H. McCoy, USN; and myself then a major.

Ed Dyess on Bataan after his attack on the Japanese at Subic Bay.

S. M. Mellnick, member of our escape group.

Leo B. Golden 21st Pursuit, my flying school classmate & roommate at Kelly Field. Died on board the "hell ship" Oryoku Maru after surviving the infamous Bataan Death March.

Bob Ibold 21st Pursuit, survived the Bataan Death March, died in a Japanese POW camp.

Charles O'Neil, flying school classmate (41-C), died in a Japanese POW camp.

Bert Bank and I in San Francisco in February 1945 shortly after he was Liberated by the Rangers from Cabanatuan.

Bob Spielman, member of our escape group and guerrilla fighter (1945).

Paul Marshall, member of our escape group and guerrilla fighter (1945).

Leo Boelens, 21st Pursuit member of our escape group and guerrilla fighter. Recaptured by the Japanese and cruelly executed.

Poem and letter were given to me by Boelens the day I left him to meet the submarine that brought me to Australia. I was instructed by Leo not to open them until I was on board the BOWFIN.

Sam

Not to be
opened until
after shove'n

Sam.– We've come a long way together,
10,000 miles or more.
To find the going tough but we've
much to be thankful for.
Our friendship was cast into brotherhood
amidst the blood and jumble,
and bound by mortar made of hardships
that time can never crumble.
Our paths diverged from time to time
common of circumstance,
but always joined at happy stands
of joyous consequence.
We have reached another junction the
sign says you must go,
Until the paths converge at a
happy stand where the pickens are good
We know.   Leo

As one buddy to another #$#T#U#UZ#I wish to express th$ the thoughts that are running through my mind, Our connection that means more than Life. We are Officers and must obey the command that confronts us, The natural impulse to act or to speak as the past has dictated is purely folly. The Commision of The United States is Of Supreme importance, and should not be questioned nor doubted. A nation is#is involved and any ques-ion that may be involved is purely personal and therefore, must be ignored. As an Officer I request that you forget any or all persona l acqua intaince and act as an Officer, Accepting#all Orders that maybe issued you by the United States# Government and acting accordingly.

All that we have been through must be forgotten and let the preent dictate the action we pursue.

Your presence will be missed more than you will ever know but your action will never be forgotten as some thing you did not desire but that you must accept.

Any thing that# is for the best and will evuntially bring us together is the path that I pursue.

Regards to those concerned and to you. Time will solve the problems we've thought about.

A Buddy L.A.B.

With Sir Cedric Hardwicke and Brenda Marshall at a War Bond show in Tulsa, Okla.
1944.

With Mayor LaGuardia of New York City and Russian diplomat at Madison Square
Garden, 1944.

At the ceremony in 1956 when the SAC Base at Abilene, Texas was renamed in honor of Ed Dyess. Left to right, Ed's father, Richard Dyess; Ed's sister Elizabeth Nell Denman; myself; and Ed's mother Hallie Dyess. The lady who painted Ed's portrait, Joan Spieler is at the far right.

Some of the few survivors of the 21st Pursuit Squadron. All participated in the Bataan Death March. Front row; left to right: Buster Court, public relations officer (unknown), Dyess AFB, Joe Ward, Carl Ruse, Sam Grashio, Herb Gregory, Omar McGuire. Back row: Henry Dominguez, I.B. Jack Donaldson, Virgil Catchings, Shorty Bohner. Taken at the Dyess Memorial Service, January 1982.

All 21st Pursuit, Bataan Death March survivors. Front row: Sam Grashio, Joe Ward, Frank Mayhue. Back row: left to right: L. J. Davault, Bob Miller, Jack Miller.

Jack Donohoe, 21st Pursuit, Death March and "hell ship" survivor.

Herb Gregory, 21st Pursuit, Death March survivor. My faithful barber in the POW camps.

Omar McGuire and Joe Ward with Ed Dyess' mother, Hallie Dyess at Dyess AFB, Abilene, Texas.

Claire Bramley, 21st Pursuit, Death March survivor and myself. Claire and other POWs made this flag from pieces of parachutes that were used to air drop supplies to them by our aircraft following the surrender of the Japanese in August 1945.

I.B. Jack Donaldson, 21st Pursuit, with General (Shifty) Austin Shofner at the Dyess Memorial ceremony in January 82.

Joe,(Whitey) Sedlar, 21st Pursuit, Bataan Death March survivor.

Allen Sly, 21st Pursuit, Bataan Death March survivor.

Bob Miller, 21st Pursuit, Bataan Death March survivor.

Harold Johnson, 21st Pursuit, Bataan Death March survivor, died in the Cabanatuan POW camp.

Ray Hunt, 21st Pursuit. Escaped from the Bataan Death March. Guerrilla organizer, co-authored *Behind Enemy Lines*, an excellent book covering guerrilla activity on Luzon.

"Jeep" Zieman, 21st Pursuit , Bataan Death March survivor, died August 20, 1942 in Cabanatuan POW camp where over 3,000 Americans died.

Anxious mothers and wives of Japanese POWs brought photos of their husbands and sons for me to identify, 1944.

Trying to identify photos of Japanese POWs. Pictures were brought to me by mothers, wives and other next of kin searching for any bit of information concerning their loved ones. This picture was taken at Detroit Municipal Airport during an Air Show in 1944.

Some of the officers of the BOWFIN and their wives prior to the BOWFIN's first patrol in 1943. Front row: Commander J.H. Willingham, Skipper of the BOWFIN. Back row: Left to right: Lt. Commander Bill Thompson, Lieutenant Dave Cone, Lieutenant Nicholson, Ensign John Bertrand.

Howard E. Clark, Ens., and his wife Vera, prior to Howie's first patrol aboard the BOWFIN.

USS BOWFIN 287, filmed on her first patrol. It was on this patrol that the BOWFIN evacuated me to Freemantle, Australia and my return to freedom.

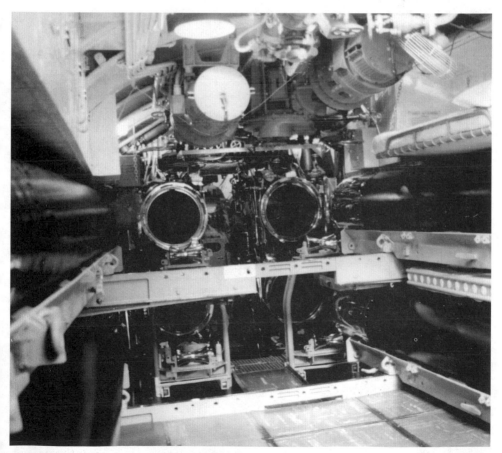

Forward torpedo room, USS BOWFIN (SS-287). I was quartered in this compartment during the 10 day run to Freemantle.

Left to right: John Bertrand, Reid Lee and myself at Reid's home in Colville, Washington. John and Reid were members of the BOWFIN's crew.

With Lt. Gen. Alexander A. Vandergrift, Marine Corps Commandant, Chicago, 1945.

With Mike Dobervich, fellow escapee, at POW Convention, Seattle, Washington, 1984.

2nd. Lieutenant Charles Page, 17th Pursuit Squadron, 1941. KIA 1/5/42 on Bataan.

Letter of condolence to Lt. Page's mother from Lt. General H.H. Arnold, Chief of the Army Airforces.

Eddie Page at the grave site of his younger brother Charles, January 1986.

Mario (Motts) Tonelli with my wife Dee in Spokane. Motts was a Japanese POW and we worked together in a Japanese prison camp in the Davao Penal Colony. He was All American Fullback at Notre Dame.

Father Richard Carberry, Japanese POW, died onboard the "hell ship" Oryoku Maru.

Father John Francis Gubbins, S.J., My boss and mentor at Gonzaga University.

General Hal George at the front porch of his bamboo Command Post on Bataan.

Canadian National Defense College students (class 15) receiving a briefing from Nehru the Prime Minister of India in New Delhi 1963.

Tour Group arrival at Manila International Airport in the early morning January 20, 1986. (left to right), John Bogle, veteran Spokane WA., Allen Sly (21st Pursuit, Bataan Death March survivor), Eddie Page, John Brownwell (17th Pursuit), Dave Oestreich (34th Pursuit, Bataan Death March survivor), Omar McGuire (21st Pursuit, Bataan Death March survivor), Robert Brown (34th Pursuit, Bataan Death March survivor), Lt. General Joseph Moore (20th Pursuit Squadron Commander,Bataan defender, flew one of the last two P-40s off Bataan, evaded capture).

Bataan Death March survivors at the Camp O'Donnell Memorial. Left to right: Omar McGuire, Robert Brown, William Cowley, myself, David Oestreich (organized tour), Stan Korczyk, January, 1986.

Jane Fredrickson and Teedie Woodcock joined me and the other members of the tour group in a moment of prayer for the over 3,000 American POWs who died in the Cabanatuan Japanese POW camp.

Myself and Bob Brown receiving a very warm welcome from Philippine Scouts upon arrival at the Manila Hotel.

My wife Dee with Magdaleno Duenas, a guerrilla fighter on Mindanao, 1986.

To SAM
MY best
wishes

Saburo Sakai, Japan's leading living ACE (64 victories). He damaged my P-40E over Clark Field on my first mission of the war, December 8, 1941.

Saburo Sakai and I next to an exhibit of his flying helmet and my Kelly Field Graduation ring on display at the Admiral Nimitz Museum in Fredricksburg, Texas.

Left to right: Aviation artist Keith Ferris, Saburo Sakai, Sam Grashio, Joseph Moore.

WILLIAM E. DYESS
First Lieutenant
Commanding

21st PURSUIT SQUADRON

The following officers whose photos appear below were transferred to the 34th Pursuit Squadron under the command of 1st Lt. Samuel H. Marett and served with that unit in defense of the Philippines: 2nd Lts: William L. Baker, Jr. (died in a POW camp, Feb. 18, 1943), William G. Coleman (KIA Aug. 15, 1944), Jack W. Hall (KIA Jan. 30, 1942), Lawrence E. McDaniel (KIA Apr. 14, 1942), Arthur B. Knackstedt (MIA Sept. 7, 1944), and Stewart W. Robb.

The following officers who appear in the photos below were reassigned to other organizations and were not sent to the Philippines: 2nd Lts: Hubert I. Egenes, Gerald W. Martin, Paul C. May, Charles Mehlert, James B. Morehead, George C. Player, Soloman T. Willis.

WILLIAM L. BAKER, JR.
Second Lieutenant

JOHN P. BURNS
Second Lieutenant

ROBERT D. CLARK
Second Lieutenant

JOSEPH P. COLE
Second Lieutenant

LLOYD A. COLEMAN
Second Lieutenant

WILLIAM G. COLEMAN
Second Lieutenant

HUBERT I. EGENES
Second Lieutenant

LEO B. GOLDEN
Second Lieutenant

SAMUEL C. GRASHIO
Second Lieutenant

JACK W. HALL
Second Lieutenant

ARTHUR B. KNACKSTEDT, JR.
Second Lieutenant

GERALD W. MARTIN
Second Lieutenant

PAUL C. MAY
Second Lieutenant

LAWRENCE E. McDANIEL
Second Lieutenant

CHARLES MEHLERT
Second Lieutenant

JAMES B. MOREHEAD
Second Lieutenant

GEORGE C. PLAYER
Second Lieutenant

STEWART W. ROBB
Second Lieutenant

SOLOMAN T. WILLIS
Second Lieutenant

BEN S. IRVIN
Second Lieutenant

21st PURSUIT SQUADRON

(Reading from Left to Right)

First Row: Master Sergeant McLean, Sherman A.,; First Sergeant Boston, Ronald O.; Technical Sergeants Griffin, Edward J.; Gross, John C.; Hightower, Porter T.; Tomlinson, Cupid D.

Second Row: Staff Sergeants Ammons, Cecil; Batcheler, John F.; Batson, Jack H.; Dabney, Edmund R., Jr.; Deering, Clyde L.; Fowler, William D,

Third Row: Staff Sergeants Gilmet, John N.; Ginnevan, Michael, Hunt, Raymond C. Jr.; Jones, Allen C.; Karlik, Jerry J.; Kolstad, Harvey T.

Fourth Row: Staff Sergeants Matisovsky, Stephen; McGrew, Charles M.; Miller, John W.; Moore, William T.; Nichols, Murray D.; Risen, Coleman L.

Fifth Row: Staff Sergeants Sedlar, Joseph; Stein, Charles W.; Webb, Charles W.; Sergeants Caldwell, Arnold C.; Hayes, Verlon O.; Kerr, Benjamin W.

Sixth Row: Sergeants Lilly, Bryce L.; Nelson, Orlando C.; O'Connell, Alfred L.; Oie, Casper J.; Roach, Geroge T.

21st PURSUIT SQUADRON

(Reading from Left to Right)

First Row: Corporals Cammarata, Joseph T.; Carpenter, James D.; Dukatnik, Robert.

Second Row: Corporals Ellis, Edward R.; Jenne, Calvin A., Jr.; McClintock, Jack; Murphy, Frank, Jr.; Rowe, Wilbert J.

Third Row: Corporals Sly, Allen N.; Yeats, Allen M. W.; Corporal Betancourt, Faustino D.; Privates First Class Clifton, Ansel H.; Cobb, J. C.

Fourth Row: Privates First Class Court, Julian C.; Farchild, Sam S.; Gillespie, James R.; Gregory, Hubert W.; Griffin, Marion M.

Fifth Row: Privates First Class Inman, Charles W.; Johnson, Cyrus F.; Privates Astorgano, Martin L.; Barber, Thomas W., Jr.; Beretini, John B.

Sixth Row: Privates Bramley, Clarence H.; Cooper, Douglas G.; Dunn, James M.; Elefther, John A.; Ellis, Asa L.

Sevent Row: Privates Galbraith, Eugene D.; Gonzales, Robert W.; Greenman, Robert L.; Jones, Joseph B.; Kuttler, Ralph D.

Eighth Row: Privates Lynch, David W.; Riner, Merrill W.; Schanz, Oscar J.; Steidle, Gordon H.; Stevenson, Harry E.

Ninth Row: Privates Thrasher, John H.; Walker, John M.; Weber, Irving; Winter, Benjamin F.

264